GASCONY UNDER
ENGLISH RULE

GASCONY UNDER ENGLISH RULE

BY

ELEANOR C. LODGE

WITH FOUR MAPS

KENNIKAT PRESS
Port Washington, N. Y./London

GASCONY UNDER ENGLISH RULE

First published in 1926
Reissued in 1971 by Kennikat Press
Library of Congress Catalog Card No: 74-118483
ISBN 0-8046-1232-3

Manufactured by Taylor Publishing Company   Dallas, Texas

PREFACE

THE first object of this book is to give a continuous account of the period of three hundred years, during which a large portion of South-western France was in the hands of the English Kings and to show the importance of this connection to England at home, as well as its influence on the relations between England and France in the Middle Ages. Its second object is to give some idea of social conditions, both in town and country, in a part of France where, despite the prevalence of feudal turmoil, a very considerable element of popular independence existed, and where the development of trade exercised marked influence on the agricultural life of the province. Economic history can most profitably be studied in special localities, and Gascony offers most interesting illustrations of serfdom and freedom in plains and mountains.

No book of this nature seems to exist at present in English, although various writers have treated fully certain detached periods of the history. In French, a small *Histoire de la Gascogne*, by Louis Puech, was published in 1914, but covering as it does the whole of Gascon history, it can only treat more or less slightly the years of English dominion ; whilst the weighty work of Abbé Monlezun has little to tell us of English rule.

The chapters on social and economic conditions generally and those on serfdom in particular are mainly the result of research in unpublished material from the Archives of Bordeaux and Pau, which are rich in *Cartulaires* and *Censiers*, and also from various collections in the Manuscript department of the *Bibliothèque Nationale*. For the political chapters, and especially the one on Government and Administration, the unpublished as well as the published Gascon Rolls have been

v

utilized to some extent, and manuscripts have been consulted in the *Archives Nationales* of Paris, as well as the important published material contained in the *Recogniciones Feodorum* and the Cartulary of Henry V and VI in Volume XVI of the *Archives Historiques de la Gironde*.

The present book is small and can only hope to form a background for more detailed work on the different subjects of which it treats, but it will have fulfilled its purpose if it shows how much there is to be done in this respect, how plentiful is the material for some sides at least of Gascon history, and how important a part was played by Gascony in mediaeval times.

E. C. L.

July, 1926

CONTENTS

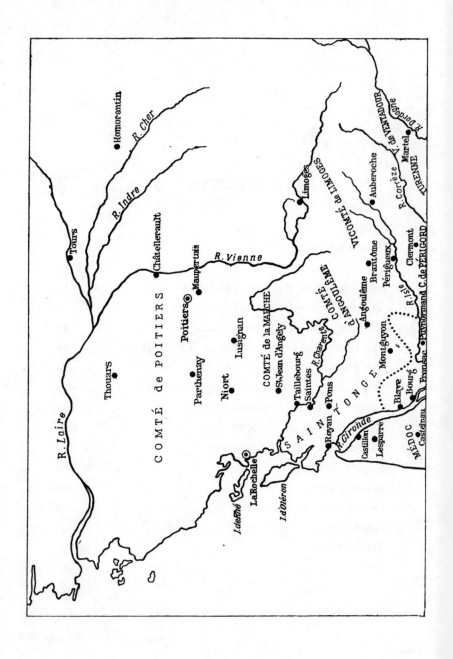

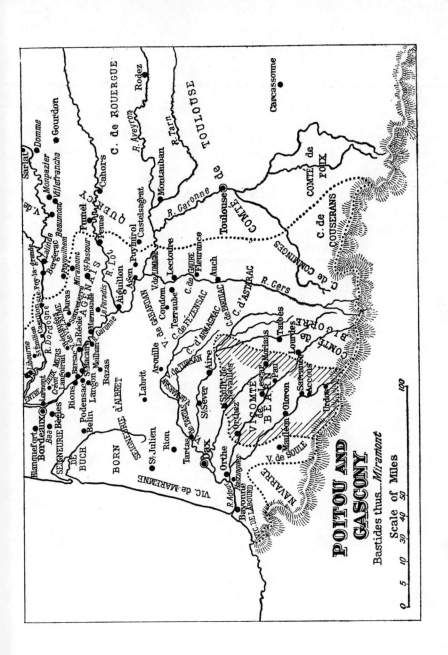

POITOU AND GASCONY

Bastides thus... *Miramont*

Scale of Miles

0 5 10 20 30 40 50 100

LIST OF MAPS

GASCONY UNDER ENGLISH RULE

INTRODUCTION

FOR 300 years Gascony was connected with the crown of England. In 1152 the marriage of Eleanor, Duchess of Aquitaine, to the young Henry Plantagenet, shortly to become King of the English, brought to him vast possessions in South-western France, of which Gascony was a part ; and a part which, through many vicissitudes, was not to be completely lost to the English till the final conquest of Bordeaux by the French King in 1453.

At first this territory was a personal possession of the English King, a feudal holding, which he treated as his private property, but as time went on the connection with England and the English people was drawn closer. Gascon nobles and burgesses visited England, English officials and traders visited Gascony ; Englishmen fought side by side with Gascons, not only in France but in Scotland ; Gascon ships came to English ports with the wine which all the well-to-do English desired, whilst English ships carried corn and other goods to the shores of the Gironde.

In the thirteenth century Gascon government was a problem which concerned England very nearly, for it was Englishmen who were sent out to act as royal Lieutenants and Seneschals. In the fourteenth century the Hundred Years' War broke out, mainly as a result of conflicts over English dominion in Gascony, and in the fifteenth century the final loss of the province was looked upon as a national disaster and humiliation.

1

The history of Gascony is a complicated one, for it is the history of a mass of feudal states, sometimes with a certain unity through subjection to one common overlord, but seldom for long together, as homage was transferred from one lord to another with apparently little compunction, and the boundary between French and English possessions was constantly altered. The name of Gascony is itself difficult to define. As Monsieur Barrau Dihigo, in an article on " La Gascogne," writes :

" According to novelists and poets Gascony includes a large part of Southern France and is the chosen home of talkers, fighters and boasters, men poor in income but rich in invention. According to experts it is the land bordered by the Pyrenees and the left bank of the Garonne, excluding Bordeaux, Bazadais and Médoc."

Neither definition, he concludes, is really satisfactory ; " if the former is too fantastic, the latter is too restricted." The problem is indeed extremely complex. If it were to be settled by language, Bordeaux and the Agenais would have to be included, for they are Gascon-speaking districts ; but, on the other hand, linguistic considerations would lead to the exclusion of the French Pays Basque, undoubtedly a part of Gascony, but speaking a distinct tongue of its own.

From the historical point of view the difficulty becomes still greater. The lands of the Dukes of Gascony have had many different frontiers. Bordeaux, Agen, and even Toulouse, have been, at one time or another, under their sway. Béarn, geographically in Gascony, was early an independent province, under its own rulers and working out its own history apart from the rest of the country.

There is, however, from the English point of view what may be called the official definition of Gascony. From the thirteenth century the name became the recognized title for the lands which the English held in the south-west of France. On the " Gascon Rolls " preserved in Chancery were enrolled the documents dealing with the government of this property. Thus Gascony came to mean a territory including Bordeaux and the Bordelais, the boundaries of which constantly shifted, which sometimes comprised less, sometimes more, than the actual geographical region properly called Gascony, lying between the Garonne and Pyrenees, and forming the southern portion of Guyenne or Aquitaine. However much the extent varied, the real core of these possessions was Gascon, and not until the English were finally expelled in 1453 did they lose the lands round Bordeaux and the lands round Bayonne.[1]

The Duchy of Gascony—or Vasconia—as it was then called, was founded in 602, but was intimately connected with the larger division of Aquitaine, the whole of the region south of the Loire. Anthropologists tell us that the early Aquitanians were a race of Iberians, which mixed by degrees with other races, and only remains in its purity among the Basques of the Pyrenees. With the coming of the Romans almost the whole of Aquitaine, except the mountain regions, became strongly impregnated with Roman civilization and Roman speech. The Roman division of Novempopulania corresponded geographically with the later Gascony proper. With the fall of the Roman Empire, Aquitania fell under the sway of the barbarians and became the scene of constant warfare. The Visigoths, established in the fifth century, were driven off by the Franks in the sixth, and the province was divided by lot among the Northern warriors. In the following century the invasion of the Vascones introduced the name which was to be adopted finally for the south-western portion of Gaul.

The Vascones were a Spanish tribe, who crossed the Pyrenees in the sixth century and overran the whole of Novempopulania, including " High Gascony " where Basque was spoken, and " Low Gascony " from the mountains to the Garonne, where Gascon, a development from the Latin, was the native tongue. The Merovingian kings exercised some sort of vague sovereignty over this region of the south-west, but its independence was considerable and it was distinctly

[1] The Chancery still, however, makes use of both terms, and in the Gascon Rolls the same man is known indifferently as Seneschal of Gascony or Seneschal of Aquitaine or the Duchy of Aquitaine. The use of the name Guienne is confined almost entirely to French writers.

separate from the rest of Gaul. After the seventh century the territories of the Dukes of Gascony extended and the term Vasconia was substituted for a time for that of Aquitaine. Then the northern part was conquered by Charlemagne and the name was once more restricted to the country south of the Garonne. The so-called Duke of the Gascons, who was allowed to retain his title after the famous defeat of Charles' rearguard in the pass of Roncevaux by the mountaineers, was probably little more than a ruler of the Pays Basque, for the rest of Gascony seems to have been administered by the Counts sent out by the great Emperor, as was the whole of Aquitaine.

Under the descendants of Charlemagne, his Kingdom of Aquitaine began to fall to pieces and to break up into a number of fiefs, very slightly controlled by the nominal ruler. In 864 the territory south of the Garonne became the hereditary Duchy of Gascony, subject in little but name to the larger division now known as the Duchy of Aquitaine.

In the tenth century the Gascon dukes began to extend their territories. Béarn claimed independence, but not always very successfully; Bigorre, Comminges and Couserans were vassal states; Bordeaux, Agen and Lomagne were held by homage from the Dukes of Gascony; Fezensac became definitely part of the Duchy. At first there was a Count of Bordeaux as well as a Duke of Gascony, but in 987 one man held both positions, and Bordeaux, from that date, became more and more reckoned as a Gascon city.

In the eleventh century Gascony became again united to the Duchy of Aquitaine. The line of dukes ended in 1032, with Sanche VI, but his sister had married the Count of Poitiers and Duke of Aquitaine, and after a time of struggle the title of Duke of Gascony became merged in that of the Duke of Aquitaine; but Béarn stood out for her claim to hold from no feudal superior and the rights of sovereignty over her were abandoned.

This was the situation when the death of William X, Duke of Aquitaine, in 1137, without male issue, brought his great dominions into the hands of his daughter and heiress, Eleanor.

By her marriage for a time to Louis VII of France, it seemed as though the separation of Aquitaine from France was early to be overcome, but her divorce and re-marriage to Henry Plantagenet linked the fortunes of the south-west with the English crown and accentuated the differences which existed between Gascony and France.

Henry II's vast Duchy was not to remain a permanent possession. The land which came to him through his wife stretched to the Loire and included, besides Gascony, the counties of Poitiers, Saintonge, Angoulême, Limoges, Perigord, Ventadour, Turenne, Quercy, Rouergue and Auvergne, besides claims to overlordship over the whole county of Toulouse. This was the Duchy bestowed on Richard Cœur de Lion, which roused the jealousy of his brothers and the bitter hostility of Philip Augustus of France. Auvergne was given up in 1189, but the rest was retained in uncertain vassaldom till the losses of John's reign and of the early years of Henry III reduced the English territory to part only of Gascony itself. But this part was to remain almost intact till 1453, and shadowy claims over the rest were to be renewed from time to time and culminated for one short period in the full sovereignty of the Black Prince in Aquitaine after the Peace of Brétigny.

Throughout this period of English possessions in France, the history of Gascony has an important bearing on that of England : its government was a constant source of difficulty to the Kings. Even when Henry II created his son Richard Count of Poitou and Duke of Aquitaine, acts were still passed in the name of the King and the ultimate authority rested with him. Queen Eleanor in John's reign was sent to rule as Duchess over her own territory, but the King went in person to receive submissions, granted charters and defined policy. The constant troubles in Gascony during the reign of Henry III added to the incessant demands for money with which that monarch burdened his people, and with the wise reforms of Edward I Gascony became a dependency of England, under a government which has been compared to our later government of India. It was undoubtedly the question of English rule in Gascony which more than any other helped to bring about the Hundred Years' War, and it was in Gascony that the struggle finally terminated. The Lancastrian losses in France during the reign of Henry VI, the effect of the long wars on the English nobles, and the disturbing element introduced into England when the disbanded soldiers returned from abroad, are all of paramount importance to a student of the Wars of the Roses.

The relations between the French and English Kings are of constant interest. The question of homage, the exact relationship which that involved, the summons of one King after another to answer for his conduct in the royal Court of France, the marriages with French princesses, are all in the main the result of this Gascon connection; and France was by no means the only country that had to be conciliated if the English were to maintain their foothold in the south-west. Aragon and Castille both had claims, which they were ready to assert when opportunity presented itself; and the wedding of Henry II's daughter to Alfonzo, Edward I's marriage to Eleanor of Castille, and the help given by the Black Prince to Pedro the Cruel, are all proofs of the need for averting danger from the side of Spain.

The reason for the efforts made by England to retain a possession at such a distance and fraught with so many difficulties lies in the commercial connection between the two countries, a connection which was all-important and which provides the key to many of the political complications of the period. From fairly early days Gascony became famous for the vineyards for which her soil was so well suited, and it was necessary for her to seek a good market for her wines. That market was provided in England, where the demand for wine was constant, doubtless far more so than in France herself, where other vintages were procurable. In those days of turbulence, also, transport over the sea with all its perils was in many ways preferable to transport through the ill-protected roads of France, with certainty of constant tolls and possibility of worse losses on passing through the many feudal estates. As Froissart says, quoting from a speech of the Sire d'Albret : " Wherever we took any excursions in search of adventures we never failed to meet with merchants, whom we squeezed, which made us gay and debonair." The commercial connection is of vital importance and was fully recognized to be so by both English and Gascons. The English Kings, in their anxiety to keep on good terms with Bordeaux, the main centre of the trade, gave the merchants who came over equal rights with those of their favoured city of London—a concession which the Londoners frequently resented with more than mere words. To maintain this important connection, one King after another offered privileges to the Gascon towns beyond any which they granted in their own home country, and this policy is the central feature of English rule in Gascony from the very earliest time. This favoured position of the towns explains, also, the fact that, despite difficulties with the nobles, the English rulers were on the whole acceptable in Gascony and that the precarious possession was so long retained. The commercial centres of Bordeaux, Bayonne and Dax were the real strongholds of English influence. A glance at the map helps to explain what this meant. The loyalty of these towns involved the loyalty of a considerable portion of outlying territory. Bordeaux on the Garonne, very near its junction with the Dordogne, was not only admirably fitted for sea-trade, but was the natural outlet for all the little towns and traders along the banks of the Garonne and the Dordogne, and the *filleules* of Bordeaux, as the smaller towns around her came to be called, were practically affiliated to her and forced to have similar interests (see Chapter VIII). Dax and Bayonne, to a smaller extent, influenced those places which could send their goods by the Adour ; but more than anything else, Bayonne was bound to the English connection on account of her shipbuilding. It was from Bayonne that most of the vessels were procured, which plied the trade between England and Bordeaux, and the fortunes of Bayonne were closely bound up with those of the more northern town. This fact of the importance of the towns and the town connection must be remembered all through the complications

of political history, for in it will be found the keynote of
the royal policy and the explanation of many facts in the
story of Gascony.

Not only, however, is Gascony important for her influence
on English history, and as the scene of constant struggle
owing to the consolidating policy of the French Kings : she
presents in herself a mine of information to the student of
social and economic history. The Communal movement in
the south-west of France is particularly interesting, because
of the characteristics of the leading towns, because of the
numerous *bastides*, which were largely the result of Edward
I's policy, and because of the peculiar independence of the
valley communities of the Pyrenees. Gascony is also a
country where customary law can be studied in the many
fors or customs, which have been preserved not only for
states such as Béarn and Bigorre, for towns such as Bordeaux
and Dax, but for tiny little rural settlements, and mountain
valleys with their almost independent governments. In the
Pays Basque the old rules of succession to property are still
clung to by the people, despite the uniformity of present
French law.

The history of Gascon serfdom is also of special interest
and helps to illustrate the influence of geography on social life.
Despite the broad similarity of social conditions in feudal times,
the serfs of the Pyrenees differed considerably from the serfs of
the Bordelais, and the commercial development of the country
led to an early commutation of services and to special conditions of agriculture and labour. As far as space will allow,
these different features of interest will be treated in detail
in later chapters.

Certain periods in the history of the English dominion
stand out more prominently than others, partly because
they are more important for general history, partly because
the historical material for them is more abundant. For
these reasons, perhaps the four most interesting sections
of the subject are the reign of Henry III with the severe
seneschalship of Simon de Montfort ; the time of Edward I,
the king who organized the government of the Duchy and

bound it more closely to England ; the period of personal rule, when Aquitaine became a Principality under the Black Prince ; and the final struggle of Bordeaux and Bayonne to resist French absorption in 1451–3. Whilst, however, we may know more about Gascon history during these periods, the trade connection and the constant problems of maintaining order and resisting aggressions in the territory are equally important throughout all the intervening years.

To understand conditions in Gascony and some of the problems of its rulers, a brief survey is required of its geographical features and of its feudal divisions. The southern portion of Gascony is made up of mountainous country, with the great barrier of the Pyrenees not yet a very exact boundary between France and Spain, since the Kingdom of Navarre extended on both sides of the mountains. The conformation of this Pyrenean chain led to the existence of numerous valleys of varying size, more or less divided one from the other, and the rarity of road-passes over the mountains rendered the whole region to a great extent poor and isolated, although the mountains sinking to the west made intercourse in that portion more possible. Through Navarre the important pass of Roncevaux was the constant route of pilgrims on the way to St. James of Compostella ; through the Vallée d'Aspe in Béarn the mountains could be crossed over the Somport, but the heights of the rest of Gascony were only pierced by paths which must often have been inaccessible and never possible except for mules and foot-passengers. At the foot of the mountains, hilly country, suitable chiefly for pasture and a few vineyards, stretches for a considerable distance, and offers a hard living to the industrious peasantry who cultivate it in the sweat of their brow. In all this part of the province the chief occupation was the keeping of flocks and herds, which were driven to the lower valleys in the winter and to the higher *ports* or pasture ground in the mountains as the snows melted and the tracks became accessible. Tradition has it that the usual practice of leading instead of driving the sheep, which still prevails, grew up in order that in passing from one pasture land to another the shepherd might not wittingly drive his sheep on to the best bits of his neighbours' land which he had to cross on his way.   Farther north the land becomes increasingly fertile, and the river valleys of the Adour, the Garonne and the Dordogne were suitable for corn land and meadows, although the increasing wine trade, and the value of the vineyards which could be grown upon the soil, led by degrees to the extension of viticulture at the expense of other forms of agriculture.   The sandy flat stretch of land on the left bank of the Gironde, known as the Médoc, became a special grape-growing district, whilst the beautiful undulating country in Entre-deux-Mers and Bénauges, between the Garonne and Dordogne, had many vineyards interspersed amongst its fields of wheat and other grain.

Between Bordeaux and Bayonne stretches the vast plain of the Landes, now well drained and fertile, but at no very remote period marshy, unhealthy and desolate.   An Italian traveller as late as the sixteenth century writes of it as follows :

" It is a country uncultivated, sterile, and very sparsely inhabited ; hamlets appear here and there where a group of trees or a spring has given them a possible site ; elsewhere it offers little either of beauty or of utility.   Travelling in it is very difficult, for either one sinks in the sand, or plunges into the muddy waters which create an endless stretch of thick bog . . . the pathway has to be sought painfully, hidden and obstructed as it is by interminable fields of tamarisk and bracken.   These plants and other thorny bushes trip up the horses and wound their feet."

Such was the inland country, and the sandy dunes on the coast offered no opportunity to fisherman or trader.   Despite the poverty of this tract of country, its political importance was great, since its situation between Bordeaux and Bayonne made it of considerable value to the overlord of the two great cities.

As the economic life of Gascony was to a great extent the outcome of its natural features, so its political life was affected by the extreme feudalization of the country and its division into numerous seignorial estates of varying size and importance, the lords of which were all ready to claim as much independence as was possible. To quote Monsieur Bladé : " Après 1039 il n'y a plus la Gascogne politique. Il y a simplement l'administration des rois d'Angleterre et des rois de France dans notre sud-ouest."

The traveller in this part of the country, however unobservant, is bound to be struck by the frequent remains of feudal castles, which seem to have been built on almost every hillock of commanding position, and which testify to the number of small lords with estates barely sufficient to yield them a precarious livelihood, whose energies would doubtless turn joyfully to the activities of war with the possibilities of booty and reward. Only the larger feudal properties can, however, be mentioned in this sketch and those great lords whose fortunes were most closely linked, either by alliance or hostility, with those of England.

The main divisions of feudal Gascony were : the Counties of Armagnac, Bigorre, Fezensac, Gaure, Pardiac, and Astarac ; the Viscounties of Lomagne, Gabardan, Soule, Labourd, Marsan, Tartas, including Dax, Tursan, Maremne, and the seigneurie of Albret. To these may be added the Viscounty of Béarn, geographically Gascon, though politically independent, or claiming to be so. From the point of view of English dominion, as well as for linguistic reasons, Gascony may be held also to include the counties of Comminges and Couserans in the south ; the Pays of Buch and Born, the Médoc, Bordelais and Bazadais in the north ; and beyond the Garonne, Bourg, Blaye, Entre-deux-Mers, Bénauges and Agenais. All this country was in every way distinct from France, speaking a different language and living under its own written customs ; mediaeval France may be said to have ended at Blaye.

To the north and east of Gascony other great estates existed, under the English rule at times, and constantly playing an important part in English and Gascon history. The Counties of Poitiers, La Marche, Saintonge, Angoulême, Périgord, Quercy and Rouergue ; the Viscounties of Limoges, Ventadour, Turenne ; and in the south the County of Foix,

which was eventually to spread its borders and to be united
with the Viscounty of Béarn in 1290 in the person of Roger
Bernard, husband of Marguerite of Béarn.   The exact relations
of these different feudatories with the Kings of France and
England, and with each other, is subject to constant changes
and exceedingly complicated, and the exact subjection which
was implied by the performance of homage, even of *hommage
lige*, was far from being uniformly defined.   The situation
was further affected by the power in the hands of great
ecclesiastics.   The Archbishop of Bordeaux, in particular, was
the ruler of wide estates, with courts of justice almost uncontrolled, and took an active part in the politics of his
day.   The Archbishop of Auch was often engaged in secular
disputes, and the great Abbeys such as La Grande Sauve
were feudal lords as well as religious bodies.

Each of these feudal states might claim a separate history
of its own ; but even the briefest sketch would over-weight
an already full programme.   Their overlords played a great
part in Gascon history, which was largely made up of private
wars and feudal resistance to central control.   Amongst
these great Gascon seigneurs, perhaps the most important
were the Lords of Albret and the Counts of Armagnac.   The
Albrets, whose original territory was in the Landes, could
block the land route from Bordeaux to Bayonne ; the Armagnacs, established in the very heart of Gascony, were constantly extending their estates and disturbing the peace,
both of their suzerain and of the neighbouring landholders.
In the thirteenth century the country was wasted by war
between the Armagnacs and the Counts of Foix ; in the
fourteenth they led the way in the desertion of the Black
Prince, which cost him his principality ; and in the fifteenth
they extended their dominions over Fezensac, Magescq,
Lomagne, part of Comminges and Rouergue in the east.

The Viscounts of Béarn appear so frequently in all the
history of the English dominions, and were so often the centre
of discontent and revolt, that a short explanation of their
independence may not be out of place.   Originally part
of Vasconia, Béarn was under its own viscounts from the

ninth century, when, according to tradition, Louis le Débonnaire made a grant of it to Centulle I, a second son of the Duke of Gascony, and its independence was affirmed in the following century, when it was declared to be possessed in full sovereignty and held from no feudal superior. Not only the viscounts, but the people claimed unusual independence. The old story preserved in a Register of customs may not be strictly historical, but it contains an element of truth:

" Once upon a time there was no seigneur in Béarn, but the people heard praise of a knight in Bigorre and went to find him and made him their lord for a year. But after that he would no longer regard their laws and their customs and the Court of Béarn met at Pau and insisted that he must recognize and confirm their ancient rights and privileges. This he refused to do, so they killed him in the Court. They then heard a good report of an honest knight in Auvergne, and him they made lord for a year likewise. But he in his turn became too proud and disregarded their *fors* and their customs, so that he in his turn had to be slain, and this was done by the blow of a sword on the Bridge of Sarrance. Once more they sought a seigneur and heard of a Knight in Catalonia who had twin sons ; and the men of Béarn, having taken counsel amongst themselves, sent two representatives to request one child as their lord. When they saw the two babies, one lay with his hands open and the other with his hands shut ; and they chose as seigneur the boy with the open hands."

This story is supposed to refer to the twelfth century, when the Viscountess Marie is said to have been deposed because she had taken an oath of allegiance to the King of Aragon. In any case, the homage demanded by Richard Cœur de Lion, when he entered into his Duchy, was steadily refused, and when Gaston later became "the man" of Edward I, it was for outlying possessions in Gascony, never for his Béarnais property. In the Treaty of Brétigny there was no question of Béarn being ceded to England with the Principality of Aquitaine. Other states aimed, less successfully than Béarn, at similar independence, and the feudal tie was weak and frequently disregarded. Certainly there was no lack of problems and of difficulties for the English to face in South-western France.

COUNTS OF ARMAGNAC

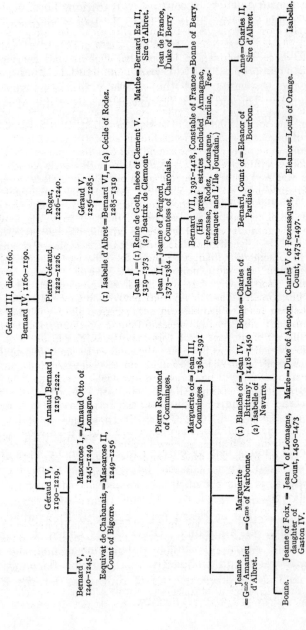

COUNTS OF BIGORRE AND FOIX ; AND VISCOUNTS OF BÉARN

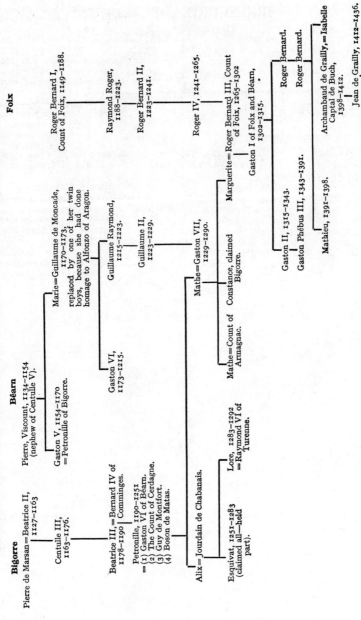

SEIGNEURIE OF ALBRET

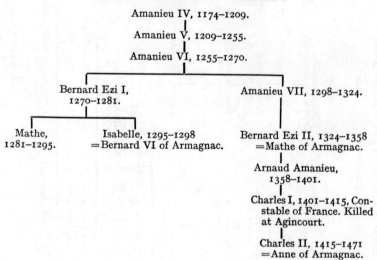

Amanieu IV, 1174–1209.

Amanieu V, 1209–1255.

Amanieu VI, 1255–1270.

Bernard Ezi I,
1270–1281.

Amanieu VII, 1298–1324.

Mathe,
1281–1295.

Isabelle, 1295–1298
=Bernard VI of Armagnac.

Bernard Ezi II, 1324–1358
=Mathe of Armagnac.

Arnaud Amanieu,
1358–1401.

Charles I, 1401–1415, Constable of France. Killed
at Agincourt.

Charles II, 1415–1471
=Anne of Armagnac.

CHAPTER I

GASCONY UNDER THE ANGEVIN KINGS

THE story of Gascony in connection with England begins with the marriage of Henry Plantagenet to Eleanor of Aquitaine, a marriage which brought many a difficulty in its train. His wife's possessions were vast, varied, distant, constantly out of hand, uncertain in extent and threatened by other claimants. Henry had not only to reckon with his own unruly vassals, but had to establish his position in regard to his overlord the King of France, and to substantiate claims of his own as Duke of Aquitaine.

Eleanor was the daughter and heiress of William X, Duke of Aquitaine, who died in 1137, and her inheritance, stretching from the Loire to the Pyrenees, from the sea to the Cevennes, included the county of Poitiers and the Duchy of Gascony, with overlordship of lesser counties and viscounties and claims to other lands, such as the county of Toulouse, which in the past had been part of the old Kingdom of Aquitaine (see Introduction, p. 5, and map). Eleanor was a wife worth seeking, and her first marriage to Louis le Jeune, directly after her father's death, bade fair to lead to an early union of Aquitaine and France, although Louis did little to assimilate the south-west to his other dominions and failed in his attempt to make good the claim of Aquitaine over Toulouse. In any case, personal feelings seem to have got the better of hopes for political advantage ; the incompatibility of the pair became very apparent when they were away on crusade and the marriage was dissolved. Although the divorce was arranged by mutual

17

consent, the attitude of Louis VII to Eleanor's new husband, whom she married almost immediately, was not likely to be cordial.

Henry II early found the lands his wife had brought him no light responsibility. His visit to the Duchy in 1156, when he received homages and organized the administration of Seneschals and Provosts, was already signalized by disturbances. At Limoges, despite a grand reception arranged in his honour, riots broke out later which led the King to destroy the fortifications of the city and also created uneasy relations with a town, which was never to settle down into complete subjection. The Church was also accustomed to great independence, and Bordeaux elected as Archbishop a man of whom Henry did not approve. Finally in 1159 a great attempt to enforce his claims on Toulouse ended in a retreat from the capital, which was defended, not only by Count Raymond, but by Henry's own suzerain, Louis of France himself.

The next ten years are full of little but feudal revolts, faced, when Henry was absent, by his officials the Seneschals of Poitou and Saintonge, but frequently demanding the presence of the King himself, until in 1169 he gave the whole Duchy into the hands of his son Richard, a boy of twelve, who was established with his mother Eleanor in the palace of the Counts of Poitiers.

Richard's period of rule was in many ways a repetition of that of his father, for revolts on the one hand and armed suppression on the other largely make up the actual events of this part of Gascon history. A few salient features, however, stand out in this complicated period, and the policy which all the English rulers were to follow with the greatest success is already beginning to appear. In Richard's case the situation was rendered particularly complicated owing to the fact that not only was he evidently subject to the authority of his mother, as well as under the direct suzerainty of the French King, but that he was also in some sort of ill-defined subjection to his father, who never abandoned his final responsibility for Aquitanian affairs, and the

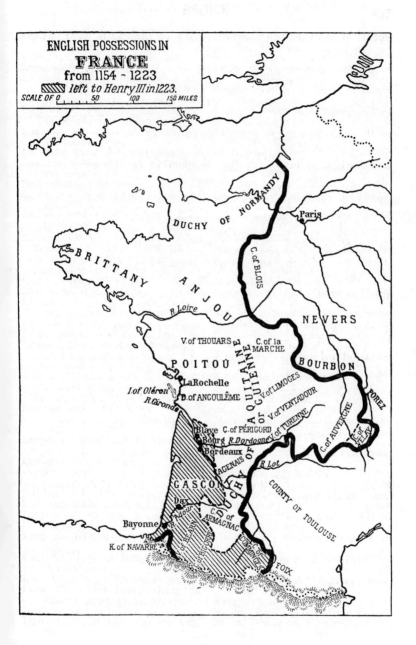

ENGLISH POSSESSIONS IN
FRANCE
from 1154 - 1223
left to Henry III in 1223.
SCALE OF 0 ..... 50 .... 100 ..... 150 MILES

DUCHY OF NORMANDY

Paris

BRITTANY

ANJOU

C. of BLOIS

R. Loire

NEVERS

V. of THOUARS

C. of la MARCHE

POITOÚ

BOURBON

LaRochelle

V. of LIMOGES

I. of Oléron

D. of ANGOULÊME

FOREZ

R. Gironde

V. of VENTADOUR

Blaye

C. of PÉRIGORD

V. of TURENNE

C. of AUVERGNE

C. of VELAY

Bourg

R. Dordogne

Bordeaux

AGENAIS

R. Lot

GASCONY

DUCHY OF AQUITAINE or GUIENNE

COUNTY OF TOULOUSE

Dax

R. Adour

C. of ARMAGNAC

Bayonne

COMINGES

K. of NAVARRE

FOIX

quarrels between the two hot-tempered men were frequent and dangerous.

From 1169 to 1173 Richard and Eleanor together ruled in Aquitaine. Eleanor was always popular in the land of her birth, and she used her influence to stir up risings against her husband, to whom she was in constant opposition. The nobles of Aquitaine were always ready to arm on any excuse, and Richard was induced to throw himself upon the same side and oppose his father, whose interference was doubtless irksome to the young Duke. The result was that Richard at the head of his Poitevin nobles joined in that great feudal revolt of 1173, which broke out almost simultaneously in Brittany, Anjou and Aquitaine, and which King Henry was able to put down with comparative ease, since no common cause bound together its various elements. To Aquitaine he came in 1174, took the towns of Poitiers and Saintes, built the castle of Niort as a stronghold in the most disaffected region, and divided the Duchy into six Seneschalships, with his own appointed officials at the head of each. Richard submitted, and Queen Eleanor was taken to England and imprisoned by the command of her husband. Henry clearly felt that the main fault lay with her and still hoped to keep on good terms with his son, for in the same year Richard was made sole ruler of Aquitaine, though considered rather as Lieutenant of the King than as the final authority. This trust for the time being was justified. Richard turned his warlike energy to the task of subduing his own turbulent vassals, and thus reduced his father's enemies to order and submission. The next few years were fully occupied in this task. The Counts of Angoulême and Bigorre, the Lord of Pons, the Viscounts of Limoges and Turenne were all in revolt and had to be defeated ; Dax and Bayonne were fortified and garrisoned to resist the young Duke and had to be humbled. One place after another was besieged and taken by Richard, castles were destroyed and the country forced into peace. This quiet was not to last long. In the last revolt an active instigator had been Bertrand de Born—" half poet, half condottiere "—and in

1181 he was stirring up fresh trouble by his songs and by his influence. The actual cause of Bertrand's hatred of the Duke seems to have been little but the usual dislike of the feudal noble for any controlling hand, and there appears no ground for the view that he was a champion of national independence against foreign rule. Bertrand and his brother Constantine shared between them the castle of Hautefort, a plan only too likely to lead to trouble. When during their continual disputes Constantine succeeded in gaining the support of Richard, Bertrand's course of action was easily decided. His idea in 1181 was to replace Richard by the young King Henry, the eldest son of Henry II who was already crowned as his successor. Henry was a man of the poorest character, a bad son and a bad brother, far less of a personality than Richard himself ; but he must have had some peculiar attraction, and his free and pleasure-loving manners appealed, it would appear, to the men of the south. However that may be, Bertrand was able to form a fresh league against Richard, with the young King as its centre, and it was only the death of young Henry at Martel in 1183 which broke up the confederacy. Bertrand's affections, however, were easily transferable, and his later poems show him ranged on the side of Richard and singing his praises during his absence on crusade. The last few years of Henry II's reign were once more full of miserable conflicts between father and son. Richard clearly felt his possession of the Duchy insecure and feared his father's evident desire to provide for his favourite son John at the expense of his elder children. He also seems to have come under the influence of the crafty King of France, Philip Augustus, Henry's persistent enemy, with whom we are told he not only stayed but shared his bed, so great was their affection, and against his father's wishes he did homage to him for all the French possessions in 1188.

The tragic story of Henry II's last years, his unwilling submission to the French King and his death broken-hearted at the news of John's treachery, is too well known to be repeated here, and too far removed from the history of

Gascony, although it concerned the Gascon ruler. Richard had difficulties of his own, besides his share in augmenting his father's troubles, for in 1188 his own nobles, the Count of Armagnac, Geoffrey of Lusignan and the Lord of Pons, were once more in arms ; and a short war was waged against Toulouse, in retaliation for the ill-treatment of some Poitevin merchants by the Count.

In 1189 his father's death placed Richard on the throne of England and he was seldom again in Aquitaine. His mother, restored to great honour, with the dowry of three queens bestowed upon her, was given Aquitaine as an apanage, and Seneschals were appointed over Poitou and Gascony to assist in keeping order. The new King's mind was turned almost wholly to preparations for his crusade, and though he visited his southern dominions it was chiefly for the purpose of gaining help in money and men for the war in the Holy Land. A few Gascons went with him, but most of the nobles preferred to look after their own interests at home ; the Archbishop of Auch and the Bishop of Bayonne were chiefs of his fleet and a few of the lesser nobles sailed with them.

Richard's long absence was too good a chance to be missed by the great lords, and the two Seneschals were constantly in arms against the rebels ; the intrigues of Philip Augustus, after his return from Palestine, increased the disturbances, and some of Richard's subjects were forced to do homage to the French King. In 1196, when Richard was set free from captivity and came back to his own country, he seems to have supplanted his mother's rule in the south-west by that of his young nephew Otto of Brunswick, the son of Henry II's daughter Matilda and Henry the Lion ; for until 1198 when Otto returned to Germany we find him holding the title of Count of Poitou. This title probably implied authority in Poitou alone, for Gascony had been given as a dowry to Berengaria of Navarre on Richard's marriage with her and was gradually becoming separated more and more from the northern part of Aquitaine. Otto's position in his Duchy was similar to that which Richard had occupied during his father's lifetime, for the King of England was still the Duke of Aquitaine and evidently kept the final authority in his own hands.

Richard's death in 1198 before the castle of Chaluz in Limousin once more gave Eleanor her old Duchy, for she hastened south to take over the government for her son John, declared by the dead King as heir of all his possessions.

It would seem at first sight that neither Henry II nor Richard had any other policy as regards their south-western provinces than that of suppression, nor any other weapon than that of force. This is not, however, the case. Already the plan of conciliation when possible, especially the conciliation of towns and the Church, is beginning to appear. The abbey of La Grande Sauve had its privileges confirmed and its rights of justice secured ; grants were made by Richard to abbeys in Saintonge and protection was decreed to the passage of pilgrims. The towns already were especially valued ; La Rochelle had its commercial privileges confirmed ; Bayonne was granted a charter of liberties and the fairs of Poitiers were secured by royal grant. In 1189 one of Richard's first acts as King was to write promising freedom of toll on the new bridge which was being built at Agen. Thus was initiated the policy which all wise Kings were to follow in the future.

The history of John's reign in the south-west is one of disaster and loss in Poitou, but of comparative security in Gascony, and the King's policy shows a curious combination of shrewdness and slackness, of ability and ineptitude.

John's character is not an easy one to understand, and all would not agree with the description of him as "the ablest and most ruthless of the Plantagenets." His Gascon policy does, however, show evident traces of ability, and on occasion John could act with the vigour and dash of his brother the Lion-heart ; but at other times his apparent apathy and lack of effort stand out here with extraordinary clearness and must have been due to more than his lack of support and distrust of all men. There is no doubt that his position was a difficult one. Philip Augustus was clearly aiming at the absorption of as much of France as possible into the lands of the crown ; in the north the claims of Arthur (son of John's elder brother Geoffrey and Constance of Brittany) were recognized by many ; and the English barons, though ready to accept John as their King, were not ready to yield him unquestioning obedience, nor help him to fight for foreign property, which to them seemed as yet of little value to England herself.

When John went to England to be crowned, Eleanor was sent back to Poitou, and was guaranteed in its possession for her lifetime, but she in her turn made over the whole of the property to John as her rightful heir and received his homage for it. It was Eleanor, however, who did homage in person for the Duchy to Philip of France, and John himself was not very often in the south. He came first as King at the close of 1199, but it was not till 1200 that he was at last recognized by Philip as the rightful heir of Aquitaine as well as of Normandy, Maine, Anjou and Touraine, and that he came to take possession of his lands in person. During this visit John took a step which may have been part of a deep-laid scheme, but which looks very like a sheer piece of undisciplined folly. He prevailed on the Archbishop of Bordeaux and other Gascon Bishops to declare his marriage with Isabella of Gloucester, a marriage which had taken place eleven years before, null and void since they were cousins in the fourth degree, and he then at once married the little Isabella of Angoulême, a child of twelve years old, the daughter of Count Ademar, so long an opponent of the English overlord. So far, no doubt, the step was a wise one and the Count of Angoulême became an adherent of the King ; but Isabella had been betrothed to Hugh of Lusignan, Count of La Marche, and had literally to be stolen from her affianced husband, an action which drove the important Lusignan family into active hostility. John made matters still worse by claiming, at the same time, the direct sovereignty over La Marche, a claim which may have been legal, but as Hugh had been left in undisputed possession for twenty years it was unexpected and misjudged; possibly John was really anxious to provoke an immediate quarrel with the Lusignans and to have an opportunity of crushing them.   The affair gave rise to a curious piece of legal history. John summoned the Lusignans to prove their right in his court by wager of battle, a perfectly legal proposal, but refused by Hugh and his brothers when they found that it was not their equals with whom they were to fight, but a body of picked men hired and trained for the occasion. They appealed to Philip, and John in his turn was summoned to answer at the royal court of France.   He refused to come in his character of Duke of Normandy, since, as such, he was exempt from French jurisdiction, but Philip replied that he commanded his attendance as Duke of Aquitaine.   In neither character, however, did John consent to obey the summons.   Eventually war broke out in the north on behalf of Arthur, and the disaffected southerners, the three Lusignans and Savary de Mauléon joined the other adherents of John's young nephew.   In the end they and he were captured before the castle of Mirebeau, which John rescued from them with one of his sudden but rare bursts of energy. For the time being Aquitaine was quiet and John left his interests to be maintained by the Seneschals whom he placed there; Robert of Turnham in Poitou, Martin Algeis, a chief of the *routiers*, in Gascony and Périgord.   His mother had been working hard in his interests all this time despite her great age, but in 1204 her death at Poitiers left the Duchy in his hands alone.

The years 1204 and 1205 were fatal to John in the south, and his persistent absence from the scene of trouble illustrates the curious slackness which came over him at times and made others unwilling to help him when he sought for aid.   From the north Philip overran Poitou and all was lost to John save the two strongholds of Niort and La Rochelle.   From the south Alfonzo of Castille, putting forth a claim based on his marriage with Henry II's daughter Eleanor, raided Gascony and was eagerly welcomed by some of the disaffected nobles, but his success was checked by the resistance of the towns which remained faithful to John. Bayonne and La Réole refused to open their gates to him, and though he nearly reached Bordeaux he was not prepared to face a siege of so strong a place and retreated over the mountains again. John's possessions were now practically confined to Gascony, but his wife's lands of Angoulême were untouched and he was still hopeful of winning back his Poitevin estate. In 1206 he at last came south and offered a free pardon to those barons of Poitou who would return to their allegiance. When a truce was made with Philip that year, he had partially regained a foothold in the country, over which he still appointed a Seneschal.

After 1206 John did not again come south in person until 1214, but he was carrying on a consistent policy all the time and a policy which showed his appreciation of the best means of securing his remaining territory. To hold these distant possessions, divided as they now were from English land, was only possible if local support could be procured, and the King carried still further the wise method of winning over adherents which his predecessors had already adopted. It was the towns which profited most from this policy, but it would appear that John was not without some power of conciliating his enemies and was not universally disliked by the nobles. An interesting instance is that of Savary de Mauléon. In arms against the King and captured at Mirebeau he was released on condition of fealty in the future and justified this step by regaining for John the important Castle of Niort in 1204. John rewarded this act by making him Seneschal of Poitou in 1205, and he apparently found the plan of employing as far as possible native officials a wise one ; doubtless his English barons were more disaffected than his Gascon subjects. In any case we find in 1206 that Reginald de Pons was to be Seneschal of Gascony and Bordeaux, Arnald de Landa custodian of the forest of Bordeaux, in 1212 Ivon de Jallia Seneschal of Poitou, and in 1214 B. de Pouy Seneschal of Angoulême. He even seems to have come to terms eventually with Hugh of Lusignan, for he made him his bailiff in Saintes, and bade his faithful men of Oléron to be obedient to him in 1214. He also sent over his little daughter Joan, to be married to him when old enough, although the marriage never took place and she was sent home again in the next reign.

It was with the towns, however, that John was most successful and that his policy was most fruitful. Bordeaux, Bayonne and Dax were closely bound to the English interest by many grants of privileges and he made great effort to keep the towns of Poitou loyal to his cause. Failure in this attempt must have been due to the fact that their trade connection was not so strong as that of the Gascon towns, and that though the English King was lavish in favours, they could make their allegiance to the French King a bribe for still more favours from him. The Gascon towns gained more than favours, though these were given generously, they gained a prosperity and commercial activity which they feared to endanger by any change of overlordship. Bordeaux was not only granted commercial privileges and had its right of minting money confirmed, but individual citizens were favoured frequently with letters of protection and leave to carry salt and wine free of royal duties and so forth. Doubtless it was liberality of this sort which had made the towns impervious to the advances of Alfonzo of Castille. This policy, though less successful in Poitou, was tried repeatedly, and John's letter seeking aid from La Rochelle is couched in terms which show how much he felt the necessity of conciliating the proud burgesses: " We beg you to take up arms in our service so long as no damage or danger to the town is involved in your so doing."

John had not given up hope of regaining lost territory in the south and re-establishing himself once more in the whole of Aquitaine. He had said earlier when urged to re-visit Philip: " Let him alone ! Some day I shall get back all that he is winning from me." His plans came to a head in 1214. The scheme was that he himself should lead an attack against Philip's power in the south, while the Emperor Otto and a great league of the Counts of Flanders, Boulogne and Holland invaded the north-western frontier of France and endeavoured to catch Philip in a vice. It seemed at one moment as though this bold scheme might be successful. John landed at La Rochelle in February and was actually welcomed by many of the fickle nobles of Aquitaine. He hurried hither and thither through the country collecting supporters, made a truce with the Count of La Marche, won over the younger Hugh of Lusignan by the promise of his daughter Joan in marriage, and came to terms with the Viscounts of Limoges and Turenne. Eventually at the head of a considerable force he marched northward as far as Angers and prepared to fight the French army under Prince Louis which was opposing him. But he had reckoned without his followers. The barons of Poitou refused to fight, either because they distrusted John, or because they were not prepared to break entirely with the French, and the discomfited King was obliged to retreat once more behind the Loire. Worse was to follow. The great combination which the King had laboriously built up in the north was met by Philip himself on the Bridge of Bouvines and completely routed. The whole plan was destroyed and in October John left La Rochelle for England, never to return. His greatest bid for victory had failed and nowhere could he look for the support which was necessary for any new effort.

During the stormy year of 1215, when John's nobles forced upon him the unwelcome Charter, the King still remembered his lands in the south, and several documents testify to the continuance of his former policy. Hubert de Burgh was for a time Seneschal in Poitou, and Reginald of Pons in Gascony, the latter taking over the two offices when the King's difficulties led to Hubert's recall. Savary de Mauléon, one of the few of John's Poitevin subjects who seems to have been persistently loyal after his first revolt, was rewarded by the privilege of minting his own money, and command was sent out that this money should be received as current throughout Poitou, Angoulême and Gascony. The King still sent messages to the towns of Poitou, which he claimed as his own despite the successes of Philip, and he still had his own Seneschal in Angoulême. As late as 1216 John wrote to the city of Bayonne begging that ships might be equipped to fight against his enemies. But whatever his hopes may have been and although Poitou was still theoretically in his hands, it was a very precarious property which was handed on to the young Henry III, when his father's death put him on the throne in 1216.

CHAPTER II

GASCONY UNDER HENRY III

JOHN'S death in 1216 left a very difficult situation for his little son, and so great were the troubles in England, with Louis of France invading the country, that the great Earl Marshal, the Regent, had little time and less money to spend on the Gascon possessions. After his death Hubert de Burgh could barely meet expenses at home, and the troubles overseas were more and more intensified. The Seneschal of Poitou, Geoffrey Neville the Chamberlain, was not a strong man and had little support from England. Louis of France when driven from England was only restrained from active steps in the south-west by a four years' truce arranged in 1220, and when he succeeded his father Philip Augustus in 1223, he prepared for aggression the moment the truce should be over. All the nobles were more or less disaffected, especially those of Poitou, and they were constantly in arms against the towns, whose privileges they considered a danger to their own authority. John had even succeeded in endangering the loyalty of the towns at the end of his reign by the seizure of wine without payment ; and the quarrels of town with town did not tend to peace and security. Bordeaux and La Réole were in frequent opposition to each other, Dax had grievances against Bayonne. Even when the towns were faithful, they were in need of money for strengthening their fortifications, and appeals to England for help met with scant response. Poor Geoffrey Neville made vain representations to the King ; he was too short, he said, of men and money to do anything, and was determined to throw up his post and set out for the Holy Land, unless better supported. An extremely delicate situation in regard to the Poitevin barons was created by the marriage of the most powerful of them, Hugh of Lusignan, Count of La Marche, with John's widow Isabella. The Queen wrote to her son to explain how completely she had taken this step for his sake. Hugh needed an heir and must marry, it was surely safer to marry her than some French heiress. The good effect on Hugh was not, however, very obvious; his opposition to English interests was generally as active as ever; but Henry, whose family feeling was strong, seems to have been ever ready to believe his protestations and pardon his past misdeeds, and his two sons, " my dear brothers," were constant recipients of young Henry's bounty. William Larchevêque, Lord of Parthenay, was another very turbulent element in Poitou. The town of Niort was urgent in its demands for help against him and begged that the King would send out a strong Seneschal. Hugh of La Marche made a truce with England on his marriage, but it seems to have meant very little; he planted armed men round the walls of Niort so that the inhabitants could not get in their necessary supplies. An effort was made to restore a stabler condition by the appointment of Savary de Mauléon as Seneschal, but the nobles were less pleased than ever, and even the towns preferred an Englishman. In 1224 when the truce with England ended, Louis VIII marched south and speedily regained the little of Poitou which was still nominally in English hands. La Rochelle was last to surrender, but she did so with only one dissentient, and Savary himself threw off his allegiance to Henry and joined the victorious party. The Isle of Oléron alone remained faithful. Again, as in John's reign, Gascony was saved for the English by the loyalty of some of the towns. In September of that year, in a letter to Ralph Neville, Bishop of Chichester, an anonymous commissioner writes of the faithfulness of Bordeaux to the English cause: " The men of Bordeaux will go on fighting for you for ever if they have money, but the presence of the King and his brother will do good."

This led to the sending out of the King's young brother Richard, now Earl of Cornwall and Count of Poitou. His expedition in 1225 was on the whole successful. He was received with honour at Bordeaux and the greater part of Gascony recognized his authority. In May he wrote to his brother that all Gascony was free from the French except La Réole, and all the nobles faithful except Élie Rydel. La Réole he took later in the year, and the new Seneschal Henry de Thouberville, who was appointed when Richard returned home in 1227, seems to have acted with vigour and some measure of success, as he was less unpopular with the Gascon nobles apparently than most of the English officials. Poitou, however, was lost all but the isle of Oléron, and when Louis IX became King in 1226 Hugh of La Marche did homage to him in spite of his relationship to Henry. The young King of England paid his first visit to Gascony in 1230, but he seems to have stayed only a few weeks and done little but borrow money; he may have thought things were quiet, but it was for a very short time. Requests for help continued to be sent to him and the money difficulty was as pressing as ever. It was not, however, till 1242 that Henry again set out to try his own hand at regaining lost ground and establishing order in these distant dominions, which must have been considered of very great value, since their retention meant vast expense and constant difficulties.

The position in 1242 was a curious one. Hugh of La Marche was once more intriguing with England. He refused to do homage to Alphonse, the new Count of Poitou, younger brother of Louis IX, who had received the conquered county as an apanage; and various other Poitevin lords also seem to have thought that a distant overlord would after all be preferable to one on the spot, and they urged Richard of Cornwall to come and regain his lost rights.

In a letter to the Emperor Frederick II, written after the event, Henry explains that he came to France hoping for a federation with La Marche and other nobles of Poitou and that his subsequent ill-success was due to their treachery. Henry might have learnt by this time how very little these Poitevin promises were to be trusted. Early in 1242 the English King began his preparations and sought help from the English nobles on the ground that Louis IX had broken the truce between the two countries ; Louis claimed, and with obvious reason, that to attack his own rebellious subject La Marche, who had broken his allegiance to him, was no breach of his obligations to England. Henry was still young and apparently burning to distinguish himself in war, though he would appear to have had little aptitude for military affairs when actually put to the test. In May the King landed at Royan and sent out a summons to his Gascon nobles to meet him at Pons with their quota of knights ; to the towns also he wrote asking for military aid in knights and men-at-arms. Horses were procured from Spain, money was borrowed right and left. The events that followed give an interesting illustration of the characters of the leading actors. Henry III and Louis IX were both looked upon as pious monarchs, devoted to the Church and fervent in their devotions, but their piety was of a very different quality. Saint Louis was an energetic actor in the history of his kingdom, prompt in war and determined in policy. At the same time he showed himself scrupulously fair to his adversaries, anxious for real settlement, not for showy success, and ever on the generous side. Henry, on the other hand, was ready to take up schemes for which he was not prepared and to thrust himself into adventures for which he was not fitted. He was no warrior and very little of a statesman, though he had the sense to continue the policy of conciliating the towns and strengthening the commercial element. His leading weakness was extravagance. He seems to have had no idea of the value of money, nor of wisely considered expenditure. He spent prodigally and hoped to be able to repay in the future. He let himself be persuaded again and again by the last speaker, whoever he might be, and his openhandedness may well have seemed to his subjects far more of a vice than a virtue. Henry had ambition without ability, pride without perseverance, and a temper which occasionally ran away with him and caused him to quarrel with his best friends. His brother, Richard of Cornwall, seems to have had rather more vigour and more warlike ability, but he was not a man of much force of character, nor a very good adviser for his brother, and he had no idea of striking out a line of policy or helping to govern Gascony. He accompanied Henry on this expedition, but he seems to have been chiefly concerned with safeguarding the King's person, and when things became uninteresting he went home as speedily as possible.

In July the French and English armies faced one another. Louis was in Taillebourg, which had been delivered to him by its lord Geoffrey de Rançon, a bitter enemy of Hugh of La Marche. Henry with his force drew up outside the town on the opposite side of the river. Here, however, there was no fighting. Richard of Cornwall negotiated a truce, according to Matthew Paris, because he feared for his brother's safety, and Louis granted one for the next twenty-four hours, that " night might bring counsel." The English force fell back on Saintes, and then the following day, pursued by Louis, they were severely defeated. The Poitevins deserted and the Count of La Marche, declaring that he had never sent to invite Henry to come over, as the King asserted, made his submission to the French King. Abandoned by most of his allies Henry beat a hasty retreat to Blaye, and although the illness of Louis prevented any attack upon him there, the campaign was over and the Anglo-Gascon army had distinctly had the worst of it ; when a truce was made in 1243, the French King was to retain all that he had taken. But Henry had not yet given up hope. He stayed on in Bordeaux over the winter, spending considerable sums of money and, according to Matthew Paris, wasting his time as well as his treasure. Perhaps he was not quite so foolish in his conduct as might at first sight appear ; in any case he did definitely continue the policy of trying to bind the towns closely to him, and though he expended sums of money among the nobles without much lasting result, he may have averted a certain amount of revolution by this un-satisfactory method. In regard to the towns he had first to conciliate Bordeaux, for having exacted military service. To the mayor and jurats he wrote to say that he quite realized that no service was due outside the diocese of Bordeaux, that any help given was an exceptional favour, and that it should not be made into a precedent. The island of Rhé was allowed to copy the charter of Oléron and to have its own mayor and jurats. The men of Dax and Bazas were forgiven for having failed to send men to his army ; the Mayor and Commune of Bayonne were given judicial privileges and the promise that no vines should be rooted up or houses pulled down in return for misdeeds, however serious. In 1243 Bayonne was given a constitution similar to that of Rouen, and a hundred *prud' hommes*, corresponding to the Norman *cent pairs*, were established to rule and guard the city.

The nobles, on the other hand, were rewarded with money rather than with privileges. Over and over again the Rolls contain notices of annual sums from the Exchequer to such and such a man " to keep him in our service," or " for as long as he remains in our service." Much of the expenditure was in repayment of loans, or for salaries of soldiers still in arrears. Besides these inevitable expenses, Henry seems to have been unable to resist the pleasure of making presents. The Viscountess of Béarn and her son Gaston were enriched without much apparent reason, presents in money were made to churches and monasteries, robes were bestowed on ladies of the Court, and knightly equipment was provided for newly dubbed knights. For his own use Henry occasionally made extensive purchases ; wine regularly and clothes on such occasions as Christmas and Easter : scarlet robes and russet robes, silks and samite from Flanders. The money from England as a rule was almost wholly pledged in advance, though occasionally large sums arrived from the Exchequer and were paid into the King's wardrobe, under the charge of Peter Chaceporc. It was little wonder that Matthew Paris speaks of the King considering England as an inexhaustible well ; and no wonder that the Gascons tried to prevent the return to England of one who was proving himself so profitable a guest.

The French nobles laughed at King Henry and his conduct in Gascony, but Saint Louis refused to be amused at their jeers. " His alms and his masses should gain him forgiveness," said the pious King, and he granted safe-conduct through France to all Englishmen who wished to return home. "Would that all my enemies might leave me so," he said to all those who objected to such generosity, "and that they should never return."

At last, in the September of 1243, the King of England sailed from Gascony in ships of Bayonne, especially prepared for this purpose, and Nicholas de Molis was left in charge as Seneschal.

The next important stage in Gascon history is dominated by the figure of Simon de Montfort, a very different man from the royal master whom he was sent to represent.

Matters were not long quiet after Henry left his Duchy. The King of Navarre (Thibaud of Champagne) took up arms to make good certain frontier claims, and was only temporarily put down by the Seneschal, who, however, found his office too heavy a burden and was allowed to resign, being replaced in 1247 by W. de Bueles, who seems to have proved himself worse than useless. Revolt was once more stirred up, this time by the much-enriched Gaston of Béarn, who had no scruples caused by past favours and who had already joined the King of Navarre. Other claimants were ready to come forward when so good an opportunity seemed to present itself. The King of Castille said that Gascony should be his, as a descendant of Alfonzo VIII and Eleanor Plantagenet, daughter of Henry II. The King of Aragon, who had married the daughter of Alfonzo IX, was also prepared to assert his rights by force of arms. The Gascon nobles, always ready for a fight, were up in arms for their own private ends, and the towns—strongholds of English influence—were torn by internal dissensions. In Bordeaux the powerful merchants were divided into warring factions, headed by the two great families of Coloms and Delsolers. The Coloms were the chief of the wine-traders, the Delsolers were almost more nobles than traders, allied with the neighbouring lords, themselves in possession of feudal property, and aiming rather at feudal independence than at trading advantages. In Bayonne the divisions were more social than they were at Bordeaux, an aristocratic versus a popular party ; but trade interests also seem to have been involved, and one party favoured commerce with Spain, whilst the other was more closely concerned with English trade and shipbuilding. In La Réole and Dax parties were opposed one to the other and were to some extent connected with the rival forces in Bordeaux. Who was strong enough to cope with such a situation ? Constant menace from France ; threatening dangers from Spain ; nobles against towns, towns against other towns, merchants against each other ; and all in very nominal subjection to England and thoroughly disobedient to the rule of the Seneschals. The Seneschals, in their turn, were hampered on every hand by lack of money and lack of men, poorly supported from home and never too sure of the favour of their royal master. The situation could scarcely have been worse, but Henry knew of one man who might be equal to the occasion. Simon de Mont-fort, Earl of Leicester, a son of that Simon who had shown himself so strong if also so ruthless an opponent of the Albi-genses, had completely adopted England as his home, had married a sister of the King and had fought well with his royal brother-in-law in the campaign of 1242. Marriages had also given Simon an interest in the south-west, and a possible source of influence. His elder brother Guy had been married to Petronille, Countess of Bigorre, who on her death actually entrusted the county to Simon's charge ; whilst his chief enemy Gaston VII of Béarn was a distant connection because he had married Mathe, a daughter of Petronille by her fifth husband : a connection which proved, however, only an added source of rivalry and dislike.

Simon was already pledged to a crusade and was unwilling to take up the heavy task of establishing order in Gascony ; but he was persuaded at last and insisted on definite terms of appoint-ment, without which he realized that success was impossible. He was to hold office for seven years ; he was to be given unlimited authority ; he was to be supplied with money, and fifty knights were to be kept in his service for a year. He was sent out to subdue by force and to suppress rebels at all costs. Armed with these powers Simon set out for his dependency in the autumn of 1248. The character of Simon and the value of his Gascon policy has been variously esti-mated. None can question his courage or his ability ; but whether the severity of his suppression was justifiable, or even if justifiable, expedient, is still open to discussion. There is little doubt that Simon thought that he was fulfilling his mission by crushing his opponents, and that he felt no scruple in breaking faith with rebels who were beyond the pale of ordinary justice; there is little doubt that he was badly treated by Henry, who shifted from praise to blame from moment to moment, and who interfered with the Seneschal to whom he had promised a free hand. There is little doubt that the task was one which required vigour and promptitude and no light hand; conciliation had already been tried and had been found unsuccessful. But when all is said, the admirers of Simon may feel that this episode in his career is one not wholly to his credit, and that permanent success could hardly have been based on a policy so open to objection.

In any case Simon went to Gascony with more authority than any Seneschal had had before him, and with a more determined policy than that of the King in 1242. The nobles were to be crushed, the towns were to be reduced to order, the trading element was to be strengthened and the popular party supported. It was to be war to the knife against the aristocrats, whether merchants or warriors, and peace was to be imposed at the sword's point. At first Simon seemed to be wonderfully successful. Gaston of Béarn was isolated from his supporters, shut off from Bigorre, which he claimed as his own, and forced to make a truce. The King of Navarre agreed to arbitration, and one lord after another submitted or was cast into prison. But this forced pacification was only temporary. Next year most of the work needed redoing, and the situation in Bordeaux became critical. Here perhaps is to be found the main difficulty of Simon's position and the clearest illustration of his policy. As has been already said the two main factions which split the town were those headed respectively by the Coloms and the Delsolers. The Delsolers believed that Simon favoured their rivals, and it is probable that he did so, for the Coloms were undoubtedly bound closely to England by the needs of their trade, whilst the Delsolers were more inclined to ally themselves with the disaffected nobility into whose ranks they were evidently climbing. The crisis came in June 1249, when a tumult arose in the town on the night before the date for the election of the new Mayor. The Seneschal, hastening to the scene of disorder, called on both parties to desist, but when the Coloms alone obeyed him, he turned his arms against the recalcitrant Delsolers and forced their leader to surrender.   Ultimately both parties were made to give hostages for their good behaviour, but the Colom hostages were soon released, whilst those of the Delsolers were kept in prison, and Rostein, the head of the family, died there. The dispossessed Delsolers, headed by Gaillard, son of Rostein, laid their case before the King in England and at first met with support, until the easily swayed monarch was gained over to the opposite side by the arrival of William Raymond Colom, Mayor of Bordeaux, who followed his enemies to London and finally achieved their abandonment to Simon, who seems to have cast them once more into prison, without going through any form of legal trial.   La Réole and Bazas also felt the heavy hand of the Seneschal, and the warring factions there were severely repressed ; after which the indefatigable Simon hurried southward to make head against a new rising of the untrustworthy Viscount of Béarn.   Gaston was taken and sent to England, but there Henry for some unknown reason pardoned this hardened offender and so practically threw over his Seneschal, although he was still nominally supporting his actions.   Meanwhile Simon was sadly in lack of money and his enemies were increasing round him.   In 1250 Matthew Paris tells us that he returned to England in sorry plight with only three squires and an emaciated horse, and told the King how impossible it was for him to continue to bear these heavy expenses of rule from his own pocket.   " Per caput Dei," answered the King, " you speak truly and I will not refuse you aid," and the Seneschal returned with some help from England both in men and money and hired soldiers from Brabant.   Matthew Paris admires the Earl, but he does not attempt to conceal his severity, and even tells us that but for the value of English markets for their wine trade the Gascons would almost certainly have broken fealty and sought another lord.

Little by little the King's faith in Simon was shaken by the many urgent complaints and accusations which were sent month after month from Gascon lords and Gascon towns. Some of these accusations were, unfortunately, true enough. Gaillard Delsoler sent a letter recounting the events in Bordeaux, putting the worst possible construction upon them for Simon and implying that Bordeaux and Gascony, prosperous before the coming of the Seneschal, were suffering materially from his actions. The town of Sault de Navailles reported that de Montfort was the first Seneschal who had refused to swear to observe their customs and had ill-treated the citizens ; Dax complained that he had burnt the town and seized the goods of its inhabitants ; Gosse that he had extorted money unjustly and forced military service which was not owed ; Bayonne also wrote of extortions and of unfair judgments. The nobles spoke of ill-treatment, of miscarriage of justice, of imprisonment without trial, of waste of land and goods. In 1251 the King determined to find out the truth of these accumulated accusations. Two commissioners were sent out to investigate the state of the country, and the chief towns and nobles were instructed to send over representatives to the royal court in England to report in person on the complaints which had been made. Simon was summoned to England to answer the statements made against him.

The trial of the Earl, which followed, ended in his acquittal. The English nobles who formed the court were in his favour and considered that his conduct had been justified by his situation and by the treachery of the Gascons. The King, however, hesitated and was not prepared to let him complete the promised seven years of his Seneschalship ; he did indeed deny his promise. According to Matthew Paris this led to a stormy scene between Henry and his outspoken vassal, who gave the lie to his royal master. " Who could believe you to be a Christian ? " said the angry Earl. " Do you ever go to confession ? " " Indeed I do," said the King. " What is the use of confession without penitence ? " replied Simon. And the two men had to be separated by their horrified friends. Despite this terrible scene Simon was once more allowed to return to Gascony, whither he went with a large band of foreign mercenaries, more hostile than ever to the unruly Gascons and determined to crush out the numerous risings which had followed immediately on his departure. The King, however, had new plans for the future. He conciliated the Gascon delegates, disappointed at their failure to convict the Seneschal, by promising that his son Prince Edward should be their ruler, despite the indignation of his brother Richard, still nominally Count of Poitou. This meant the final removal of Simon, and the King was obliged to give him money as compensation for the end of his Seneschalship and to promise that his Gascon debts should be paid; the deeply offended Earl withdrew to France.

It appears from this chapter of Gascon history that Simon de Montfort was far more of a soldier than an administrator; that he was hot-tempered, inclined to violent measures and ruthless to his enemies; but he had defenders even in Gascony, amongst the people rather than the nobles, and he had a definite policy of backing up the party which was bound to England by trading interests, and of gaining the support of the popular element. The task of a Seneschal was always more difficult than that of a King; for Gascon nobles only recognized the authority of the overlord himself, in so far as they recognized any authority at all; and no official had sufficient available money to pursue any policy with real vigour. Simon did not succeed, for his absence from the country was invariably followed by renewed troubles; only his personal presence and his armed hand could maintain any kind of order, and even the allegiance of the towns was shaken; but it is hard to judge of his efforts when he was never properly supported from home, and when the King was always ready to thwart his policy. That there was justification, however, for many of the complaints which were made against him is only too obvious; the ordinary methods of justice and of fair dealing with his enemies were evidently disregarded and Simon's rule was merely high-handed suppression with little sign of constructive statesmanship.

In the autumn of 1253 Henry prepared to travel once more to his troublesome province before handing it over to his son.

Alfonzo of Castille was again threatening and Gaston of Béarn was once more in alliance with him. Simon's old enemies the lord of Albret and the Viscount of Fronsac were in arms. So alarming was the whole situation that the King on his arrival actually begged his disgraced Seneschal to return to help him, and Simon generously consented. He was persuaded to this step by Bishop Grossetête, Paris tells us, who urged him to return good for evil ; but he can hardly have failed to feel some elation at Henry being forced to take so humiliating a step. Henry's invitation to him was indeed a very humble message : " We beg you to come and discuss affairs with us and show us what you would wish to be done," wrote Henry. " If you find that you cannot stay, you shall be allowed to return with honour. As we know that it is dangerous for you to undertake the journey, we send an escort to bring you to us in safety."

The Earl evidently elected to stay, and together he and the King besieged and took the strong places which were fortified against him, La Réole and Bénauges surrendered, and some semblance of order was introduced. The King had a trump card to play, which no Seneschal could have employed. He sent an embassy to treat with the King of Castille and to arrange a marriage between Prince Edward and Eleanor, Alfonzo's half-sister. It is characteristic of the King's shifty character that he wrote home for aid under the pretence that Alfonzo was actually invading Gascony, when the negotiations were well under way. His wife and son had written to him that only such danger as that would induce the English barons to vouchsafe their help. It was doubtless the removal of this outside supporter which led the Gascon nobles " drop by drop " to make their peace with Henry ; but the King also renewed his old policy of conciliation, of endless payments and promises of money : while at the same time—possibly through Simon's advice—he garrisoned all the important castles which were in his hands and put them in the charge of trusted Constables. Many of those nobles and burgesses whom Simon had offended in the past were now won over and compensated ; money and lands were restored, prisoners were released and debts were condoned. In December 1253 Amanieu d'Albret was pardoned all his transgressions when he came to the King's peace. Early in the following year a truce was made with Gaston of Béarn, and in August 1254 Henry proclaimed to his barons, knights, seneschals, reeves, bailiffs and all faithful men that peace was made between himself and the Gascon barons and that all were to observe it.

This peace followed the formal agreement with Alfonzo of Castille, signed in April 1254, and it was at his request that some of the worst offenders and his constant supporters were restored to favour. Alfonzo gave up all his claims to Gascony, Prince Edward was to be sent over for his marriage with Eleanor of Castille and to receive knighthood at the hands of the Spanish King. This treaty was a great success and removed a very active source of danger. Henry was able, on the whole, to hand over a fairly satisfactory dominion to his young son. The towns had to be pacified as well as the nobles, and the King made some measure of concession to the hostile factions. The Delsolers were pardoned and restored to the greater part of their property, and the corresponding parties in the smaller towns were also brought back. But the King did not reverse Simon's policy of friendship with the wine-traders in especial, and the Coloms in Bordeaux still had the predominant power in the town. In Bayonne the King, under colour of concession, was able to extend his authority and to influence the choice of members of the municipality. The hundred *prud'hommes*, who, like the *cent pairs* at Rouen, were given an important share in town government, were all chosen from the party of his supporters ; and the office of Mayor was actually filled, with the consent of the citizens, by a royal nominee, Bertrand de Podensac, an outsider and a knight, who was connected with the main wine-trading families of Bordeaux. For the time peace was restored and " Gascony with all its appurtenances " given to Prince Edward, " saving our allegiance so that it may never be separated from the crown of England."

The King travelled home through France, paying on the way a visit to Saint Louis, back from his first crusade. The two Kings met rather as allies than as enemies ; and the

French King is reported to have said, as he kissed Henry on both cheeks at parting : " If only the peers and barons would consent, what close friends we should be ! " As a sign of friendship he bestowed an elephant on the English King, while the Queen gave him a jewel shaped like a peacock. In 1259 this friendship was sealed by a treaty which at any date would have been unusual, for Louis ceded to the monarch he had defeated in arms, not only Gascony, but all his own rights in Quercy, Limousin and Périgord, with the reversion of Saintonge and Agenais should Alphonse of Poitiers die without heirs ; in return for which the English King gave up any claims to Normandy, Anjou, Maine, Touraine and Poitou, and was to hold his southern possessions by liege homage from the King of France. Perhaps there was sound policy in the reply Saint Louis made to the barons of his Council who questioned this concession : " I give these lands to the King of England in order that there may be love between our children and his. And it seems to me that I am making good use of the property which I give him, for he was never truly my man in the past and now he is to do homage to me."

CHAPTER III

GASCONY UNDER EDWARD I

HENRY III had done something to put Gascony in order before he left for England in November 1254, but nevertheless it was no light task which faced his young son when he returned from his marriage in Spain and entered Bordeaux on 15 December 1254, to begin his personal rule in the Duchy. Edward was only fifteen years of age and he had to tackle a problem which had proved too much for many a full-grown man. He had, moreover, a position which required tact of an unusual kind. At first it seemed as though his father wished to throw off the responsibility which Gascon rule involved and to leave his young son to do the best he could unaided and untrammelled; but this was not permanently the case. Henry soon began to take part once more in Gascon affairs and Edward had no free hand, but was obliged to act through him and under his authority, though still at his own expense. It was even possible for Edward's actions to be repudiated by his father and himself scolded for delay in carrying out his father's instructions. It must have been humiliating to the young man when in 1258 he had to explain to his uncle Guy of Lusignan that the gift which he had just made to him of the Isle of Oléron and the office of Seneschal had been bestowed in error and must be revoked. This interference of Henry in Gascon affairs was so constant during the following years that it looks as though the King had been anxious to get rid of all difficult responsibility in 1254, whereas after his advantageous peace with Saint Louis in 1259 he felt proud of his success and wished once more to exert authority.

Not only was Edward subject to interference before he came to the throne, he was also unable to give undivided attention to his troublesome possessions in Gascony, for he had also received in gift the whole of Ireland, the Earldom of Chester, the Islands of Jersey and Guernsey, besides such lands in Wales as the English King was at that time able to bestow, and he was needed at his father's side in England on more than one occasion.

The history of the Barons' War and the part played by Edward both for and against Earl Simon is not part of the present subject, but such happenings meant that the Prince was unable to spend long in his Gascon lands and had to trust a great deal to the rule of his Seneschals. The amount that he actually did, despite his youth, his father's interference and his own absence, is still remarkable, and as King his reign, full though it was of other activities and difficulties, is one of the most important periods in the story of English rule in Gascony. The periods which Edward himself spent in Gascony before his father's death were as follows : from June 1254, except for the six weeks which he spent in Spain in the autumn the same year, till the 26 October 1255 ; from December 1260 till December 1261 ; and in 1270 he crossed the province on his way to embark for the Holy Land. Edward became King while still absent on the crusade, and before returning to England he hastened to Gascony to see that order was established in his most distant property ; this time he stayed from August 1273 to May 1274. In 1286 he again came to France in August, visited Oléron in October, and reached Bordeaux on 1 November ; this time he made a considerable stay and was not back in England until August 1289. This was his last opportunity of visiting Gascony in person, and through the troublous years which followed his place had to be taken by others ; but from 1254 to 1307 his connection with affairs was continuous ; he kept in close touch with his officials, was applied to on every matter of importance, and was the very real ruler of his Duchy. The state documents concerning Gascony began to be separately enrolled in his reign, and these " Gascon Rolls " show how much personal attention was

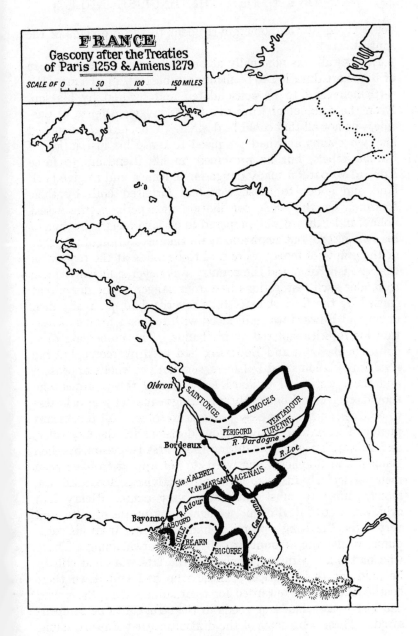

FRANCE
Gascony after the Treaties
of Paris 1259 & Amiens 1279

SCALE OF 0   50   100   150 MILES

Oléron   SAINTONGE   LIMOGES
                              VENTADOUR
         PÉRIGORD   TURENNE
                  R. Dordogne
Bordeaux
                          R. Lot
         Sie. d'ALBRET   AGENAIS
         V. de MARSAN
                  R. Adour
Bayonne
         LABOURD   R. Garonne
         SOULE   BÉARN
                  BIGORRE

47

being given by the home government to the problems of the south-west.

In 1254 all was nominally at peace, but the peace had been of too short duration to be firmly established, and Henry III's settlement had to be consolidated and secured by his son. Even the conduct of Edward's father-in-law, Alfonzo of Castille, was not all that could be desired. True, he had renounced his own claims and had promised to cease his instigation of Gascon rebels, but he presumed on his friendship to force Edward to pardon many dangerous enemies and to give back land and goods to those who had forfeited both by their treason. On the whole conciliation was, perhaps, the wisest policy, and Edward was prepared to go far in that direction of his own accord, but again and again the restoration of property or the grants of money were said to be made at the request of the Spanish King, and the country was never sufficiently loyal to render such restorations free from danger. The discontent caused by the Earl of Leicester's severity had not really died down and Edward was still faced with requests for compensation for injuries suffered at his hands. The immediate difficulties in Bayonne and Bordeaux had been overcome, but the rivalries of Coloms and Delsolers were not yet wholly appeased, and the question of Gaillard Delsoler and the treatment he should receive was constantly appearing year after year in letters to officials, and was no easy problem to solve. All this meant plenty of work and many anxious decisions for the new ruler, and Edward's Seneschals during those first two years, Stephen Bauzan and Stephen Longsword, do not appear to have been men particularly fitted to lead and to advise ; above all, the money difficulty must have been very acute. Henry had achieved a good deal of his settlement by means of gifts, and very often the King's promises had to be met from his son's purse, whilst the amount of debt was overwhelming. Those who had sided with the English in the late wars had still to be paid for their services ; those who had laid down their hostile arms to be rewarded for their submission ; those who had lost houses, lands, or goods in the struggle to be compensated. These were some of the difficulties that Edward found awaiting him, and the fact that his retinue was ill-treated by the townsmen as he travelled through Saint Sever on his arrival from Spain showed that the people were far from subdued and that he needed to work hard to establish a claim to respect and obedience.

Bénauges and La Réole had been centres of opposition in the late wars, and in the latter town the church, one of those strongly fortified buildings so frequently in the south the strongest portion of town defence, had been destroyed by English orders. Edward hastened to secure these places by putting his own official in command of the castle of Bénauges, and by sending money for the rebuilding of a church in La Réole ; other castles from which danger might be feared were put in the hands of trusty followers, and those that were restored to their former owners were given with the proviso that they must be surrendered to the ruler in time of war when he needed them for his own defence. Some of Henry's debts were repaid, or the creditors were furnished with pledges that regular sums should be secured to them from the customs of Bordeaux. Pardons to individuals or to towns, inquiries into complaints and evil customs, the sub-infeudating of land on easy terms, or the payments for homage, are the chief matters which figure in the Gascon rolls for these first years of Edward's rule. All this meant very heavy expense, and we find the Prince busy over plans for increasing his revenue. The Constable of Bordeaux, an official who was the head of the financial department, was appointed and given instructions for the collection of the great and little customs of Bordeaux, and new officers were put over special districts to collect a *focallagium* from agriculturists ; for each pair of cows or oxen five sous were demanded ; for one ox two sous and six *deniers*, and those who had none were to contribute one sou and three *deniers*, unless their evident poverty excused them. The towns, on the whole, seem to have been won back to allegiance fairly easily. The Prince saw to it that concessions were made to them, especially trading concessions. The Mayor and *prud'hommes* of Bourg and Saint-Émilion, for example, were to be free for five years from royal *prises* on

their vines, and various small places in the Landes were promised privileges and protection ; but some of the powerful
individuals who had nominally submitted to his father needed
very careful handling. Those who were still disaffected, such
as the Viscounts of Fronsac, Castillon, and Bénauges, were
living at the Court of King Alfonzo of Castille. The others
were gradually won over. The Count of Périgord did homage
and received 3,000 Bordelais pounds a year ; Amanieu d'Albret
was pardoned, and granted permission to arrange the guardianship of his own lands ; he was paid 80 marks sterling in recompense for the use of his castle, which Henry III had occupied
according to agreement. Gaston of Béarn was one of the
least trustworthy of these newly won allies. He had restored
to him castles confiscated during the' wars, and was granted
full pardon, but his daughter Mathe was taken for four years
as a hostage, and later history soon showed that his submission
was only nominal. He was quite ready to set off on his old
tack when opportunity presented itself.

Before peace could be properly restored, not only the rebel-
lions against England had to be suppressed, but also the private
wars of noble with noble, of townsman with townsman, for
there was general anarchy and disorder throughout the Duchy.
The Viscount of Soule was at open war with Arnaud of Tardets ;
Gaston of Béarn with Auger of Soule, and these were only a
few of the many quarrels. The adversaries were forced to
submit to the arbitration of the Seneschal and some sort of
agreement was generally patched up. An account of the
arbitration which followed a long series of quarrels of factions
in Dax gives some idea of the sort of disturbances which
were only too usual in the towns at that time. In 1272
arbitrators were appointed by mutual consent of the rival
parties. These were three knights, one citizen of Dax, and
the royal commissioner Martin Bonet de Saint-Quentin. The
heads of the two factions were Raymond Arnaud, sometime
Mayor of Dax, and Auger Robert, a leading citizen. The
climax of the quarrel had been reached during the mayoralty
of Raymond Arnaud, when his adversary had rushed at him
and struck him on the head, while another citizen had dealt

him a cut with a knife on the arm ; the Mayor had himself
struck one man in the face with a knife, and in return for a
small wound in the neck by another rioter had dealt a still
worse one in the face. Several men were killed in the course
of this unseemly brawl, one of whom was a clerk, but in many
cases the author of these crimes was not forthcoming. The
arbitrators went very carefully through these different items ;
some of the blows were said to cancel out each other, but for
most of them proportionate fines were imposed. The murder
of the clerk was a more serious matter, and seven men upon
whom suspicion fell were sentenced to banishment until one
of their number should confess his guilt and the Bishop should
decide his punishment. For other murders the leader of each
faction was to pay the money due and also to make compensation to the relatives of the slain. Both parties were
alternately to swear peace and good-will and to renounce any
intention of forming confederacies or leagues. Such were the
sort of quarrels which were hindering town development and
giving the ruler an opportunity to assert his authority. Clearly
two separate lines of policy were necessary. The towns must
be won over, they must be conciliated, they must be bound by
strong ties of gratitude to the ruler, and by profitable trading
benefits to England ; but on the other hand they must be
controlled, complete independence was dangerous, a powerful
commune was fully as troublesome a vassal as a powerful
noble. This double policy was to be the secret of Edward's
success in his treatment of the towns. Already before he was
King he was advancing in this direction.

Bayonne was already a more or less royal town, and Bernard
de Podensac, the King's nominee, was not only Mayor but
provost and chatelain. The quarrels of the Delsoler and
Colom factions gave Edward his opportunity in Bordeaux.
Henry III had made a fair settlement before leaving Gascony
in 1254. Gaillard Delsoler had been pardoned and allowed to
re-enter Bordeaux (Aug. 1254) ; both parties had given hostages and submitted their disputes to arbitration (Oct. 1254).
By the King's decision it had been decreed that all causes of
quarrel were swept away, all hostile oaths and confederations

annulled, and that marriages were to be made between the rival families, " though these should not be forced, as marriages ought to be entered into freely " (13 Oct. 1254). Prince Edward had received an oath of fealty from Gaillard, to whom all forfeited property had been res.ored. But, as usual, a forced peace was not altogether satisfactory, and Gaillard Delsoler was stirring up fresh troubles in 1257 and was arrested by the Mayor. Both parties were summoned to London to settle their differences, but their refusal to go ended in the arrival at Bordeaux of the Prince himself and the drawing up of statutes which, while maintaining the privileges and the prosperity of the town, went far to diminish its independence. The Mayor in future was to be nominated by the Prince ; in each parish the Prince was to appoint two persons to supervise his rights ; the Prince or his delegate should decide the amount of rent due from each citizen, and no noble should in future become a citizen save with the authorization of the Prince ; should the statutes need revision he must choose the persons empowered to revise them ; military service should be due from the town (though this was only to be according to old custom), and all citizens must be entered on a city roll, one copy of which should be kept by the Prince and another by the Commune. This measure was exceedingly important. It meant that for the time being the political power of Bordeaux was considerably curtailed, although her commercial progress was favoured and continued to increase without abatement.

Edward had made a good beginning. The country was quieter than it had been for many years, and when the English troubles were also over after the death of Simon de Montfort and the close of the Barons' War, he was able to set out on the crusade, leaving Gascony under the charge of Seneschals, who he hoped would now be able to maintain the order which he had apparently restored.

Edward's real policy can better be studied when his accession to the throne gave him full control of his foreign possessions, but there is no doubt that he learnt much from his period of subordinate rule, and that during that time he thought out and to some extent initiated the policy which he was to carry out with more vigour in later years. It was difficult enough to reduce the turbulent country even to temporary order ; it was a far more difficult problem to discover how peace and good government were to be made permanent and effective. Edward in the first half of his reign approached more nearly to this ideal than any of his predecessors.

In 1272 Henry III died, and Edward succeeded without question. Before returning to his own country he came to Gascony to settle troubles which had arisen during his absence and to receive the homage of his Gascon vassals. The years that follow are interesting in more ways than one, and concern not only the history of Gascony but the history of England. The connection of Gascony with England was closer than ever before, and perhaps for the first time it could be considered an English possession rather than merely an outlying bit of royal property. The events in Gascony naturally affected the King's position in England ; when things went well he could look to Gascon soldiers to help him in Wales and Scotland ; when things went ill he had a burden on his shoulders which hampered him at home and gave his barons an additional handle against him. But the interest of this period is concerned more with general policy and administration than with actual events, and Edward may have learnt from his experiences, not only how best to act in Gascony, but also how best to meet some of his English difficulties. His inquest into tenures in Gascony preceded his *quo warranto* inquiry in England ; the Gascon towns were in many ways more advanced than English towns of the same date, and burgesses were meeting with prelates and nobles to vote taxation, not perhaps before his Parliament of 1275, but certainly before the better known meeting of 1295. Some of the King's problems in the south-west were different from those at home, and he needed to walk even more warily with regard to the clergy and nobles there than in England, but in both countries we see his strict insistence on his own feudal rights, with, at the same time, an equally punctilious regard for the feudal rights of others ; in both countries he aimed at maintaining, where possible, his supreme right of justice and the authority of his own courts, and where he had to recognize the jurisdiction of his vassals he let this appear more as a favour than a right ; in both he suppressed crime and disorder with severity and justice.

When Edward took up the real reins of government he had various matters to occupy his attention besides the immediate disorder in the Duchy.   His attitude to the French King had to be considered in view of the fact that all the conditions of the peace of 1259 had not yet been carried out, and the government had to be strengthened in a way that would enable him to leave the country unvisited for long periods at a stretch ; his time would be less his own than ever.

Edward's first need was to know how he stood in regard to his fiefs and to estimate the help that he might be able to reckon upon from the services due to him from the lords.   With the object of obtaining this information he caused a thorough inquest to be made into his own demesne property and into the tenures by which his immediate vassals held their lands. Proclamation was sent out through the Duchy summoning all the vassals of the King to come in person to do homage to their overlord, who received them at three different centres, Saint-Sever, Lectoure and Bordeaux ; and there before the royal notaries they were forced to declare on oath the nature and extent of their property, the character of their services and the courts of justice which they were bound to attend.   (On the nature of tenures as shown by this Inquest see Chapter X.) Edward's tenants-in-chief included almost all classes : great prelates, counts and viscounts, knights and *domicelli*, as the younger nobles were called who had not yet obtained the rank of knighthood, towns as corporate bodies represented by their leading men, individual burgesses and the King's special freemen, groups, that is, of countrymen who held immediately under the Duke of Gascony and had special privileges from him.   The answers made by the different vassals are most instructive, and there is no wonder that Edward felt the need for emphasizing and enumerating services which might very easily have been forgotten, and indeed already were so in many instances.   The Churchmen, as a rule, had no doubt as to their position. In almost every case they claimed to have allodial property, and to owe no feudal service of any description, though they might be expected to pray for the King's soul. Many of the great lords claimed the same, and declared that beyond homage and fealty they had no obligations on their lands ; others owed military service, but rarely more than that of a single knight or his equivalent in men-at-arms, whilst a few held simply at a money rent. Burgesses in some cases held noble fiefs and were responsible for the knightly service, whatever it might be, but in the majority of cases the King's urban tenants held from him in return for money rent and money *esporle* (see p. 197). The statements made by the communes are interesting as showing that the King not only expected money support from them, but also military service. This service was always limited in time and often to a special district unless the King was willing to take over the whole expense, but the military value of the Gascon towns is one very special feature of the country.

The declaration made by Bordeaux is characteristic of the proud attitude adopted by that commune, even after the King's control had been secured in 1261. The Mayor and twelve *prud'hommes* made their declaration in the Cathedral of Saint-André. First the King and Seneschal had to swear to observe the customs of the town, and then, and not till then, did the burgesses take their own oath of fealty. The town was said to hold no fief properly so called from the King, though it held from him its use of the public ways, empty places, walls and ditches ; most of the houses and vineyards were claimed to be allods, over which, however, the King could exercise justice and receive escheat and forfeiture. To the King the town owed guard of the city and military service for forty days in the year throughout the diocese of Bordeaux, and this service was to be done in person by the head of each household should the King himself be present with the army. Finally the declaration ended with the claim that all their liberty was a natural right and must be safeguarded. As to the King's freemen, though some money and military services were due, it is clear that the tenure was more advantageous to the vassal than profitable to the seigneur.

Besides the obvious value of this Inquest as throwing light on tenurial conditions, there is no doubt that it was an important event at the time, and that Edward's future policy was to some extent at least determined by it. He had obtained a good knowledge of his property and an insight into the difficulties which he had to face. He had learnt which of his subjects were prepared to recognize him as their overlord and he could judge what line of policy it was most expedient to adopt. There were certain great lords who must be won over to his service, and although the mass of the nobles were poor and owed him very little tenurial duty, they could make themselves very dangerous if they formed themselves into leagues against him or were won over by the French King. Thus the nobles must be conciliated and must be made to see the value of loyalty to their English overlord. It was to the towns, however, that he must look chiefly for any real help, and therefore the commercial element was all-important. Trade must be encouraged in every way, disorder put down and merchants protected, and towns must be increased both in number and strength ; fortified centres would protect the country and the grant of privileges would bind the people to him. From this time, therefore, Edward set steadily to work to organize a strong administration, to confirm commercial privileges and to create bastides (see Chapter IX).

Edward's policy in Gascony, as in England, though of the greatest importance, was rather a development and strengthening of the old system than the establishment of anything original and revolutionary. The King was himself the mainspring of the government. When he was able to visit Gascony in person he travelled indefatigably from place to place, supervised every branch of the administration, did justice and settled disputes. During his longest stay he took with him his Chancellor, half his Council and half his Chancery, whilst his Wardrobe with its Treasurer acted as a sort of " travelling Treasury " ; from it was provided the King's heavy expenditure and through it were audited the accounts of his local officials. When the King was in England the chief matters concerning the Duchy were still constantly referred to him, and he sent out directions on endless affairs, sometimes even on what would appear to be quite small local business : such, for example, as a quarrel concerning a wall of partition between two properties, or street fighting between rival town factions, or the appointment of minor officials and many other such matters. From time to time, when he himself was absent and very much occupied, he sent out some vicegerent or Lieutenant with full powers to represent him and to act as though invested with royal authority ; otherwise he governed through a Seneschal who acted under his orders and was responsible to him for his conduct, although his power was considerable and his position one of very real importance and influence. Among his Lieutenants we find leading men such as Robert Burnell, the Bishop of Bath and Wells, his trusted Chancellor, Otto of Grandison, a Swiss, who had been with Edward in the Holy Land and was a devoted friend and servant all his life, the King's own brother Edmund of Lancaster, who died in Gascony, and Maurice, the lord of Craon and Sablé, a son of Henry III's half-sister Isabella of La Marche. The Seneschals were also men of some standing and of knightly rank, but not great lords as were the King's Lieutenants. As a rule Edward sent to administer the Duchy men who were not connected with the country, and could thus stand outside its rivalries and factions. The greater number were English, or belonging to families which had taken up their residence in England, such as Luke de Thanny, John Havering and John of Saint John; but we also find a younger son of the Duke of Brittany, and John de Grailly, member of a noble family in Savoy. Under the Seneschals of Gascony Edward had minor officials, sub-seneschals of provinces within the Duchy, Saintonge, Périgord, including Limousin, Rouergue and Quercy, the Agenais, and for a short time Bigorre ; bailiffs and provosts of towns and districts and custodians of royal castles. These offices were as often as not filled by Gascons, and it would appear that whenever possible his foreign subjects were encouraged in their loyalty by positions of some value and

importance.   This policy was a move in the direction of amal-
gamation of the two peoples, was successful in conciliating
some of the nobles and was popular without being too dangerous, so long as the main authority was in the hands of the
King himself.

This use of Gascon officials for all but the head posts was
accompanied by very careful organization of the whole administration and constant supervision of the working of his ministers.   The Constables of Bordeaux, at the head of the financial
administration of the Duchy, were controlled by the Exchequer,
and were frequently changed ; few held office for more than
two years, and some were only one year in the post.   The King
kept in very close touch with all his officers.   From time to
time inquiry was made into their conduct—at once if any
complaints were lodged against them—and they were removed
if found guilty of any injustice or infringement of local customs.
Edward made frequent use of special commissioners whom he
sent over to hold inquests, to arbitrate in disputes, or to carry
out any particularly important transactions.   The Bishop of
Saint-Quentin is found on several occasions acting with the
Seneschal or other commissioners on such business as framing
an agreement for the King with the turbulent Viscount of
Fronsac, coming to terms over rights to Bigorre with the
Bishop of Le Puy, or arranging to free the poor from any
royal taxation on account of scarcity of crops and mortality
of beasts.

The supervision and control of justice was a difficult task,
for the chaos of local jurisdiction was greater in Gascony even
than in England ; the lords were so numerous, their rights of
high justice so uncontrolled, and the communes also claimed
privileges of justice and their own courts under Mayor and
jurats.   Edward and his Seneschals did what they could to
supervise this chaos.   The lay nobles were under royal jurisdiction, and appeals could generally be made from other judgments, although such cases were not very numerous.   Sometimes Edward shared jurisdiction in towns and districts with
the Bishops and other lords ; but when possible he retained
the royal right over high justice and limited subordinate juris-

dictions to the smaller cases. Sometimes even great offenders had to come to England to answer for their misdeeds, instead of submitting to the jurisdiction of the Seneschals. In all courts of justice the King seems to have increased the professional element when possible at the expense of the feudal, and to have done what he could to centralize and unify judicial procedure when it could be done without offending his difficult vassals.

Besides his careful organization and control of all matters of government, Edward's policy towards the towns was particularly noteworthy. As has already been seen, he realized that whilst the important towns must be conciliated and favoured, they must be prevented from obtaining dangerous independence ; he was not the man to have his authority set at naught by communes any more than by feudal lords, and thus he took into his own hands the appointment of that most important of all municipal officials, the Mayor of Bordeaux ; and extended a similar system to other towns such as Saint-Émilion. In the case of new towns or fresh grants of charters the practice of nomination instead of election was always introduced. After times of unusual stress, such as had heralded his rule in Bayonne, he put in some foreign mayor and gave him very strong authority ; Bertrand de Podensac occupied the threefold position of Mayor, Provost and Constable of the castle. In Bordeaux occasionally an Englishman was appointed, but as far as possible Edward nominated someone likely to be popular with the burgesses, so long as he was not heading a warring faction and augmenting instead of soothing town jealousies and family rivalries. Complete peace and order were never secured, but, on the whole, the King seems to have had success in his policy, and the burgesses were bound to his cause by the re-confirmation of old privileges and the addition of new, especially of trading privileges and freedom from toll.

Not only were the older towns kept faithful by carefully regulated favours, Edward was directly or indirectly responsible for the creation of the many little fortified towns or bastides of which the traces are still so numerous throughout the whole

country. Here again Edward was no innovator. Some bastides had been constructed by Alfonzo of Poitiers, others were
formed by the French King in the parts of the south-west held
by him, some were created by the nobles themselves, and
others sprang up round monasteries or won their own privileges
from their feudal overlords ; but the greater number of these
strongholds in Gascony dated from the reign of Edward I, and
many were the result of the direct action of the King, who
commanded their erection or arranged for it by a treaty of
pariage with the lords of the district, or gave permission to his
own officials to form fortified centres and to issue charters of
privileges to attract inhabitants.

The benefit of these bastides to Edward was obvious. They
were valuable for military purposes, they helped to protect the
inhabitants from invasion and private war and to safeguard
rural industries and markets ; the burgesses or *voisins* were
anxious to secure their advantages by good behaviour, and
were likely to be loyal to the ruler of the country who had
granted or confirmed their charters (see Chapter IX).

All the time that Edward was striving to strengthen his
government, improve the conditions of the country and secure
the people to his obedience, he was coping with continuous
difficulties of one kind and another. Some of the nobles were
very hard to hold, and above all was this the case with Gaston
of Béarn, whose promises of loyalty were of very little value,
though occasionally he would fight on the King's side when it
was made worth his while to do so. When Edward returned
from the crusade he found that this unruly neighbour had
begun to give active trouble once more, had disobeyed the
summons of the Seneschal to appear before him at the Court
of Saint-Sever and had shut himself up in the castle of Sainte-
Quitérie ; while at Orthez violence had been done to the King's
envoys. As usual he was lavish in promises ; as soon as the
King himself marched against him, he declared his willingness
to obey the decision of the royal court and to hand over his
castle and men of Orthez, especially those who had been found
guilty of seizing Edward's messengers. The withdrawal of the
hostile troops from Sainte-Quitérie, however, speedily changed

Gaston's mind, and entrenching himself at Orthez he appealed from Edward to the King of France. After a long period of negotiation, recrimination and delay, Gaston was advised by Philip to present himself in England, which he did, sued for pardon, and became a paid follower of the English King. This, however, did not prevent some very questionable actions on his part later. In 1255 the death of the Count of Bigorre, which Gaston considered left his own daughter Constance heir to the territory, gave him the opportunity to hurry his daughter to the capital, to get her recognized by the Estates and to force the nobles to do homage to her, disregarding entirely the claims of Edward, the direct overlord : an action which produced long and complicated negotiations and much dispute until Bigorre was finally handed to the English in 1360. The impatient Edward showed unusual patience in dealing with his unruly Gascon vassals, a wise policy, but one which it must have needed great self-control to adopt ; the case of Gaston was only one amongst many. The King wrote bitterly in 1279 in regard to the Archbishop of Bordeaux, that he had so often excused himself and not kept his promises that it was impossible to believe in him ; but again and again he gave pardons, restored property and made many grants as gifts or recompense. He came to terms with the Viscount of Fronsac, almost a greater offender than the Viscount of Béarn, and gave all his old rights to his son in 1284 ; knights of Fezensac were commanded to recognize the overlordship of Géraud, Count of Armagnac, and to do their homage to him (1279) ; in 1289 the nobles of Agen were promised that a careful inquest should be made into possible encroachments and usurpations made by his officials and so forth. Nevertheless the situation in regard to the nobles needed constant vigilance, and even the towns were endlessly giving trouble through internal brawls and disorders. So bad was the state of things in Bayonne that in 1287 the town had again to be put under a military governor, and Hugh de Broc became Mayor, Provost and Chatelain as Podensac had been on a previous occasion. The men of Dax behaved so badly to the Seneschal that they were only admitted to peace on very humiliating terms. Not only was the

King in future to nominate the Mayor, but the town was forced to make formal submission to the offended Seneschal. All the men of Dax were ordered to meet him outside the town, barefooted and clad only in under-tunics, without caps or girdles, and there to beg his pardon on bended knee, whilst for the expenses of the trial the town was to pay him a thousand Bordelais pounds.

Perhaps Edward's greatest difficulties, however, were caused by his relation to the French King. In vain did the English lawyers draw up elaborate statements to prove that the whole of the Duchy was allodial property and that the King ought to own it as his independent possession. The claim was never substantiated and Edward had to hold Gascony as a fief from the French Crown. An active overlord could give a great deal of trouble on occasion, and Edward was punctilious in fulfilling his own feudal obligations as he was severe in enforcing them on others. But it was not only feudal obligations which pressed hardly on the English King : his overlords were not only exacting, but also unscrupulous. Thus the promises made by Saint Louis to Henry III in 1259 were still unfulfilled by his successor when Edward came to the throne. There were Bishoprics in Limoges, Cahors and Périgueux which had never been handed over and the territory of Saintonge, Agenais and Lower Quercy which should have reverted to the English on the death of Alphonse of Poitiers in 1271 had been calmly appropriated by Philip III. Edward did his homage in 1273 in very guarded terms : " for the lands which I ought to hold from you " was the form he used. Edward was not the man to submit tamely to the loss of what was rightfully his. He kept up a constant negotiation on the subject of his promised possessions, and in 1279 more or less satisfactory terms were arrived at by the Peace of Amiens. Philip was forced to hand over the Agenais to the English and also to renounce a preposterous claim which he had made, that all Edward's Gascon subjects should swear allegiance to himself. Quercy was not ceded at the time, but the matter was put into the hands of a commission of inquiry, and a good deal of the southern portion was later adjudged to Edward. In return the English King gave up any claims which he might have from past days on the lands of the French King. Edward's longest visit to Gascony in 1286-9 was largely occupied with the affairs of his Agenais property, receiving homages, creating bastides and putting the land generally into order. It was a rich and important portion of his dominions and geographically valuable as linking up Gascony proper with Périgord and commanding the valley of the Garonne.

In 1285 the accession of Philip the Fair presented Edward with a still more crafty and dangerous overlord. He had again to complain of the unsatisfactory fulfilment of the terms of the treaty, and when he went through the ceremony of homage in 1286, he said : " Jeo devint vostre home des terres que jeo tenuz de vous de ceala, solone la forme de la pees que fu entre noz ancestres."

Whatever the terms of the homage, however, Philip had no doubt as to how he meant his overlordship to be interpreted. He appointed French officials in those parts of the country not very clearly separated ; so that we find both a French and English Seneschal, for example, in Périgord, and there was constant friction and encroachment. The lands ceded by the treaty were not all given up, and the French King held them pending any inquiry into the right of the case. Appeals to the French court were encouraged as much as possible, and Edward had often to keep proctors permanently in Paris to act for him in the cases which arose concerning his Gascon subjects, and at other times to pay large sums for the expenses of his Seneschal and Constable in Gascony to travel to Paris to supervise the business. Relations were getting more and more strained when the climax came over trading disputes and grants in 1293. There had been constant skirmishes between ships from Normandy and ships from Bayonne, backed up by the English. Piracy and reprisals turned into something like real war when La Rochelle was attacked by the Bayonnais, and the Norman fleet defeated off Cape Saint-Mathieu in 1293. Philip furiously demanded that the guilty ringleaders in this affair should be given up to him, and that his agents should occupy Bordeaux and the Agenais. Finally a summons was sent to Edward, as the King's vassal, to appear before his court in January 1294 : " to answer for all these evil deeds and to do justice." "Whether you appear or not," ends the French proclamation, " we shall proceed against you despite your absence." The time was most inopportune for the English King, occupied as he was by troubles at home, and he sent as his accredited representative his brother Edmund of Lancaster to attend Philip's court in Paris and to see that justice was done. The chronicler Walter of Hemingburgh suggests that Edmund was not considered a sufficient substitute, and hence the negotiation failed, but this can scarcely have been the case, for in February a treaty was arranged, which was agreed upon ostensibly by both parties. Twenty Gascon hostages were to be given up to Philip and six fortified places in Saintonge and Agenais ; the rest of the Duchy was to be in possession of the English, although the French King was to be allowed to send one or two Frenchmen into the principal towns. In return for these very considerable concessions, all threat of confiscation was revoked ; Edward was to marry the French King's sister Margaret, and the Duchy to be given in perpetuity to their issue, while a safe-conduct was to be issued for the King to come in person to Amiens. As usual the English King hastened to fulfil the terms of the treaty ; towns and hostages were delivered and warlike preparations which had already begun were ordered to cease. Philip's actions were, perhaps, equally characteristic. It was not one or two men that he sent to enter the Gascon towns, but a regular army, and when challenged by Edmund to observe his promises he replied that his court was against it. Edward never received his safe-conduct, nor did the Princess Margaret consent to marry him ; in consequence he did not appear at Amiens as had been arranged, and was proclaimed a contumacious vassal by his crafty adversary (19 May 1294) and his whole fief was declared to be forfeited to the French King. Edmund returned home and sorrowfully admitted to his brother that he had been a fool. Edward wasted no time in blaming him, he summoned a Parliament, vowed that had he nothing but a boy and a horse he would pursue his right to the death, and was supported heartily by his indignant subjects. Messengers were sent to France renouncing all homage and obedience. " As none of the treaties with ourselves nor with our brother Edmund have been kept, it seems to us that we are not bound to be your man and do not intend to be so," wrote the King, and steps were immediately resumed for gathering a mighty army to recover the Duchy which had been almost entirely taken over by the French. The English were commanded to render the service they owed to the King, writs to the sheriffs summoned the lesser barons, and the prisons were emptied of malefactors, who were given the chance of showing loyalty and repentance in the French wars. Appeal was made also to Gascon lords and towns, but the terms of summons here were different. The Inquest of 1274 had shown how small was the actual feudal service due in return for the land, and Edward now begged the nobles to come with as many men as they could bring and of their kindness to help him regain the land so unjustly seized from him. Ships and sailors were also collected in considerable numbers ; William de Leybourne was made Commander of the English fleet, and Barrau de Sescas, Admiral of Bayonne. Judging by the names of those who were paid for their services the response to the summons must on the whole have been satisfactory, although some of the Gascon nobles were won over by French promises, and even Bordeaux, after its first reluctance to admit the French, seems to have been fairly submissive to its new rulers, whom it forced to recognize its old customs and privileges. Doubtless also the French garrison was particularly strong and impossible to resist in a place so important for its wealth and position. The town chiefly distinguished in this war for loyalty to the English was Bayonne, which early became the head-quarters of the troops and a great supporter of the English cause, both with money and men.

In October 1294 the English army set sail from Portsmouth. The King was occupied in Wales and was unable to go in person, but the army was led in two divisions by John of St. John and John of Brittany. As the fleet of armed men sailed up the Gironde, Castillon in Médoc and Macau were taken, Bourg and Blaye and Rions were occupied, but an attack on

Bordeaux was repulsed.   Eventually the army was landed and John of Brittany was left at Rions, whilst John of St. John proceeded to Bayonne, where the burgesses received him gladly, and the French garrison holding out in the castle was speedily forced to capitulate.   So far things had gone fairly well for the English, but in 1295 the tide was turned by a large French army under the King's brother Charles of Valois, who took Rions on Palm Sunday—" with lances, not with palms," says the chronicler—and captured Saint Sever after a long siege, where " Frenchmen died like pigs in the heat."   Fresh efforts were needed, and a new army was sent out from England, under command of Edmund of Lancaster, early in 1296.   His career in Gascony was a short one.   In June of the same year he died at Bayonne, " lacking money and spirit," and Henry de Lacy, Earl of Lincoln, became chief Commander in his place.   The records of actual fighting are not of very great moment. Hemingburgh has a curious story to tell us of the treachery of an English knight, Thomas de Turbervile, who had been sent as prisoner to France, and there made terms with the King for his own release on the grounds that he could gain command of the English fleet, and would put up a flag in any port where the French could enter without difficulty.   He returned to England on these terms, but though kindly received by Edward, he was unable to secure for himself the position he desired, and the French fleet cruised about in vain looking for the welcoming flag, and met with disaster when landing was attempted. Other treacherous negotiations were eventually discovered, and Turbervile met the fate he deserved at the hands of the executioner.   Henry de Lacy meanwhile was getting considerable support from the Gascons, who seem on the whole to have shown a majority in favour of the English, but he did very little of value, failing in the siege of Dax and being badly defeated by Robert of Artois early in 1297, on occasion of a sortie from Bayonne.   On the 9th of October of the same year, however, a truce, concluded at Vyve-Saint-Bavon and renewed year by year till the final peace was made, ended active hostilities. This truce was largely the result of continuous efforts made by Cardinals sent out from Pope Boniface VIII, and was also no doubt not unwelcome to Edward, whose expedition to Flanders, besides his constant troubles in Wales and Scotland, were enough to give occupation to the most active of Kings, especially when both clergy and nobles were unwilling to help on the war by money contributions. Nevertheless a truce was no certain security, and Edward still had to keep an army in Gascony, mercenaries were hired and strong men were given positions of authority. From 1297, when the truce was first signed, to 1303, the date of the peace which ended the war, Gascony was practically divided between the French and English on the basis of the *status quo*. Bordeaux was still held by the French, as was the greater part of the Agenais, but the English had Blaye and Bourg in the north, as well as Bayonne and most of the southern part of the Duchy. Negotiations were going on for a long time before actual peace was concluded, and the delayed marriage of Margaret and Edward was accomplished in 1299. In 1302 special guardians of the truce were appointed by each party to see that order was kept, and Edward gave Amadeus of Savoy, Henry de Lacy and Otto of Grandison power to treat upon terms with Philip. Finally on 20 May 1303 a treaty was signed in Paris. By this Philip promised to restore all that he had taken in the Duchy, all prisoners and hostages were to be released, and the King of England was to do homage and be in fealty and obedience to the King of France, " purely, simply and without condition." Eventually it was arranged that the young Prince Edward, who was betrothed to Princess Isabella of France, should be the King's proctor to perform this homage (though it seems likely that the ceremony did not actually take place until 1308), and in 1306 his father made over to him the whole Duchy of Aquitaine, " to have and to hold with all liberties, customs, lands, homages, services, rents, etc., as we and our progenitors have held it."

The war was ended, but restoration and reparation were never completely made ; Edward II succeeded to a very troublesome and very ill-secured inheritance, and the definite outbreak of the Hundred Years' War was only a question of time. The war of Edward I's reign was a very direct step

towards the later struggle, and the efforts towards consolida-
tion, so marked a feature of the policy of Philip the Fair, were
certain sooner or later to lead once more to active strife. The
remainder of Edward I's reign, as far as Gascony was concerned,
was spent in the endeavour to repair the damages caused by
the French occupation and the long struggle and to restore the
Duchy he had ruled so successfully to something like order and
contentment. This was no easy task and the expenses must
have been prodigious. Edward had to pay heavily to both
friends and foes. There were arrears of pay to be made up to
those who had fought for him, and they expected also that the
losses they had incurred in the war should be made good ;
compensation had to be made incessantly for horses killed and
for lands ravaged and confiscated by the French. In some
cases Edward had to maintain at his own cost those whose
lands were not yet restored by Philip, despite the terms of the
treaty. Not only arrears of pay were made good, but in some
cases rewards were given to show that loyalty was a good
policy. Offices were bestowed, castles and fortified strongholds
were permitted ; pasture rights, hunting privileges, rights of
high justice were granted, or restored to those who could prove
that they had suffered loss or encroachment ; any misdoings
of his own officials were dealt with severely ; and many of
those who had fought most bitterly against him were pardoned
and allowed to regain their holdings. Townsmen were particularly favoured, and as far as possible the numerous loans which
had been made to meet the expenses of the war were gradually
repaid. The towns themselves had suffered severely, and many
of them had to be largely rebuilt, or at least re-fortified. All
round the region of Bordeaux this was the case, and large sums
had to be provided for the restoration of Bourg, Blaye, Rions,
and many other places. It was a great opportunity for the
Gascons to make something out of past troubles, and petitions
were constantly sent to Edward, who did all that was humanly
possible to meet the demands, to provide compensation and
to investigate through his commissioners alleged cases of loss
or misusage. But this was not all. The country had become
sadly demoralized as a result of the constant fighting, and

private wars continued when the main struggle had ceased. Quarrels of noble with noble, and of townsman with townsman, disregard of justice and disobedience to officials kept busy Edward's Lieutenants and Seneschals, even the loyal Bayonne began to give trouble when peace was once made, and Bordeaux was a good deal out of hand. And thus ended sadly a reign which had begun so successfully, and which had seen Gascony better administered and in a more contented condition than at any other period of the English dominion. Edward's reign, however, had shown that much could be done by a policy of strict justice tempered with conciliatory measures ; that Gascon officials could be employed with advantage in all but the highest positions in the government of the Duchy, and that towns great and small might be controlled as well as privileged when the King could appoint the Mayor or Provost. England and Gascony were becoming far more closely connected than they had been in the past ; not only merchants plied their trade between the two countries, but Gascon soldiers fought in Edward's war in Wales and Scotland ; young nobles came over to England to be trained in methods of administration before taking up official duties at home ; and Englishmen were found settling in Gascony and being given land and houses, as well as offices and guardianship of castles. Edward II might still have made something of his Continental possessions had he had even a fraction of the character or the ability of his father.

CHAPTER IV

THE BEGINNING OF THE HUNDRED YEARS' WAR

EDWARD II was not the man to succeed where his father had failed, and his marriage with Isabella of France did not prevent his royal relatives on the French throne from being just as anxious to regain the south-west of France as they were before. Added to this he was always in trouble over homage. In 1308 he performed it in person to Philip IV, but in 1314 there was a new King, Louis X; and before the new ceremony was performed, Louis' death in 1316 and the accession of Philip V made still another occasion for homage, when Edward declared that affairs in Scotland made it quite impossible for him to cross over to France. At last after long delay, which gave an opportunity to the French King to threaten forfeiture of his vassal's possessions, Edward did succeed in doing homage in person. In 1322, however, a fresh change of sovereigns and the succession of Charles IV brought the whole matter once more to the front. This increased the difficulties over Gascon affairs and never allowed the question of the exact relationship of lord and vassal to be forgotten. Meanwhile the position of affairs in Gascony itself was as embarrassing as ever. The terms of the 1303 Treaty had never been properly carried out, for one excuse or another, and the whole of the country was never really restored to English control. Complaints were constantly being sent to England of the damages done by the French in town and country, and the demands for compensation or for arrears of payments were still very frequent, despite all that Edward I had done before his death. It is evident that what the French King had not achieved by direct conquest he still hoped to do by gradual

70

encroachment. Bayonne sent to Edward to protest against its citizens being summoned to justice at the " court of France " (i.e. the Parliament of Paris), when such justice should only be the result of their own appeal ; nobles claimed that they were under the court of the Seneschal, not the court of the French King ; Bordeaux told the tale of a Frenchman who got into the town as a private individual and then produced a wand of office, which had been hidden between his shirt and his doublet. Edward II, although always anxious for a quiet life, was moved to complain to Philip V that his Seneschals of Périgord and Toulouse acted as though they were sovereigns in the Duchy, and stated that he meant to maintain the rights which were his according to the treaties his ancestors had made. At last this perpetual friction led to the actual outbreak of war in 1324, the immediate occasion being the affair of the bastide of Saint-Sardos. This was built by the Lord of Montpezat, but the French claimed the site and took possession of it ; the English Seneschal came to the aid of Montpezat, and together they attacked the little place and massacred the French garrison. This gave excuse for a fresh sequestration of the whole Duchy. The war which broke out was not of very long duration. Edward, now aroused, talked a great deal about coming, but eventually sent his brother Edmund, Earl of Kent, to command his forces, whilst the French army was under the leadership of Charles of Valois. The English held out for a long time in the strongly fortified town of La Réole, but in the end the town surrendered, and only the strip of land all along the coast remained in the complete possession of its old ruler.

Negotiations began and peace was at last made by the intervention of Queen Isabella (3 May 1325), but not a peace which did much to restore English prestige. Until homage was done French officials were to hold the Duchy, and the English were to retire to Bayonne and the Seneschal to take oath to the King of France, who was also to retain that land in the Duchy which he held at the time.

Following a very frequent precedent, Edward II sent out his young son to perform this homage and invested him with his lands of Gascony and Ponthieu, although he himself claimed to act meanwhile as Governor and Administrator of the Duchy of Aquitaine. The interpretation of the treaty, however, was not apparently what the English King had hoped, and he was furious at the French claim to retain La Réole and the Agenais as conquests of Charles of Valois. The quarrel which ensued once more led to the declaration that the Duchy must be sequestrated, and French troops again marched south to take possession. Preparations for war were begun in England, but little could be done in Edward II's reign, for Isabella had taken advantage of her stay abroad and of the presence of her son at the French court, to plot with Mortimer for her husband's overthrow, and in 1307 the young Edward was King of England as well as Duke of Aquitaine. The events of the reign had been little more than added links in the chain which was to lead to open and prolonged warfare.

One effort of importance was made, however, to cope with the difficulties of Gascon administration. In 1323 the King's Council drew up a series of ordinances in regard to Gascony and its government, which show that the organization as formed by Edward I was to be maintained, and regularized as far as possible. The Seneschal and Constable were to be kept at their old salaries, and together with the Council in Gascony to have the right of advising on the nomination of a Chancellor of the Duchy, and of other officials, Seneschals and Judges, whose salaries were fixed and the places filled. The list shows that whatever the actual facts of the case the English claims to the Agenais, Périgord and Saintonge were still as strong as ever, and that the plan for their administration was to be maintained as before.

The young King began his reign with an apparent desire for peace, but also for retention of the property still left in English hands. His first action was to appoint new officials in Gascony, John Hanstede being put for a time in the place of the old Seneschal Oliver of Ingham, and towns and nobles were summoned to take the usual oath of fealty to his commissioners. His second step was to send over proctors to negotiate peace with the King of France, and terms were agreed upon by which both sides consented to the restoration of lands wrongfully held, and to the pardon of rebels. Some of those, including the old Seneschal Oliver of Ingham, who were sentenced by the French court to the penalty of death for stirring up movements against France, were to be given their lives, but to be banished from the country—a sentence afterwards remitted. At first sight it would appear that the young King of England was going to submit fairly easily to French demands, and to rest content with the strip of country from Saintes to Bayonne, which was all that remained to him after the losses of his father's reign. But Edward III was more ambitious than this, and his character was to display a vigour and energy which he did not inherit from his easy-going father, although he did not show the practical ability of his grandfather, nor did he know so well how to consolidate his possessions by good government and sound organization.

The English possessions in France were indeed in considerable need of attention. They were not only reduced in extent, but many of the nobles were far from reliable in their allegiance, and although the towns, as before, were anxious to maintain the English rule, insidious attempts were being made on the part of the French to shake this loyalty and to stir up distrust. Events at the close of Edward II's reign show very clearly the need for greater energy on the part of the King. The Constable of Bordeaux wrote repeatedly to Hugh the Despenser to implore for speedy help, for better officials, for the repair of fortifications, and for the sending out of ships, arms and provisions. Evidently loyalty was beginning to be seriously shaken, for advice was given that there should be a regular campaign of propaganda throughout the country to make known the evil deeds of the French, and that warm thanks should be sent to those nobles who had served the King faithfully in the past. Edmund, Earl of Kent, had not been a very tactful Lieutenant, it would appear, for he was to be warned to be more affable to all classes of men and to summon more Gascons to the Council. In 1326 two burgesses of Bordeaux wrote that news was being spread throughout the country to the effect that Edward intended to abandon the Duchy and that in consequence Bordeaux was in great distress and many of the inhabitants, both English and Gascon, were preparing to fly. Money had been pledged right and left and there was never sufficient for the ordinary business of the Government.

The young King Edward III set to work at once to repair some of the negligences of the former reign. He wrote in March 1328 to his new Constable and Seneschal to declare that he was determined to recover his rights, and that they must take every means in their power to win over the disobedient nobles and to promise pardon and advancement to any who would make their submission. Already, in the previous year, he had written to thank the Lord of Albret for his services in the past, for it was of the greatest importance to keep this powerful family on his side ; and this letter was followed by others to less well-known nobles and to the leading towns of the Duchy ; trading rights were reconfirmed, and promises of protection to foreign merchants renewed. Meanwhile he did all in his power to win over old opponents, and grants of indemnity and peace were made to such formidable enemies as the Count of Armagnac, the Viscount of Lomagne and Gaston, Count of Foix. Obviously Edward was anxious to conciliate all his subjects, both high and low. His officials were severely reprimanded when any evil deeds were complained of, they were forbidden on any consideration to seize beasts or goods for their own use ; damaged churches and monasteries were restored and trading privileges granted.

But meanwhile Edward was faced by a still weightier problem, which was to colour all his later policy and to affect his attitude towards his Gascon lands.

On 1 February 1328 Charles IV of France died, leaving no male heir, but a widow whose child was shortly to be born. In the interval Philip of Valois, cousin of the late King, was appointed regent, and when the expected child turned out to be a daughter he was placed on the throne as Philip VI. The barons of France declared that no woman could succeed to the throne, and that as a result, neither could her son—thus putting on one side the rights which would otherwise have passed to Edward III. The fact that no woman could succeed had been established by precedent, for in 1316 one had been passed over in favour of Philip V and in 1322 for Charles IV. On that point there was no hesitation ; as for the right which might be handed on through a woman, that was still disputable, and Edward III proclaimed himself the rightful heir.

This is not the place to tell the story of the Hundred Years' War, nor to discuss how far Edward was in earnest when he made the claim, which at the time he was not ready to uphold ; but it is necessary to show Edward's relation to the French King in so far as it influenced the history of his Gascon lands, and to consider to some extent how far he was serious in his desire for the throne, or how far his main object was to establish himself firmly in the south-west. There is no doubt that Gascony played a very large part all through the tortuous history of intrigue, negotiation and war.

Philip VI's accession meant the need for the renewal of Edward's homage for Gascony, and at the end of 1328 the French King sent to summon him to come to France to perform his feudal duty. The summons had to be renewed in the following year, and confiscation was threatened before Edward made up his mind to obey the summons. The peers of France agreed in Council that the revenues of the Duchy should be taken into the King's hand and that disobedience meant forfeiture.

The situation was a perplexing one : if Edward ever meant to dispute Philip's claims the ceremony of homage would seem to put him in the wrong ; but the young King had already much on his hands, and though he is said to have protested privately that his claim was maintained, he did go to France in June 1329 and went through a rather doubtful form of homage at Amiens. Although Froissart is mistaken in saying that he did not place his hands between those of the French King, the English King was not prepared to allow that this was liege homage until he had returned to England to look into his privileges ; and both Kings protested that none of their old rights were renounced. Knighton is doubtless true when he writes that they were " friends only according to the outside of their faces."

The later history and the causes of the Hundred Years' War are too well known to recount in detail. Trade disputes and skirmishes between French and English sailors helped to embitter the already strained relations. The economic situation and the jealousy engendered by the Flemish demand for English rather than French wool, the help given to the Scots in their incessant hostility, the insinuations and the encouragement of Robert of Artois when he took refuge in the court of England—all doubtless were so many aggravations of the enmity which led to the proclamation of open war and to the definite assertion of the English claim to the throne. But with due allowance for the great accumulation of causes, the rivalries in Gascony still remain entitled to the first place. The war might have been more local and less extensive in character but for all the other causes, but war of some sort was inevitable and something more violent and more decisive than the almost incessant bickerings which were going on between the English and French Kings in the south-west. The English territory was more valuable and more desirable than it had been in earlier days, and the whole question was a far bigger one than when Gascony was merely a piece of royal property, a personal rather than a national possession. It is true that the Gascons and the English were none too friendly, that London and Bordeaux were constant rivals, that trade connection could antagonize as well as unite. Nevertheless Edward I's policy had knit the two countries together as they had never been knit before. Gascons lived in England, they served in English armies in Scotland and Wales, they were educated in the methods of English administration. Not only were English officials established in Gascony, not only was Henry de Galeys Mayor at one time of London, at another of Bordeaux, English families settled down in the country for trading purposes, and English nobles were given lands and houses there as reward for services. The connection was close and the value of the connection was obvious, though perhaps still more obvious in Gascony than in England ; for the Gascon towns knew that they could get better markets for their wine in England than in France, and the nobles on the whole preferred their distant overlord to one nearer at hand. But as the country became more prosperous, and as towns and trade increased, so did the French Kings feel more and more anxious to extend their sway over this outlying province ; and from the time of Saint Louis onwards the French Kings pursued the constant policy of consolidating and unifying their dominions. Even had the feudal relationship of the two monarchs been a satisfactory one, sooner or later the union of the country was bound to be fought for, and, as it was, the relationship was about as unsatisfactory as it could well be. On the one hand the English King resented the interference of the French King with the justice administered in the courts of the Duchy : whilst the French King, anxious to assert his authority, found it nevertheless difficult to insist on feudal obligations, which could scarcely be enforced on the sovereign of a neighbouring country. The position was bound in the long run to be an impossible one, and by the fourteenth century both sides were hopelessly involved in a struggle, the rights of which are difficult to disentangle. Edward I had certainly been unfairly treated, and since his time treaties had been made which had never been completely carried out by either side. French officials in the surrounding provinces were always ready to extend their sphere of jurisdiction, and by gradual encroachments much land, which according to treaty terms should have been in English hands, was occupied by the French. The English Kings were not prepared to accept the position of subordinate vassals, and considered that they did not even receive their due rights as vassals, and were not properly treated as peers of France.

Such was the position, and now in the reign of Edward III things came to a head. The King was determined that Gascony should not be given up, and war for its possession was inevitable, whilst its possession on old terms was so unsatisfactory, that some better solution was worth a struggle. Then came the possibility of the French throne. If fighting was to come in any case it was better to fight for the greatest gain, even if it were not very likely to be achieved, and the mere claim to be King of France at once settled the vexed question

of appeals from Gascon courts to those of the superior overlord—Edward could and did insist that all appeals went to
him.   The fact that after a successful war, peace was made by
the grant of extended territories in the south-west to be held in
full sovereignty, and not as a vassal fief, makes it appear probable that the desire for this full sovereignty was the prevailing
factor in Edward's policy, and its satisfaction was sufficient
compensation for abandoning a claim to a throne which he may
have very well realized he could never have held in peace.
During this reign, in any case, Gascon affairs (taking the word
in its widest geographical significance) loom large in the
history of the Hundred Years' War.

After the temporary settlement achieved by Edward's homage in 1329 both Kings began to concentrate their energies on
Gascony, and to intrigue for support in the struggle which
they knew was bound to follow.

Edward not only enjoined on his English subjects the practice in the use of the bow, which might have been to prepare
them for war against the Scotch or Welsh ; he also enjoined
the learning of French by all classes, in order that they might
be of more use in war.   In 1329 he granted safe-conduct to
various Gascon nobles to visit him in England, and in 1330
he sent out commissioners to Gascony " to treat with nobles
and commons in all that concerned the tranquillity of the
Duchy," and he made further grants both of lands and money
to the Lord of Albret, indeed a proposal was even mooted for
marrying Amanieu d'Albret to a daughter of the Earl of Kent.
Meanwhile Philip on his side was allowing French troops to
continue their depredations in the territories of his vassal.
In 1331 he was forced to make some amends.   " His dear
cousin Edward," he proclaimed, had written to him to complain of the damage done to the castle and *bourg* of Saintes by
his dear brother the Count of Alençon, but that his dear
brother had rightly done owing to the great misdeeds
committed by the town against the Frenchmen.   Nevertheless
for peace and concord he agreed to give up the castle and
bourg and to pay heavy compensation.   Saintes was not, however, the only place to complain of ill-treatment, and Agen and

other towns actually laid their grievances before the Pope, citing various ill-deeds of French officials and claiming that the ministers of the King of France had no right to exercise justice over them nor to force them to come to courts of justice other than those of the King of England.   Besides these secret encroachments the responsibility for which could be made to rest on the officials themselves, Philip tried to win over the southern lords.   Gifts were made to the important Count of Armagnac, proceedings against Gaston of Foix for a supposed murder were stopped, and money payment was made to his brother Roger Bernard of Castelbon.   Meanwhile open nego- tiations, ostensibly for peace, were going on between proctors of the two Kings ;   restoration of territory and remedy of griev- ances were promised by both sides, and Edward even went over in person in 1331 to obtain some concessions.   But these measures were merely a postponement of the struggle, whilst underneath preparations were continuing ;   and it was as early as 1330 that Edward wrote to his officials in Gascony that he was determined to defend his rights against the King of France, and urged them to prepare their defences, and to encourage the support of the native nobles, since he believed the French King might send an army that winter into the Duchy.   It was not, however, until 1337 that the first actual campaign was fought in Gascony.

The immediate cause of this outbreak may be found in the events of 1336 ;   but these events were merely the final spark set to a train already long laid.   In 1336 a dispute which had arisen between Edward and one of his subjects, the Lord of Navailles, was brought for judgment before the Parliament of Paris.   Edward was said to have ravaged the lands of Navailles and was, in consequence, commanded by the Parliament to compensate his vassal by a large sum of money, and pending the payment of this debt French troops were sent to seize the Castle of Puymirol and to hold it in pledge.   The resistance made by the townsmen to this occupation gave the French King the excuse for sending troops to put down opposition. In July 1337 two French Constables were sent and took some small places in the Agenais, and the seizure of the whole of

Guienne was decreed. Edward was not taken unawares. He had already in England begun active preparations for war, ships of Bayonne were to be equipped against the enemy ; requests for help were sent also to Bordeaux, Dax and Saint-Sever, and to various individuals. Bernard d'Albret and Oliver of Ingham were appointed his Lieutenants in Gascony, Walter Manny and Bartholomew Burghersh Admirals of the fleet. In August 1337 Edward issued a proclamation reciting his many offers to keep the peace, his visits to the French King in person, and the futility of his efforts. He pointed out that according to the words of the ceremony of homage he should as Duke of Aquitaine be a peer of France, but that never was he given the due investiture, his seat in the French Council, nor his command in war. Many lands promised him had never been delivered and those handed over had been ravaged and despoiled. In October of the same year he finally adopted the title of King of France and sent out his letters of defiance to Philip of Valois. The war had definitely begun.

The events of the war in Gascony from its outbreak in 1337 to the truce made in 1341 are not very striking. Bernard d'Albret as Lieutenant kept faithful to the English despite repeated efforts on Philip's part to win him over and to gain him for the French army. Robert of Artois also fought for a time in command of English troops. Several places fell to the French arms. Blaye was taken by a trick ; the French in disguise pretended to bring provisions into the city and then letting their laden wagon stick in the gateway enabled their ambushed fellows to rush into the town. Penne and Tartas both fell to those Gascon nobles, who had adopted the side of Philip when the strong town of La Réole was captured after a fine defence. Affairs seemed to be going well for the French, and many of the inconstant nobles were prepared to go over to the winning side. Those who still remained faithful to Edward seem to have done little but enclose themselves in their own fortresses and were happy if they were able to keep their own lands intact. But Philip's allies were more interested in their private quarrels than in the dispute between French and English, and rivalry between Foix and Armagnac did not encourage harmonious working together on the same side.

The next outbreak of war was of a more serious character, and added greatly to the strength of the English position. The Duke of Normandy, eldest son of Philip VI, was sent in person to command the French army, and his successes round Bordeaux were beginning to threaten the English possessions in their strongest point. In 1344 a deputation of Gascons came to England to demand more help from their Duke, and declared that " his good friends and his good city of Bordeaux were badly comforted and supported." The result of this appeal was the sending out of a stronger English force under the King's cousin Henry of Lancaster, Earl of Derby, who was given the fullest powers to act as the King's representative in the Duchy, to make treaties and alliances, and to conduct the campaign to the best of his powers. An English Judge was also appointed in Gascony with power delegated to him from Edward to hear all appeals from Gascony directed to the " King of France." Edward did not wish his subjects to feel that their judicial rights were more difficult to obtain from a court of appeal in England, than from looking to Paris as the supreme arbiter of their quarrels.

The Earl of Derby conducted two campaigns with great success, not only judged by the standard of the time, which looked upon the capture of towns and booty as the main object of a really active leader, but because he showed true military ability and made the English power far more real and substantial than it had been before his coming. Derby's appointment as Lieutenant of the King was made in April 1345, but it was July before he was able to set sail for the scene of his labours, owing to contrary winds which delayed him after ships and men had been collected. He landed eventually at Bayonne, a town which had shown itself especially loyal all through these troublous times, and thence marched to Bordeaux, where he was received with joyful processions and lodged with all his men within the city. His first military act was the taking of Bergerac, a town of great importance owing to its position on the Dordogne, and where the French, commanded by the Count de L'Isle, were strongly established.   The attack was made by water, and if Froissart is to be trusted the garrison was so much alarmed by the harm done to their fortifications that they slipped away by night to La Réole, leaving the inhabitants to surrender at will, which they promptly did, swearing allegiance to the English King.   " Qui merci prie, merci doit avoir," said the Count, " qui fut moult noble et gentil de cœur," and the town suffered no injury at his hands (15 Aug.–2 Sept. 1345).   The English followed up this success by further captures in Périgord, which had been almost entirely lost to the English.   The campaign ended with a victory at Auberoche, which, after having accepted the English rule, was besieged by the Count de L'Isle during the absence of Derby.   The inhabitants, again according to Froissart, sent out a messenger to endeavour to get through to the English army—to seek for aid—but the unlucky youth was captured by the French and hurled back into the town by a catapult.   Despite this disaster Derby's forces came in time to save the town (21 Oct.).   From 13 November to 26 January 1346 Derby was at La Réole. Froissart (whose general account of these campaigns is, however, singularly incorrect) gives an amusing account of the recapture of this town.   After a siege of some weeks, the English are said to have built great wooden belfries on wheels, covered with boiled leather to resist the enemies' missiles, and with various storeys each with 100 archers, besides other soldiers armed with all sorts of weapons to break down the walls. These great moving forts, placed up against the walls of the town, enabled the archers to shoot right over the fortifications, and the terrified inhabitants hastened to submit, whilst the French captain, Agos des Baux, took refuge in the castle.   The undermining of the castle, however, made this retreat insecure, so that Agos wished for other quarters. According to Froissart he put his head out of a window and demanded to speak to the leader ; then courteously saluting Derby and Sir Walter Manny he made this extraordinary speech :

" It is true that the French King put me here to guard and defend this fortress, and I have done that to the best of my power ; but we cannot always live in the same place, and I and my companions would prefer to live somewhere else if you will permit!"

However the surrender was actually accomplished, Derby did make the strong town of La Réole his head-quarters for a time, and did not, as Froissart would have us believe, constantly return to Bordeaux to be fêted and made much of by the delighted inhabitants.

Derby's campaign of 1346 was full of victories and the capture of important fortresses (again Froissart's account has to be read with very great circumspection). Little by little he reconquered the Agenais for England ; Monclar, Miramont, Villeréal, Monpazier and Villefranche one by one fell into his hands. The warlike Bishop of Beauvais, the Duke of Bourbon and the Duke of Normandy all came south in hopes of checking the English advance. From April to August, Walter Manny and the Earl of Pembroke were besieged in Aiguillon, and Edward III's expedition in 1346, which resulted in the victory of Creçy, was primarily intended, so it is said, to come to the south and to help in the relief of Aiguillon. However that may be, the Duke of Normandy was recalled by his father to support him in the north, and Derby himself caused the siege to be raised on 20 August. Walter Manny, wild to get to the King and share in the excitement of the northern campaign, was given a safe-conduct to pass through France, but, despite it, was captured at Saint-Jean d'Angely. This caused Derby to hasten northwards ; he captured Saint-Jean (29 Sept.), released the prisoners, and taking many places in Saintonge and Poitou finally captured Poitiers, where it is said that he was angry with his followers for their wanton destruction of houses and churches. Early in 1347 the Earl was back in England, and a truce that year gave a momentary relief to the warring country. Almost the whole of Poitou, Saintonge and Périgord was again in English possession. The town of Bergerac with all its tolls and dues was bestowed as a reward on its conqueror, and letters of thanks were sent out to the Gascon communes which were then loyal to the English—Bordeaux, Bayonne and Dax, which had never been lost, La Réole, Libourne, Saint-Émilion, and others which had been regained by Derby.

Possessions in Libourne were given to the adventurous Walter Manny, who was to continue his activities in the later Gascon campaigns.

In 1350 the death of Philip VI put the Duke of Normandy on the throne as King John, and once more the truce was renewed between England and France.

The new King was a fighter and without doubt eager to renew the struggle and to repair the crushing disasters of Creçy and Calais. He began to intrigue with the southern nobles and made very special efforts to bind to his cause Gaston Phébus—then ruler of Béarn-Foix (he had succeeded Gaston II in 1343)—and the young Charles of Navarre, who might make themselves very unpleasant neighbours to English Gascony. Both of them, together with Bertrand, Count de L'Isle-Jourdain, were made Lieutenants of the King in Languedoc. Charles of Navarre gave the greatest trouble. He had claims himself to the French throne, and he was constantly negotiating with the English and bargaining to come to terms. King John sacrificed all he could to keep his allegiance. In 1351 he married him to his own little daughter—a child of eight ; he made peace with him in 1354, despite his boasted share in the murder of the French Constable Charles d'Espagne ; and in 1355 he concluded the Treaty of Valognes with him to win him back from an alliance actually concluded with the Duke of Lancaster. Even during the normal time of truce, the distracted Duchy had little rest, for it was full of marauders and disbanded soldiers, who wasted the country irrespective of party or of peace ; and many places suffered as severely from their ravages as they did from the passage of hostile armies. Froissart writes of the *routiers* :

" Those who were in Gascony, Poitou and Saintonge, as well French and English, never kept the truce or respite, and they often had fine adventures ; they became so rich that some of them were worth 60,000 crowns."

In 1355, however, war began again in real earnest : the war of ravages and sieges, which are a blot on the fair fame of the Black Prince, who was responsible for them, and which do little credit to his real military capacity. A French historian writes that this was one of the saddest episodes in the war, the English forces were so small and the damage done so great ; the enterprise was absurd in itself and was successful chiefly owing to the stupidity of the French, whose numbers were far superior to those of the English. It is only fair, however, to remember that the expedition may have been intended to divert attention from the north, and to divide the French King's forces, that such warfare was looked upon as both legitimate and honourable, and the chief chronicler of the time has nothing but praise for the leading actors in the drama. John Wingfield, in his letter to the Bishop of Winchester after the events of 1355, writes with pride : " Never was such loss nor destruction of France since this war began."

The sending of the Black Prince was partly the result of a deputation of Gascon nobles, who came to England in 1354 to complain of danger threatened from John of Armagnac, whom King John had made his Lieutenant in Languedoc. " Sire," quoth their leader to the King, " for God's sake you know well that thus it is, that in Gascony the noble and valiant knights cherish you so greatly that they suffer great pain for your war and to gain you honour, and yet they have no leader of your blood. Therefore if you were so advised as to send one of your sons they would be the bolder." For the time being there was a truce with France, but it expired in April 1355, and in July the Black Prince was appointed his father's Lieutenant and set sail from Southampton on the 8th or 9th of September. On the 25th of the same month he was at Bordeaux, and before the assembled nobles and burgesses in the Cathedral of Saint-André he read to them the letters patent of the King granting him office and powers, and took the oath to be good and loyal seigneur and to defend their rights with all his might. Quite a number of Gascon nobles were ready then to welcome the Prince, and on 5 October, followed by a mixed force of English and Gascons, he left Bordeaux, and for eight weeks marched through the south " grieving and destroying the country." The Prince himself, when he was back in Bordeaux for Christmas, wrote a letter describing the campaign,

and details of it can be fully worked out.   His aim at first was
to damage the lands of the Count of Armagnac as severely as
possible, and then to advance into Languedoc and through the
county of Toulouse, where resistance might have been expected
from Armagnac himself, who was stationed there, but Froissart tells us that Toulouse revolted against him, and he was
obliged to escape secretly and in haste, which may account for
his extraordinary inactivity.   Wherever the Prince's army
marched towns were burnt and destroyed, some prisoners were
taken and much booty.   The *bourg* of Carcassonne, "greater,
stronger and fairer than York," was captured, but the *cité*
with its triple fortifications was impregnable.   Narbonne,
which Wingfield described as "a city little smaller than London," was taken by storm.   Here the Prince seems to have
turned and marched back rather farther north with only a
few skirmishes, through Limoux, Carbonne, Castel-jaloux and
Meilhan, and came to rest at La Réole on the 2nd of December.
During the winter the Black Prince was for the greater part
of the time at Bordeaux, where he found "gaiety, noblesse,
courtesy, goodness and largesse"; his troops were encamped
at no great distance.   Warwick took up his quarters at La
Réole, Salisbury at Sainte-Foy, and Suffolk at Saint-Émilion ;
Chandos and Audeley, together with the constant friend of the
English the Captal de Buch, apparently considered a winter
rest unnecessary, and spent their time in various enterprises
and raids.   Wingfield writes that the two English adventurers
captured and took up their quarters in Castelsagrat, "where
they have victuals all but fresh fish and greens, so that you
need not bother about your good folk."

   The early months of 1356 seem to have been partly spent
by the Prince in receiving the submission of still more Gascon
lords, and he did not absolutely take the field till August.   His
first march was through Périgord.   Leaving La Réole on
4 August he reached Bergerac the same day, entered Périgueux on the 7th, and then on through Brantôme into the
Limousin and Berry, burning and pillaging *en route*.   The
citadel of Romorantin held out for some days against him, but
was finally taken, together with its two commanders Bouci-

quaut and Amaury de Craon.   He then followed the Cher and reaching the Loire, which he was unable to cross, remained facing Tours for some days and then crossing the Cher and the Indre reached Monbazon on 11 September.   Here the Prince heard news of the real French army, for King John had vowed vengeance for the damage that had been done, had collected a great force at Chartres, and was now marching at full speed against the foe.   The tidings, says the Herald of Sir John Chandos, seemed to the Prince " good and fair." Certainly he made no attempt to escape a battle, but hearing that the French were at Chauvigny he pursued them there, and then set out across the country for Poitiers, whither King John was said to have directed his course on leaving Chauvigny. At last, in the neighbourhood of Poitiers, the two armies came in sight of one another, so close were they that " they watered their horses at the same river " (the Miausson, a stream running near the battlefield).

Before the battle great efforts were made for peace by Cardinal Talleyrand de Périgord, whose influence had already been vainly exerted on earlier occasions.   King John consented that negotiations should be attempted, although he was determined to stand out for his due rights : " Never will we make peace," he is reputed to have said, " unless we get into our keeping the castles and all the land that he has wasted and ravaged, wrongfully and sinfully, since he came from England, and are also quit of the quarrel for which the war is renewed."   The Prince was equally determined, although he consented to negotiations between the two parties, but peace he could not make, he said, without the consent of the King his father.   Hostilities were postponed till Monday, 19 September, but the delegates sent out from the rival parties could come to no agreement, and were probably not very serious in their endeavours.   The Cardinal was blamed by both English and French for causing unnecessary delay, and he rode in tears from the French camp.

The accounts of the battle vary to some extent in the different chronicles, but the main features of it stand out with considerable clearness.   The French far outnumbered the

English and had little doubt of success; it was to be war to the knife, for no quarter was to be given, and only the Prince's life to be spared should he be captured. King John had all his sons in the army. Louis, Count of Anjou, and John, Count of Poitiers, were with their eldest brother the Duke of Normandy in the first "battle" just behind the two Marshals and their forces; the little Philip fought all the day gallantly by his father's side and was captured with him when the day was lost. King John led the last battle whilst in the centre his brother the Duke of Orleans took command. The Prince marshalled his little force of English and Gascons with great care and undoubtedly some anxiety. The Earl of Warwick and the Lord of Pommiers commanded the vanguard; the Earl of Salisbury was placed in the rear by a gap where a road bordered by thick hedges led up to his position. The Prince stationed himself on a small hill covered with vines and brambles and guarded his flank with pillage wagons. The Captal de Buch eventually led an attack on the flank of the French army, which did much to assist in the ultimate victory. Indeed the great deeds of the Gascons and their share in the triumph are attested by all.

The opening of the battle showed the rivalry and lack of discipline which worked such havoc in the French feudal array. The two Marshals, Clermont and Audrehem, began the day with a quarrel. The Prince's movement to his new position on the hill made the French think for a moment that he planned a retreat, and Audrehem, in command of his advance-guard, shouted that they must attack at once lest the enemy should escape them. Clermont, with a corresponding advance-guard, disagreed and said that they need not hurry. "Your delay will make us lose them at this time," quoth Audrehem. Clermont did not brook a suggestion of slackness. "You will not be so bold," he cried angrily to his fellow-marshal, "as to acquit yourself in such wise that you come far enough for the point of your lance to reach the rump of my horse." Both dashed forward, followed by their horse soldiers, and rushed without order or consideration down the narrow lane which Salisbury was facing, at what was at first supposed to be the rear. Crowded up between the two hedges the dense throng of horses and men formed an easy target for the English bowmen, and were shot down and thrown into hopeless confusion. Meanwhile Warwick and the Captal de Buch had discomfited the force under the King's sons, all three of whom fled from the field. The main body of the army under King John himself joined battle with those of the Black Prince. The Herald of Sir John Chandos—a very trustworthy authority on the whole of this episode—relates the Prince's prayer before leading his men to the attack : " Mighty Father," he cried, " right so as I believe that Thou art King of kings and didst willingly endure the death on the cross for all of us, to redeem us out of hell, Father, who art true God,·true man, be pleased, by Thy most holy name, to guard me and my people from harm, even as Thou knowest, true God of heaven, that I have good right " ; and then : " Forward, forward, banner ! Let each one take heed to his honour." The end of the battle is well known. There was hard fighting, and brave deeds of arms were done on both sides, but the issue was not really doubtful. The French had made all the mistakes possible. They had attacked on horseback by an impossible route ; now the main bulk of the army had dismounted and was ridden down by the cavalry of the enemy. There is no doubt that warriors of the day actually enjoyed a hard-fought struggle. Froissart writes of the Prince that he was " comme un lion fel et cruel et que ce jour avoit très grand plaisance à combattre ses ennemis." His friend Sir John Chandos at last begged him to desist, for the day was his and because, the chronicler quaintly adds, he was so very much overheated ! King John was captured, surrendering at last to Denis de Morbesque, although many claimed to have had the honour of capturing him, and there was a long trial later over the claims of Bernard de Troy. All are agreed as to the courtesy with which the conqueror treated his fallen foe ; but indeed both men vied with each other in chivalrous politeness. " Fair, sweet cousin," so King John is reported to have addressed the Prince, " by the faith I owe you, you have to-day more honour than ever had any Prince on one day." " Sweet sir," was the reply, " it is God's doing and not ours, and we are bound to give thanks to Him therefor, and beseech Him earnestly that He would grant us His glory and pardon us the victory." Together the two departed the next day for Bordeaux, where the winter was spent, with feastings and ceremonies of rejoicing, but also in the business of drawing up a truce, in which the Papal Cardinals were able to play a more satisfactory part than they had before. On 20 May 1357 a truce was concluded at Bordeaux which was to last till Easter of the following year, after which time it was again renewed till Easter 1359. The truce was to be observed throughout the whole Duchy of Guienne and Languedoc, which included Gascony, Limousin, Quercy, Périgord, Agenais, Poitou, Saintonge, Angoumois ; and also in Berry, Burgundy, Normandy, Flanders, Artois, and Picardy. The allies on both sides were brought in to the agreement, and guardians of the truce were appointed in all the districts involved.

The Prince and his captive had already left the country, for on 24 May they reached London, and were received with all the rejoicing and all the courtesy which the men of that time could invent.

The English King, despite the truce, did not intend to abandon his enterprise. The King of Navarre, so long an uncertain ally of the French King, was won over to the English in 1358, and agreed with Edward III to share with him the Kingdom of France, the lion's share of which was to go to England. In 1359 a secret treaty was agreed upon in London between the captive King of France and his conqueror. In this treaty Edward no longer called himself King of France, but stipulated for an enormous portion of that country : not only the whole of the south-west, much as it had been held by Henry II, but also Touraine, Maine, Anjou, Normandy, Ponthieu, and Calais, with the neighbouring country. Those lands formerly possessed by Kings of England were to be held as they had held them ; those lands acquired now from King John to be possessed as freely and completely as he had possessed them on the day that Poitiers was fought. Detailed arrangements were made about the King's ransom, about the castles to be delivered in pledge, about the hostages to be sent to London, and many other matters. This treaty was, however, rejected by the Regent Charles of France, and its rejection resulted in a new English expedition into France at the close of 1359, led by the King and his eldest son. Papal Legates, however, again took up the cause of peace, and in 1360 from 1st to 7th of May a conference was held at Brétigny, five miles distant from Chartres, followed by a truce signed on the 8th by the Regent and the Black Prince, empowered to do so by their royal fathers. On 14 June the agreement was confirmed in London by King Edward and King John, and finally the Treaty, known commonly as the Treaty of Brétigny, was formally drawn up and signed by both Kings at Calais on 24 October 1360.

The Treaty of Calais differs but slightly from the Treaty of Brétigny ; but some very important promises were made on 24 October, which are worth consideration, for on the failure to carry out these promises rests the pretext for the renewal of hostilities in 1369. Both Kings agreed to accomplish the cession of territories which they had promised before St. John the Baptist's Day, or at latest before All Saints Day 1361, and that being accomplished, to send their letters of formal renunciation to Bruges by St. Andrew's Day of that year. This exchange of letters of renunciation was to complete the formal acceptance of the Treaty terms. The general tenor of this Treaty is well known. Edward was to abandon his claim to the throne of France in return for certain territories to be his in full sovereignty. The following are those territories in the south-west, which were now to be added to what he already held in Gascony, and to constitute the Duchy of Aquitaine or Guienne :

Poitiers and all the county of Poitou with Thouars and
    Belleville, Saintes and the old county of Saintonge,
Agen and the Agenais,
Périgueux and Périgord,
Limoges and the Limousin,
Cahors and Quercy,
Tarbes and the county of Bigorre,
The county of Gaure (in Armagnac, between Auch and
    Lectoure),

Angoulême and the Angoumois,
Rodez and Rouergue.

Should any lords, such as the Counts of Foix, Armagnac, L'Isle, Périgord, or the Viscounts of Limoges, hold lands within the aforesaid places, they must do homage and due service for the same to the King of England.

The formation of this great principality opens a new chapter in the history of Gascony. The next few years are occupied with the problem of how to obtain it, how to govern it, and how to keep it.

CHAPTER V

THE PRINCIPALITY OF AQUITAINE

WHATEVER may be thought of King John's action in agreeing to the cession of so large a part of France to Edward of England, he seems to have come to terms in all good faith, and as far as he was concerned to have been prepared to fulfil his promises. He appointed commissioners to hand over to the English those places which had been added to their possessions, and some of his letters still exist requesting peaceful submission to the new lord. Neither Edward III nor his eldest son went at first in person, but Sir John Chandos, already well known in Gascony, and the best friend and adviser the Black Prince had, was sent over with full powers to receive the ceded territories, and given the title of Constable of Aquitaine, a separate and more important office than that of Constable of Bordeaux. Under him as Seneschal was first Richard Stafford, and later John Chevereston. Chandos seems to have acted with great circumspection, and the English rule began with some prospect of success, although his task was far from an easy one.

The country had been wasted by the ravages of military companies, as well as by the widespread attacks of the Black Death, and some nobles and towns were prepared to accept a new ruler hopefully with the prospect of peace in view. This was not, however, universal, and some of the places hesitated to make their submission and argued that the final sovereignty must still rest with the King of France, to whom they always wished to have the right of appeal. The province of Rouergue was one of the most reluctant to " become English." Rodez held a council and agreed that it was essential

93

to be able to appeal to France ; the consuls of Cahors wept and lamented that they were abandoned to a stranger ; other towns in Quercy closed their gates and refused to admit the English King's delegate.   But there was no support for this resistance, and one by one the towns had to submit and the English arms were painted on their gates.   Amanieu de Fossat was made Seneschal of Rouergue, doubtless with the idea that he would be more popular than an English official.   La Rochelle was another unwilling victim, and seven or eight months passed before it was put into the hands of its new governor.   But Chandos governed well.   He appointed Gascons to offices when he could, and he did much to secure the country from the ravages of the Great Companies.   There is an interesting record of the delivery of the county of Bigorre to Adam of Houghton, who acted as the King's representative at Tarbes.   First he had to swear to observe the privileges and liberties of the country, an oath which was taken on the cross in the name of the King of England.   Then the officials of Tarbes, and various barons and knights, swore to be faithful to Edward, Seigneur of Guienne ; and they were followed on subsequent days by clergy, burgesses and others, who took oath to render the same duties to the King of England as they had done to the King of France. A similar ceremony took place in various other towns, and when the Castle of Lourdes was handed over to Adam, the bolt of the door was placed in his hands as a sign of possession. At Millau (Rouergue) the ceremony of submission was still more elaborate.   The consuls held a conference with Chandos through the closed bars of the gate ; then the keys were handed out and, after the unlocking of the gates, ceremoniously returned to them ; when he had made his entry the Constable of Aquitaine was given presents of hens and pigs and calves from the rural town.

The rule of Chandos was only a short one.   On 19 July 1362 the King gave the whole of Aquitaine and Gascony as a Principality into the hands of his son Edward.   The grant runs as follows : " You shall be true Prince by honour, title and appellation as long as you live ; and we give, grant, and in our own person transfer to you cities, castles, towns, places, lands

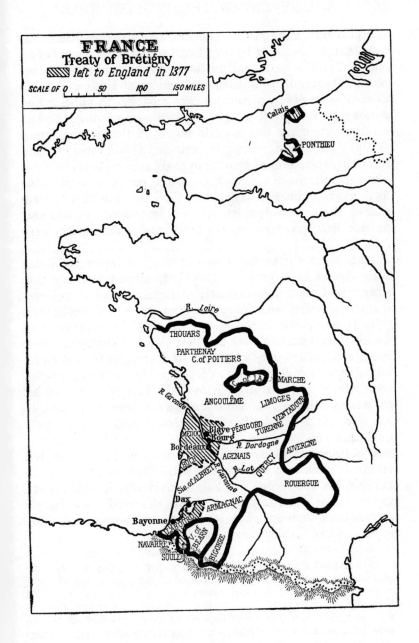

FRANCE
Treaty of Brétigny
left to England in 1377

SCALE OF 0   50   100   150 MILES

Calais
PONTHIEU

R. Loire
THOUARS
PARTHENAY
C.of POITIERS
C. of LA MARCHE
R. Gironde
ANGOULÊME   LIMOGES
VENTADOUR
Blaye PÉRIGORD
MEDOC   Bourg   TURENNE
R. Dordogne
Bordeaux   AUVERGNE
AGENAIS
R. Lot   QUERCY
Sie.of ALBRET R. Garonne   ROUERGUE
Dax
Bayonne   ARMAGNAC
NAVARRE   V. of BÉARN
SOULE   BIGORRE

95

and provinces aforesaid." This rich territory the Prince was to hold from his father by liege homage and the payment of an ounce of gold a year; but his own powers were almost complete. He was to be able to give and grant lands in domain as well as in fief; to coin his own money; to appoint and remove officials of all kinds; to grant new privileges and to confirm old rights, and to do in fact " all that a true Prince should." The King, however, retained the sovereignty and the right, therefore, of hearing appeals. Even later, in 1368, when the Prince was himself given the power of holding the final court of appeal in Aquitaine, the King is careful to state that his rights are only suspended, not renounced, and he seems to have been prepared to hear any complaints from his son's own officials.

Thus began the period when Gascony, or rather Aquitaine as it should more properly be called, existed as a separate state, ruled more independently of England than it had ever been before, and with, practically for the first time, its own ruler permanently on the spot. Many of the advantages of the English dominion were now lost as far as the nobles were concerned. They may for a time have enjoyed the splendour and glory of a court in their midst; but there is no doubt that the absence of their English overlord had been one of his charms in the past, and that the Black Prince soon began to lose some of the popularity which he had earned by his knightly qualities.

The Prince made a romantic marriage with Joan, the fair maid of Kent, and together with his Princess came over to take up his new duties more light-heartedly, it would seem, than such an important responsibility deserved. The Herald of Sir John Chandos gives no bad description of his period of rule before misfortunes began.

" He reigned seven years in Gascony, in joy, in peace and in pleasantness, for all the princes and barons of all the country round about came to do him homage; for a good lord, loyal and sage, they held him with one accord, and rightly if I dare say, for since the birth of God such fair state was never kept as his, nor more honourable, for ever he had at his table more than fourscore knights and full four times as many squires.   There were held jousts and feasts in Angoulême and Bordeaux ;   there abode all nobleness, all joy and jollity, largesse, gentleness, and honour, and all his subjects and all his men loved him right dearly, for he dealt liberally with them."

The court of the Black Prince was certainly a scene of great magnificence and great costliness, of chivalrous courtesy and knightly pleasures.   The revenues of the country could hardly have lasted out, even without the disastrous expense of the Spanish campaign later undertaken by the Prince ; but it is not fair to consider that nothing was done for the country during this period, and that feasting, merry-making and fighting were the sole business of the ruler of Aquitaine.   A good deal was accomplished for the government of the country, attempts were made to maintain justice and order ; and the Prince must have had considerable occupation in the appointment and supervision of his large bodies of officials, and in trying to keep on good terms with his new subjects.   Though not always successful, he was on the whole fair and just ; but he had nothing of his grandfather's good sense and political foresight.

The Prince's difficulties must not be underrated.   Some of his extravagance may have been necessary for the preservation of friendship ; some of the feastings and joustings at his court were obviously an attraction to the nobles, who were ready to resent a court at all.   And he had to make both ends meet from his own resources ; Edward III had given him Gascony and did not wish to spend more money on it, and the country had been more impoverished by the long war than he fully understood.   He was still to some extent in subjection to his father, and instances of interference were not unknown and were more galling than ever before.   The country and the towns needed peace, but the lords on the whole found peace irksome and craved the excitement of war.   Altogether the possession of the Principality of Aquitaine was not a wholly unmixed pleasure.

The description of the government will be given in a separate chapter.   The main difference between Prince Edward's government and that of previous rulers was due to the establishment of the court, the increase of court officials—mostly, however, of military character—and the gradual centralization of authority in Gascony itself.   The Seneschal and Constable still continued, brought more closely into touch with their sovereign, and to that extent diminished in power and importance. Far more money was needed, and besides the usual rents, dues and feudal revenue of all sorts, more definite taxation was imposed than before ; above all, changes were effected in judicial courts.   At first appeal was still made against the decisions of the Prince's tribunals to King Edward and the English Parliament ; but in 1365 the King handed over the right of final jurisdiction to his son, in order to save the Gascons, so he said, from the long journey to England—probably in hopes that a court of justice near at hand would obviate the danger of the discontented still trying to bring their appeal before the King of France and the Parliament of Paris.   This led in 1370 to the establishment of a special *Cour Supérieure* to be the final court of appeal for the Duchy.   The centralization of government might have been less unpopular had the Gascons had more part in it, but the Black Prince was inclined to give all offices to his own friends and followers and to employ Gascons, if at all, in inferior positions.   This and his heavy demands for money were the two greatest mistakes made by the Prince, although he did make efforts at good government and for a time things seemed to be going well.

The Prince's first work when he reached his Principality in 1363 was to travel through the country to receive the formal homage of his new subjects.   Each lord knelt before him without belt or cap, took the oath of fealty and liege homage for all his lands and goods, and kissing the book and the cross promised to do all that a liege vassal should for his true lord. To this the Prince responded by kissing his vassal on the mouth and receiving his homage " saving the rights of our lord the King."   On 9 July 1363 the long ceremony began in the Cathedral of Saint-André of Bordeaux, and the important Lord of Albret, Arnaud Amanieu, headed the procession : he was followed by nineteen other great barons, twenty knights and eighteen esquires, including one burgess, Pierre Caillau, who

owed the service of one knight to the King's army.   Afterwards the Mayor and jurats of Bordeaux took the oath of
fealty, and representatives were sent to do the same for the
chief towns of the neighbourhood, Saint-Macaire, Bazas, La
Réole, Langon, Saint-Émilion, Bourg, Blaye, Agen, and many
others.   Bordeaux was the chief centre, and the ceremony continued day after day till the end of the month ; on 4 August
the Prince went on to Bergerac, where a similar ceremony took
place.   On 10 August and the following days he was at
Périgueux, whither came the nobles of Quercy and Rouergue
as well as those of Périgord : on the 18th he was at Angoulême,
on the 22nd at Cognac, the 24th at Saintes, on the 26th at
Saint-Jean d'Angely, and on the 27th at La Rochelle.   The
work was still going on in September.   The Prince seems to
have taken particular trouble to go to different places in Poitou, even though very few vassals appeared at each—here
doubtless his possession was newer and more precarious ; he
was for a long while at Poitiers, from 13 September till the end
of the year, with occasional intervals, and from day to day a
few homages were done to him, a good many from noble
ladies holding in their own right.   In January 1364 the Prince
went to Agen, and here on the 12th came the very important
noble, formerly an adherent of France, Gaston Phébus, Count
of Foix and Viscount of Béarn to do homage for what he held
in Aquitaine.   Great care was taken to make clear that Béarn
was in no way included in this homage, which was due only for
Marsan and Gabardan.   Gaston Phébus was a great sportsman,
and earlier he had written to beg the Prince to be sure that
Chandos' dogs were on view, as he much desired to see them.
From Agen once more the Prince returned to Poitiers and
Angoulême.   Many of these submissions were unwilling and
meant but little : as Fillongley, to whom we owe the full
account of them, says : an oath is of little value " quant al
fine home dit alas ! "
Even quite steady friends might be tempted away in these
troublous times, and Froissart tells us that the Capital de Buch,
being given lands in France, actually took an oath of allegiance
to the French King ; when he returned to Gascony, however,

he was very soon shown the error of his ways, and blushing he declared that he was not very closely allied to France and that he would give up the gifts and renounce his homage. All would not have been so scrupulous.

One very unexpected complication arose from the establishment of the Prince's court at Bordeaux and Angoulême, the two centres which he most frequented ; the Gascon wine merchants found that they could get a good price for their wares at home, and were far less eager to ship their barrels over the seas. Efforts were made to encourage the trade with England, and when the exportation of most goods was being forbidden, merchants of Bordeaux and Bayonne were urged to buy herrings, peas, beans and corn of various sorts in return for wine. Some demands were doubtless increased by the greater number of English in Gascony, and there were frequent licences to the merchants of English towns, Hull, Dartmouth, Bristol, etc., to carry out cloth of various kinds and colours, and also to Cornish ports to send dried fish. In every case they were urged to bring back wine in exchange. The question of trade, however, was rather a difficulty at home than abroad, and the Gascon towns must have gained something from the increased demand for their goods. Bordeaux was proud of her position, and was loyal later to the Prince's little son born within her walls, Richard of Bordeaux.

The question of new coinage and of taxation to meet expenses was considered as early as 1366, but the Prince did not act on his own authority alone : money was voted to him by the three estates of Aquitaine meeting that year. His real trouble, however, did not begin until after his disastrous expedition to Spain in 1367 to replace Pedro the Cruel on the throne of Castille, from which he had been driven by his illegitimate brother Henry of Trastamare. The Prince's intervention was chivalrous, but mistaken ; on the other hand, however, his Gascon vassals were far more likely to keep loyal to him and on good terms with one another, with war to keep them occupied than idling at home after the first excitements of the new court were over. That argument may, however, have had little weight with the Prince, who was always ready himself to

53827

go on adventures, and was clearly won over by the plausible tale of Pedro, and his feeling in favour of a legitimate ruler—especially as against a bastard. The whole story of this Spanish campaign is well told by the Herald of Sir John Chandos, who was himself probably a member of the expedition, but for Gascon history the results are more important than the actual events, which need only be told very briefly for sake of completeness, and because their effects were so far reaching. Pedro wrote asking for the Prince's help and then came himself with his daughters to Bayonne, where he was met, not only by the Black Prince, but also by Charles of Navarre, who was won over by promise of important lands to break the alliance already made with Henry of Trastamare. Here the agreement to help was given and backed up by Pedro's formal promise to pay a large sum of money to the Prince, as well as to remunerate his followers (23 September 1366). The young Duke of Lancaster came from England to assist his brother in his enterprise ; the armies crossed the Pyrenees, were victorious at Navaretta or Najara (3 April 1367), placed Pedro the Cruel on the throne, and then waited for the promised reward. Nothing was paid. The Black Prince, unable to believe in such treachery, delayed till he and his whole army were striken down with illnesses caused by the heat of the Spanish summer. At last, abandoning hope of Pedro fulfilling his promise, he led his forces once more back to the Duchy, and set about getting money together himself to pay what was due to his followers ; faith was to be kept with them at all costs. This was the cause of the famous *fouage*, or hearth tax, of 1368, which is generally taken to be the main reason for the revolt of the French nobles, and the subsequent loss of almost the whole of the English dominions. This *fouage* may have been the last straw, but it was certainly not the only cause. It was not an unusual form of taxation, nor the first of its kind levied by the Black Prince, and it was not arbitrarily imposed. In January 1368 the Estates of Aquitaine met at Angoulême and voted a *fouage*, or hearth tax, of 10 sous on each hearth for five years. The people submitted apparently without difficulty. The nobles resisted. Discontent with the Prince's rule had been growing steadily. From the first the allegiance of certain lords and certain places had been unwilling and unreliable. The Counts of Armagnac and Périgord had always been French at heart. The Lord of Albret had been foolishly offended by the Black Prince on the eve of his departure for Spain. Edward had demanded from Albret more troops than he was prepared to bring for the Spanish campaign, and he refused. " The Sire d'Albret is a great lord indeed when he wishes to break the ordinance of my Council," exclaimed the angry Prince. " By God things shall not be as he thinks. Let him stay at home if he likes, I can do without his 1,000 lances." Chandos and Felton managed to smooth down their angry master, but relations were strained after that time with one of the biggest landholders of the country.

The whole situation was a difficult one. It was impossible without more money to endow the Gascon nobles as they wished ; unless they gained pecuniarily from the presence of an overlord in the country they much preferred him absent. It had been difficult enough in the past to keep the peace in Gascony itself, even dominated as it was by the chief towns ; in the extended dominion now held it was wellnigh impossible. The Prince had returned already sickening of the illness which was to prove fatal to him ; patience was never his strong point, and now his temper was hopelessly out of control. The King of France had a fine opportunity and he was the man to take advantage of it. In 1364 King John had died in England and was succeeded by the Regent, his eldest son, now Charles V. The new King was very different from his father. Pale, sickly and unfitted for the life of a warrior, he had a good deal of wisdom and a great deal of cunning. He was improving the government of his own country, and he was quick to see and to make use of the weak spots in the rule of his adversaries.

To Charles V the Gascon lords appealed in 1368, and he soon found a way of turning these appeals to good account. The Chandos Herald feels that it was the Prince's illness and his own trusting character that gave the crafty nobles their chance.

" Very soon after this [the Spanish expedition] it befell that the noble Prince of Aquitaine came to Angoulême, and there, of a surety, the malady began that thereafter lasted all his life, whereof it was pity and hurt. Then began falsehood and treason to govern those who ought to have loved him, for those whom he held for friends then became his enemies ; but this is no great marvel, for the enemy that is ever on the watch quicklier harms a valiant man than a wicked ; and on this account, as soon as it was known that the noble Prince was ill, in peril of death, his enemies were agreed to begin the war anew, and began to treat with those whom they knew of a certainty to be his enemies."

The Count of Armagnac refused to pay this new *fouage*, and in 1368 he was in Paris pouring his complaints into the ear of King Charles ; and he carried with him in his revolt the Lord of Albret, the Count of Périgord and the Count of Comminges. Many of these appeals and the answers to them are preserved in the *Archives Nationales* in Paris. Not only did the nobles complain of the heavy taxation and the ill-treatment of the King's officials, but also that the English were badly in arrears with certain payments and rents which they owed to the four nobles, and that their promises were not kept : they appealed to King Charles as " seigneur souverain de la duchée de Guienne et des autres terres baillées au roy d'Angleterre par le traitie de la pais."

The King received the rebel lords with the greatest honour. Arnaud Amanieu d'Albret was married to Margaret of Bourbon, a sister of the French Queen, and on 30 June 1368 a secret treaty was made between the King and the Counts of Armagnac, Périgord and the Lord of Albret. By this it was agreed that Charles would receive the appeal, would send aid if the English went to war, and would never give up the sovereignty of the country. On their part the nobles promised never to enter into obedience to England without the consent of Charles ; to help him in arms in the outlying counties of Auvergne, Berry, Touraine and Toulouse at a reasonable salary and to take their oath to him. Never, so he promised, should they be forced to pay *fouage* during the next ten years, unless they themselves wished and their various privileges were confirmed. For the sake of form the question of sovereignty was laid before a body of barons and lawyers, a majority of whom decreed that the King of France still retained the sovereignty, and a special body declared unanimously that he must accept the appeal made to him.

The decision was based on the non-fulfilment of the terms of the Treaty of Brétigny. Official letters had never been exchanged ; ceded places had not surrendered, but had been entered by force, and the English delegates had never met the French delegates at Bruges as had been arranged. Hence, declared the lawyers, Edward III and his son were guilty of breaking feudal law, and were justiciable before the Parliament of Paris. The example of the nobles was followed by some of the towns lately ceded. Montauban was incorporated into royal demesne because it had resisted Prince Edward. Villeneuve-en-Rouergue had its privileges confirmed by Charles V and " became French." Other places in the same neighbourhood followed suit.

The French King followed up the decision as to his sovereignty by summoning the Black Prince to appear before the Parliament of Paris to answer the complaints against him. His reply is well known : " I will indeed come to Paris, but it shall be with helmet on head and 60,000 men at my back." Early in 1369 he published a letter to nobles, clergy and commons of his country, showing the evil actions of the Count of Armagnac and accusing him of ingratitude in stirring up revolt. In June of the same year the French King sent a declaration of war to England, by a mere kitchen scullion, according to Froissart, and Edward replied by resuming the title of King of France. Meanwhile war had already broken out in the south-west, the province of Rouergue was regained by the French in 1369, and the English Seneschal Wetenhale killed. In May 1370 the Parliament of Paris declared Prince Edward guilty of felony and the whole of Guienne forfeited to the crown of France. The Prince was too ill to take much active part in the war, but his followers, especially the brave Sir John Chandos, now made Seneschal of Poitou, were in arms, and won some successes in Périgord and Poitou. It was a great loss to the Black Prince, both from the military and from the diplomatic point of view, when Chandos was struck down with a mortal blow in a skirmish at the Bridge of Lussac and died at Mortemer on 2 January 1370.

King Edward inflicted some severe humiliations upon his stricken son. In November 1369 he ordered him to give up the *fouage*, and in July 1370 he sent out his younger son, the Duke of Lancaster, almost as though to supersede him. All was going badly, the Dukes of Anjou and Berry, and the famous Bertrand du Guesclin were all concentrating on the Principality. Agenais fell to them, and the French forces almost reached Bordeaux. The final blow to the Black Prince's pride came when Limoges surrendered without resistance to the Duke of Berry, who made a secret agreement with the Bishop and the inhabitants. Edward's fury knew no bounds. Ill as he was he ordered his men to carry him in a litter to take revenge, and having undermined the wall of the city, he and his men rushed into the place and massacred the people without compassion. The latest researches have tended to minimize the general estimate of the massacre of Limoges, but it was no unusual proceeding in those days of violence ; nor was it out of keeping with the Prince's character to stop the slaughter on seeing the brave defence made by three French warriors. Whatever the real truth may be, the massacre of Limoges has long been regarded as the greatest blot on the Prince's chivalrous fame. " No one," writes Froissart, " however hardhearted, would not be forced to tears by the misery that was there wrought and the many innocent people killed : may God receive their souls, for they were indeed martyrs."

In January 1371 the Prince's health made it impossible for him to struggle longer to hold his fast-disappearing province. He set sail for England, and the Duke of Lancaster was left in command. The next year he gave up his power into his father's hands and ceased apparently all connection with the land in which he had been both so famous and so unfortunate.

Things went no better after the Prince's departure. The best English commanders were dead, Lancaster was not so much of a warrior as his brother, and no longer could they count on the support of the country. Meanwhile as opponent not only did Charles V in the background know how to advise policy which would wear out the English, without allowing them to fight pitched battles at which they were so generally victorious, but they had in command against them Bertrand du Guesclin, undoubtedly the finest soldier of his age.   Things were going none too well at home in England, where neither the King nor the war was any longer popular, and where Parliament was becoming restive under heavy taxation and uncontrolled expenditure.   France, on the other hand, had a more organized government and greater possibilities under the present King than under the warlike John or the rather colourless Philip VI.

John of Lancaster returned to England early in 1372, after a marriage with Pedro's daughter Constance which gave him a claim to the title of King of Castille.   John, Earl of Pembroke, was appointed Lieutenant in his place, but he was captured outside La Rochelle before setting foot in the Duchy, in a naval battle against the Spaniards known as that of Espagnols-sur-Mer (23 June 1372).   Great was the consternation in the country ; the French army took place after place, and in August 1372 the important town of Poitiers, which had been attacked by both Du Guesclin and the Duke of Berry, surrendered.   On the 25th of the same month Sir Thomas Percy and the Captal de Buch, who was still faithful to the English, were captured, and La Rochelle submitted to the French King, who guaranteed the inhabitants exemption from taxation and pardon from the Pope for breaking their oath of fealty to Edward.   The urgency of the occasion stirred up the failing vigour of Edward III, and the Black Prince, ill as he was, determined to make one more effort to re-establish the falling fortunes of the English.   Together with a fresh force they took sail for Gascony, but for weeks they could make no progress owing to adverse winds, and when at last they returned home, having achieved nothing, the French boasted that God was on their side in the struggle.   Thomas Felton in 1373 became Seneschal and tried courageously to conduct the defence.   The Black Prince had now restored the province which he was unable to defend into his father's hands, and some efforts were made to remedy past mistakes. The Court of Appeal was composed almost entirely of Gascons, and though the Seneschals of the various divisions were generally Englishmen, other offices were more frequently filled with natives than in the past.

The King, however, gave up all hope of himself undertaking the control of the war, and Lancaster as his Captain-General was sent out in June 1373 with powers almost as great as those which his brother had had in his capacity of Prince. Lancaster's expedition was a series of misfortunes. He chose the month of July for a long march through the heat of central France, he was constantly harassed by the French, but never given the chance of a real battle ; he went through Auvergne, a province bare, bleak, and little inhabited, and it was impossible to supply his troops with proper food ; it was not till the end of the year that he arrived by the valley of the Dordogne at Bordeaux, with but a poor remnant of his original army. The accounts of the Constable of Bordeaux, 1373-4, which give a list of the bows and arrows supplied to the different garrisons of defence, show that the towns round Bordeaux were still holding out, sometimes under Englishmen, sometimes under Gascons ; but they were fairly desperate. All this while the emissaries of the Pope had been still striving for peace, and now they held conferences with Lancaster and the Duke of Anjou. The result was the signing of a truce in 1375 (27 June) which was to last for two years.

Just before the truce expired Edward III died, and so ended in disaster the great ambitions of the King, who had lost not only lands, but esteem and popularity. The Black Prince had succumbed to his maladies in the previous year, and the faithful Captal de Buch had perished of melancholy in a French prison, from which Charles V refused to allow him to be ransomed. The accession of Richard II was followed by the end of the truce, and still further misfortunes in the south. Bergerac was finally occupied by the French, and an English force defeated at the little town of Eymet, about fifty miles from Bordeaux, where Thomas Felton the Seneschal fell into the enemies' hands. All that was left of the great Principality of Aquitaine in 1377 was Bordeaux and the surrounding country, which was practically under the sway of the town ; and farther south the two other loyal towns, Bayonne and Dax, with the French Pays Basque, which comprised the little provinces of Labourd and Soule.

Richard of Bordeaux never revisited the country of his birth. John Neville was made Lieutenant, in what was still called the Duchy of Aquitaine (20 June 1378) ; Archambaud de Grailly, the new Captal de Buch, did homage for his territories to the English overlord ; Matthew de Gournay was appointed Seneschal of the Landes, though little actual territory could be said to be held there, and in 1379 John of Lancaster, King of Castille, was made " our principal chieftain and general in France in our seigneurie of Aquitaine." The Court of Appeal in Bordeaux still functioned, and was largely composed of the few loyal Gascon nobles ; a paid army was kept in the south, partly Gascon, partly English, and various payments were made to lords and others who had done good service in the late war. Meanwhile Commissioners were treating for peace with the new King of France, Charles VI, who had succeeded his father in 1380, and in 1382 it was ordered that, pending negotiations, no war was to be carried on in Aquitaine. In 1384 (28 January) a formal truce was made with France, and the leading nobles of Gascony who were loyal to the English, together with the Mayor of Bordeaux, were made guardians responsible for seeing that peace was kept. All through his reign Richard II was working for peace, and one truce after another postponed any active renewal of the struggle.

The chief event of interest in Gascony during the reign of Richard was the attempt to establish Aquitaine once more as a Principality held by liege homage from the English King. In 1390 Richard bestowed it with full powers on his uncle John of Gaunt for his lifetime, retaining, however, to himself and his descendants as heirs of the King of France the direct demesne and superiority over the whole land. He reckoned, however, without allowing sufficiently for the Gascon pride. Bordeaux, and afterwards Bayonne, tried to prevent the landing of Lancaster, and eventually he was only allowed to lodge in Bor-

deaux pending the results of a delegation sent to England to
dispute his right. Certain nobles and men from Bordeaux,
Bayonne and Dax carried to Richard their claim that they were
direct vassals of the King of England and could not be given
over to any other lord. In vain the King pointed out that
he had not given away his supreme powers, nor was the grant
made for more than his uncle's lifetime. This was all very
well, but the Gascons were not satisfied, perhaps they dreaded
the re-establishment of a court and a ruler in their midst.
In any case the Duke soon felt that his position was an unten-
able one and none too dignified. He returned to England, his
admirers say, unselfishly anxious to avoid possible disturbances
so bad for the country and for his nephew's welfare ; more
probably because he could not secure a faithful following
amongst the Gascons. His return was shortly followed by his
death.

In 1396 Richard's long efforts towards peace were rewarded
by the signature on 9 March, amidst scenes of great magnificence and display, of the Truce of Paris, which was completed
by the King's own marriage with the little Princess Isabella on
19 September of the same year. Conservators of the peace
were appointed by both sides throughout the whole country.
" Agenais, Gascony, Bordelais, Bayonnais, and the whole
Duchy of Guienne and Languedoc " were put by the French
King in the charge of Bernard, Count of Armagnac, his Constable, and Louis de Sancerre his Marshal. Richard made the
Seneschal of Gascony, the Constable of Bordeaux and the
Mayor generally responsible, but Gascon lords were also ap-
pointed over each separate district to prevent war—the Sire de
Caumont, the Sire de Mussidan, the Captal de Buch, and others.

Three years later Richard's reign and his life ended disas-
trously. The Lancastrian period which followed witnessed not
only a new and more serious effort to gain the throne of France,
but also the final loss of the Gascon dependency.

CHAPTER VI

THE END OF THE ENGLISH DOMINION

THE Lancastrian reigns, and the victorious career of Henry V, were of far less importance to Gascony than the wars of Edward III. The objective of the King seems really to have changed : Henry V was far more determined than his predecessor to obtain the throne of France, and with that in view to strengthen his foothold in the north of France and to work from Normandy as his base. Gascon events have been, therefore, as a rule less noticed by historians of this period, and so much was the country left to its own devices that a French writer (Ribadieu) calls his chapters on the fifteenth century " La Guyenne sous la Commune de Bordeaux." Certainly the part played by the Gascon capital at this time was remarkable. It had formed its confederation of *filleules*, and was the centre of the little towns of the neighbourhood ; it took the lead in all the political events of the period and was the chief mainstay of the English dominion. But although not the scene of the greatest battles, nor the centre of negotiations during the Lancastrian reigns, Gascony, even reduced as it was in extent, was still a very important possession for England, and the war was more continuous there than in any other part.

When Richard II fell there seemed a possibility that Gascony might break away from the English on its own initiative, for Bordeaux was furious at the treatment of the Prince born within its walls, and was for the moment unwilling to recognize Henry IV as the rightful sovereign. In the end, however, material advantages outweighed sentiment, and the burgesses of Bordeaux reflected on the flourishing trade which the English connection brought them, and on the heavy burdens which the French Kings put upon their lands : " Encore nous vaut il mieux," they said (according to Froissart), " être Anglais qui nous tiennent francs et libéraux, que en la sujétion des Français. Si les Londriens ont déposés le roi Richard et couronné le roi Henry, que nous touche cela ? Toujours avons-nous roi. Nous avons plus des marchandises, de vins, de laines et de drap aux Anglais que nous n'avons aux Français ; nous y inclinons par nature mieux. Gardons que nous fassions traité nul dont nous nous puissions repentir." Henry IV, evidently, was anxious about his hold on Gascony, and he did his best to conciliate the towns and win himself support, until little by little the English dominions began slightly to extend, and the stretch of the Landes between Bordeaux and Bayonne once more united the two main centres of English strength.

Henry's first acts were very diplomatic. He retained some of Richard's officials—Henry Bowet, for example, as Constable of Bordeaux—and he appointed a good number of Gascons to important posts. Gaillard de Durfort, Lord of Duras, was first made Seneschal of Agen, and then of Aquitaine itself ; Jean de Béarn was Seneschal of Bigorre ; the Court of Appeal was almost entirely officered by Gascons, and in 1400 proctors were appointed for the rule of the Duchy, amongst whom were the Archbishop and the Mayor of Bordeaux. In 1401 pardon was issued to any burgesses or officials of Bordeaux who had opposed Henry's rule, and a new grant of privileges was made to the town : the municipality had no longer to account for its expenditure to the King. He had easily grasped the need for keeping Bordeaux loyal at all costs.

Henry was not long to remain in peaceful possession of his foreign dominions. The French King's brother, the Duke of Orleans, was eager to take advantage of English disturbances, and in 1401 he sent out a challenge to the new King to fight him in person, a challenge which the careful Henry was able to refuse with honour, since, as he replied, a King was not able to undertake wager of battle against a simple Duke. In September 1403, however, an attack was made on Gascony by a French army, in 1405 an active war on the sea was carried on, facilitated by the fact that the English King was occupied by the rising of Owen Glendower, and in 1406 Orleans was made Lieutenant in Guienne and marched down to what he, hoped would be an easy conquest. Henry had his hands very full in England, where revolt after revolt was disturbing his precarious hold upon the throne, but he sent out John Neville as his Lieutenant (1406) and various other English officials whom he may have thought more trustworthy than the Gascons in time of real war; the Mayors of Bordeaux were generally Englishmen. But Gascony did well in its own defence. Orleans was bent on obtaining possession of Bourg and Blaye, which were practically the keys of Bordeaux and Gascony on the north. Blaye was under the seigneurie of a woman, the daughter of the Lord of Mussidan, and she is said to have treated with the Duke, and promised to surrender should he be successful at Bourg. Whether this is true or no, Blaye did not surrender, for Bourg resisted bravely, thanks to timely help from Bordeaux, which sent out ships to attack the French who were blocking the town by sea and land. Orleans retreated early in 1407, nominally because of the illness of his troops and the floods of winter rain, which were rendering the camps very uninhabitable, possibly because, his own affairs were pressing. The victory of Bordeaux at Becd'Ambès had saved Guienne, and the name of the brave jurats who had taken part in the rescue of Bourg have been preserved in honour in the registers of the Municipality. In 1407 truce was declared between France and England in Aquitaine, and the Seneschal, the Mayor and the Constable of Bordeaux were made conservators of the peace.

A word of explanation is necessary here, as to the state of things in France at this time; for the internal troubles of the country are largely responsible for the events of later history, and part at least of Henry V's astonishing success must be put down to the lack of unity and patriotism among his enemies.

The throne of France was since 1380 in the hands of the unfortunate Charles VI, whom an ill-trained youth and one or two violent shocks had left subject to periodical fits of madness, and hopelessly unfitted to keep any sort of control of his "overmighty subjects." The two great rivals for power in France were the Dukes of Burgundy and Orleans. The opposition began between Philip the Bold, son of King John, who had been given the Duchy of Burgundy, and the Duke of Orleans, brother of Charles VI. Strife continued more violently than ever when Philip's lands passed to his successor Jean sans Peur in 1404. Both lords had vast dominions under them, both had great need for money and both looked to the treasury of France to augment their own incomes. Their outlook on foreign affairs was another cause of opposition. Orleans was all for a vigorous offensive against England : Burgundy, with an eye to the value of English trade, was anxious for peace. In 1407 a reconciliation took place between the two which was obviously unreal and unlikely to last, but the climax was worse than could have been expected. The Duke of Orleans—a friend both of King and Queen—was returning one night from a visit to the latter along the narrow Rue des Francs Bourgeois, in what was then fashionable Paris, when a horde of roughs fell upon him from a side alley and left him lying dead in the road (23 November 1407). Jean sans Peur, in a fit of remorse or out of sheer bravado, confessed to having instigated the deed, and was not unnaturally denied his place in the royal Council. The young Duke of Orleans, son of the murdered man, joined a party of adherents, prominent among whom was Bernard VII of Armagnac, whose daughter he married, and whose name was adopted for the whole party. This connection meant that the Gascons hostile to English rule were likely to back up the " Armagnacs," whilst Burgundy turned for his supporters to the Low Countries and the frontier nobles of Germany. The country was wasted in a true war of factions, and the hostility of Burgundy to Orleans was a far stronger feeling than any hostility of French against English. So completely lacking were both parties in any feeling of nationality or patriotism that they both began to intrigue for the English alliance. In 1411 Jean sans Peur actually came to terms with Henry IV, who promised him help against his rivals. In 1412 an embassy was sent over from the Orleans party, which went still farther, and promised the foreign King that he should be restored to his possessions in Aquitaine. Certain fortresses, they said, should be at once delivered over to him, and they would aid him to regain the rest, parts of which were to be granted out to the confederated Princes to be held as vassals of the English King. (Berry was to be Count of Poitou, Orleans of Angoulême and Périgord, Armagnac was to have four castles in return for homage.) As a result of this extraordinary compact, Thomas, Duke of Clarence, was sent out by Henry IV as his Lieutenant in Aquitaine, to receive the ceded territories, and to regain all he could of the rest.

For the moment Burgundy took up the rôle of defender of the kingdom, and it does not appear that the promises of 1412 were in any way fulfilled. Circumstances were changed by the accession of Henry V and his sheer determination to win the crown of France, not merely a property, however valuable, in the south-west. Again Burgundy— possibly anxious to be on the winning side—was negotiating with England, but the final event which riveted the English and Burgundian alliance was the murder of Jean sans Peur himself on the Bridge of Montereau. Orleans had been made prisoner at the battle of Agincourt, Bernard VII of Armagnac, Constable of France, died in 1418, the Armagnac party was headed by the Dauphin, and he planned a conference with the Burgundian Duke, to end presumably in reconciliation and a united effort against the invading foe. Whether or no the murder was planned it seems difficult to determine ; it may have been that the Dauphin's followers thought the Duke's gestures suspicious and struck him down in fear for their Prince's life ; but a premeditated crime would be by no means an impossibility. In any case Jean sans Peur was dead, and the Burgundian party, for better or worse, adopted the side of Henry V, who by the Treaty of Troyes in the following year was given the title of Regent during the lifetime of Charles VI, was married—as he had long wished—to Catherine of France, and was named as successor when his father-in-law died.

These events have taken us some way from the history of Gascony, but the story of the internal rivalries amongst the French Princes, helping as they did the victorious career of Henry V, the ambitions of that King which led him to aim higher than the mere possession, however independently held, of the Duchy of Aquitaine, and affairs which concentrated English attention rather in the north than the south, explain the apparent neglect of Gascony by the Lancastrian Kings, and the way in which Gascon history in the fifteenth century seems to be more isolated than before from general events and royal policy. When, after Henry V's death, Bedford was ruling in France, his hands were too full to allow him to take any personal part in the effort to save the old property of England ; and the later period of Henry VI's reign was so full of internal troubles, from the quarrel between Beaufort and Gloucester onwards, that very little active help was forthcoming to back up the really wonderful effort made by Bordeaux and English Gascony to resist the inroads of the French.

Before beginning the story of the final struggle it might be as well to consider some of the principal actors in it, and to explain the attitude they adopted in the events which follow. Of Bordeaux there is little to add to what has already been said. The town was desperately anxious to remain English. Never was she more independent and more privileged than in the fifteenth century, whilst in France generally the towns were nearly all declining before the progress of the monarchy. Bayonne and Dax were bound to the same cause, though perhaps less fiercely " English " than the still more prosperous trading centre. The heart and soul of the English party in Bordeaux—at least until after the first surrender in 1451—was the Archbishop, Pey Berland as he has come to be called.   The Archbishops always occupied a position of great importance, both as the practical rulers of their own large diocese, the head of the Church Court, and among the richest landholders in the country ; but they were also great political magnates, members of the royal Council, and as a rule of the High Court of Appeal in Aquitaine, besides being put constantly on commissions of arbitration and justice.   Not always, however, were the Archbishops actually devoted vassals, but Pey Berland believed that the English rule was the safeguard of the city, and he did all he could to hearten up the citizens and to keep them loyal through thick and thin.   The son of a peasant in the Médoc, Pey Berland was one of the many instances of an able man who had risen to the highest position through the avenue of the Church.   He studied theology at Toulouse, became secretary to the Archbishop of Bordeaux, François Hugouino, and was chosen as his successor in 1430.   He was very popular amongst his fellow townsmen, took a lead in all the events of the day, and in 1442 was the chief founder of the University of Bordeaux, established in order to enable the young Gascons to gain their education without leaving their native land.

The chief of the nobles, who was consistently on the side of the English, was the Captal de Buch, at this time Gaston I of Foix-Grailly.   The seigneurie of Buch had been given in the fourteenth century to the family of Grailly, the descendants of John de Grailly, the Seneschal of Edward I, whose name came from the little seigneurie of Grailly in the Pays de Gex.   The Captal de Buch was uncle of the Count of Foix, Gaston IV, and father of Jean, Count of Candale, as he is generally called (in reality Earl of Kendal), who fought with him against the French.   Two brothers, Bertrand and Pierre of Montferrant, also played very leading parts in these final scenes.   Bertrand, the elder brother, had the castle and title of Lord of Montferrant, he was a member of the royal Council in Aquitaine and at one time Captain of Bourg.   The younger brother Pierre took the curious title of Souldic or Soudan de la Trau, a poor seigneurie in the Landes which came to him through his mother (the best-known possessor of this title was one of the warriors of the fourteenth century), but he claimed the castle and property of Lesparre, which had been bestowed on Henry VI's Lieutenant, the Earl of Huntingdon, in 1438, and although the long processes on this question never gave him what he sought, he is sometimes called the Sire de Lesparre. He married an illegitimate daughter of John, Duke of Bedford, and hoped for great things from the connection and from promises which Bedford made, but which he had no time to fulfil before his death.

The position of the Count of Foix, in this period, was to some extent ambiguous, since in 1422 he was made Governor of Languedoc for both Henry V and Charles VI, and the Councils of both countries gave him grants for his expenses. This was, however, when Henry was Regent and recognized heir. When war actually broke out later in Gascony, Foix was leading troops on the side of the French. Both Foix and Béarn were now in the hands of the Grailly family. The marriage (in the thirteenth century) of the daughter and heiress of Gaston VII of Béarn to Roger Bernard III, Count of Foix, had connected the two states : the marriage of another daughter and heiress, Isabelle, in the fourteenth century, to Archambaud de Grailly, Captal de Buch, had brought the new dynasty into possession. The eldest son of this marriage succeeded as Count ; the younger Gaston as Captal de Buch. From 1412 to 1472 Foix and Béarn were ruled over by Gaston IV, son of Jean and nephew of the Captal. Still another son of Archambaud de Grailly was Mathieu, Count of Comminges, who, unlike his brother Gaston, fought with his nephew on the side of Charles VII. The brother of Gaston IV, Pierre, Viscount of Lautrec, also supported the French cause.

Neither Armagnacs nor Albrets had been really regained to the English cause since their desertion of the Black Prince in the fourteenth century. Count John IV, who had succeeded Bernard VII, the Constable, in 1418, hesitated between the two parties, and was nearly won over to an English alliance (as will be seen later) in 1442, but his son the Viscount of Lomagne was fighting all the time in the French army, and he succeeded his father as Jean V just before the final loss of the English possessions (1450). The Albrets played an important part all through the final stages of the war on the French side. Arnaud-Amanieu, as has already been seen (p. 103), had married Margaret of Bourbon after his desertion of the Black Prince ; his son Charles I became Constable of France, and the next Lord of Albret, Charles II, was one of Charles VII's chief commanders, and was assisted in the war by his two sons Tartas and d'Orval. Certainly the wealthiest and more powerful nobles were now on the side of French rule in the south-west ; but England was still supported by the wealth and power of the towns.

To return to the history of the province itself after the truce made in 1407, when the timely aid sent by Bordeaux to Bourg had saved the situation, and Orleans had retired to meet his unexpected death in the same year. One of the last acts of Henry IV in regard to Gascony had been the treaty he had made with the confederated Princes in 1412.

In 1414 Henry V entered into negotiations with the King of France, and the embassy sent from England demanded from him " all that part of the Duchy of Aquitaine which our relative of France detains." The term " relative of France " was significant that Henry did not mean to recognize his title of King ; and the large offers made at the time did not hinder his preparations for war : Agenais, Bazadais, Périgord, Bigorre, Saintonge, Quercy and Rouergue were not enough for him.

In 1414 war had broken out in Gascony, the Duke of Bourbon commanding the French, and the Duke of Clarence the English armies ; but the truce of that year postponed active trouble for a time. The next move was made by Bordeaux. Although Bordeaux had surrounded herself by a circle of loyal *filleules*, three very important towns were in the hands of the French since 1377, Saint-Macaire, Rions and Bazas, and were very dangerous indeed to the Bordelais trade on the Garonne. The Captain of Saint-Macaire made himself especially obnoxious, and revenged a refusal to provide him with arms by the seizure of boats and burgesses belonging to Bordeaux. In 1420 Bordeaux could bear the situation no longer, and on her own authority levied an aid for war and summoned soldiers to fight. The forces of the town were successful in the capture of Rions and then turned their arms against Saint-Macaire. This town was one of the strongest fortresses of the day. It stood high over the river surrounded by a triple band of fortifications, and crowned with a massive castle. But the Bordelais were determined. Privileged and unprivileged alike took up arms, they chose John Ratcliffe, the English constable, as their leader (he became Seneschal in 1422), and after a month's siege an attack was made with such energy, and such a perfect hail of stones and bullets, that Saint-Macaire yielded, and La Réole followed suit, thus leaving the Garonne free for the commerce of Bordeaux. Fighting continued for some time after this, all conducted from Bordeaux; Bazas was regained and other neighbouring towns. The burgesses showed the utmost zeal to remain English; patriotic contributions were voted, freewill offerings were brought into the treasury from poor as well as rich, and townsmen vied with nobles in their warlike deeds. Bordeaux had once more not only saved the English possessions from destruction, but strengthened them amazingly by taking the offensive.

It was not till 1442 that regular war broke out again in Gascony, but that was far from meaning that the country was at peace. The Gascons themselves sent out bands of *routiers* to raid the neighbouring provinces, whilst they in their turn suffered from the depredations of Rodrigo di Villandrando (a Spanish *routier* supported by the French King) in the north, and the Lord of Albret in the south. The Count of Foix as governor of Languedoc should have done something to protect the province, but he was really an adherent of France, not of England, and proclamation was made in 1433 that no English subject was to take pledges or hold fiefs from either the Count of Foix or the Count of Armagnac. But apparently the English King had not yet grasped the fact that Foix was disloyal, for in 1439 he was especially commissioned to guard the town of Bazas against the men of Villandrando and Albret.

In 1442 a very interesting attempt was made to strike a real blow at the power of France in the south by winning over the great house of Armagnac to the English alliance. Things were obviously desperate. Edward Hull had returned to England early in the year with a heartrending account of the condition of affairs in Gascony and with the news that a French army was in full march for Bordeaux.

It was urgently necessary that something should be done. The Count of Armagnac had already made proposals for a truce with England as early as 1437, a result, it was said, of a quarrel with Charles VII; what was more he had three marriageable and, if rumour spoke truth, beautiful daughters; the young King Henry was unmarried. Henry's Council felt that the opportunity was too good to be lost. Thomas Beckington, later the Bishop of Bath and Wells and sometime tutor to the young Henry, was sent over, together with Sir Robert Roos, one of His Majesty's carvers (a post of great honour at Court), to negotiate the match, and were joined later by Sir Edward Hull. The marriage was a political move and was clearly planned as such, but for once the poor King felt that he must assert himself. He wrote privately to his ambassadors, a letter which he said was to override all other instructions, begging that they would send him portraits of the girls, in order that he himself might choose which of the three should be the royal bride. He writes :

" At your first commyng thider, in al haste possible, that ye do portraie the III daughters in their kertelles simple, and their visages, lyk as ye see their stature and their beaulte and color of skynne and their countenances, with al manner of features ; and that one be delivered in al haste with the said portratur to bring it unto the Kingé, and he t'apponte and signe which hym lyketh."

The marriage, however, desirable as it was, was destined never to be accomplished. The ambassadors arrived at Bordeaux, and sent repeated messages to Armagnac, but they never reached his Court nor saw his daughters. Sir Edward Hull brought out a Dutch artist, who managed to reach Auxerre and got so far apparently as the portrait of one daughter, but by some excuse or other the matter was dragged on to an interminable length. Armagnac and his Chancellor Batute outdid themselves in excuses and pre-varications : " The country is so unsafe it will never do for the ambassadors to undertake the journey," " a safe-conduct from the King of France is necessary for you, we are expecting it daily," " the painter is hard at his task, but the weather is so cold the colours won't work," and so on and so on. Beckington and Roos lost patience, and their letters were distinctly more pointed than those of Armagnac, especially since his son Lomagne was meanwhile fighting actively under the banner of the French King. The ambassador wrote pretty plainly to the Count's Chancellor :

" It appears to me that when the King, our Sovereign Lord, shall be correctly informed of the war which the Viscount of Lomagne has carried, and still daily carries on against him, he will not agree to the business which you are aware of. After the arrival of our army from England I make no doubt that their first attack will be on you."

In January 1443 Beckington embarked to return from his vain mission. Roos and Hull had become actively in-volved in the great struggle against the French which was all this time in progress.

In 1442 Charles VII undertook in person the effort to recover Gascony, and it was an effort which threatened to be successful, such was the vigour of the attack and the difficulties of defence. The English King's Lieutenant at this time was the Earl of Huntingdon and the Seneschal Sir Thomas Rempston. In February 1442 they had occu-pied the town of Tartas, the possession of which they hoped would defend Dax and their southern frontier. The town submitted, but only on condition ; the garrison would repudi-ate the contract and again take up arms should the French come to their rescue before 24 June. The time came nearer and nearer and hope seemed almost over, when three French forces converged on Tartas : Charles himself marched from Toulouse, another section of the army arrived under Constable Richemont, and a third under the Viscount of Lomagne. On 23 June the town was handed over to the French King, who marched on to Saint-Sever, where not only the town but the English Seneschal fell into his hands, and in July he laid siege to Dax, the third most important of the English towns. Charles made no mistake this year about the vastness of the task before him ; he had a very strong army under him, and was accompanied by his own son, as well as leaders such as Clermont, Albret and Gaston IV, Count of Foix, who was now quite definitely enlisted on the side of the French. Dax defended itself with considerable vigour, but it could not withstand the fury of the attack, the mining of the walls, and the projectiles flung over the ramparts by enormous engines of war. On 2 August the King made a triumphant entry into the fallen city. Bordeaux was in something very like a panic at the ill news which was being brought in. The inhabitants feared that the next objective would be their own town, and a false message, spread by a certain John Goer, that England no longer cared to trouble herself about Gascony, roused a spirit of despair which almost led to immediate surrender. The Mayor at the time, Gadifer Shorthose, an Englishman, was a very feeble reed, the Constable was ill, and the two chief Gascon nobles in the town, the Captal de Buch and Montferrant, were in rivalry with each other and unwilling to let either take the command ; whilst the fortifications were weak and dilapidated. The situation was saved by the Archbishop. Pey Berland summoned the people to meet in the Cathedral Church ; he read to them the real letter from Henry VI which the two ambassadors for the marriage had brought with them, and he inspired them with something of his own zeal and courage. A new spirit pervaded the town, young and old, rich and poor flocked to the ramparts to start the work of reparation, and in a week the town was once more

in a state of defence and ready for the enemy. Meanwhile
the Archbishop set off on an embassy to England to hasten
the sending of help and to rouse the slackening energies of
the English. He carried with him a letter from Roos and
Beckington, which painted the position of affairs in dismal
colours :

" We cam to this your noble cite of Bordeaux on Monday the XVI
day of Juil, where at our first commyng we founde as sorrowful a town
and as gretly dismayed and discoraged as any might be in th' erth."

It then went on to show how the enemy had taken Tartas
and Saint-Sever, were besieging Dax, and from thence meant
to proceed first to Bayonne then to Bordeaux, whilst another
force was gradually approaching from the north. At first
the Archbishop met with but a poor reception, for England
was more concerned with the quarrel of Beaufort and
Gloucester than with events overseas, but at last he managed to get the ear of the King himself, and his plea was
strengthened by the arrival of fresh news of misfortunes,
including the fall of Dax, brought from Bordeaux by a pil-
grim, who had carried the letters sewn up in the hem of his
gown. An expedition was planned to be sent out under
the Duke of Somerset, and a few troops under Sir Edward
Hull set sail at once, to restore the flagging hopes of the
English and Gascons in Bordeaux.

Meanwhile the French had been making steady progress.
After the fall of Dax, the Castle of Orthe had been seized,
which meant the control of a great part of the Landes ;
in Agenais many important towns had fallen and the
Garonne was no longer guarded from the French ; even
the town of La Réole was captured (8 October), although
the Castle of the Quatre Sos (Soeurs) held out till December.
In the absence of the Archbishop and the illness of the Constable (Sir Robert Clifton ; he died 20 September) Sir Robert
Roos had been chosen Regent, and he and the Captal de
Buch had done all they could to save the English cause ;
but they had a very difficult task and there was disaffection
where they might have expected help : especially was Gadifer

Shorthose a real danger, occupying as he did the important position of Mayor. He had been given in the past the guardianship of Bergerac, when he received a letter from the Regent urging him to take measures for its defence, " he carelessly kicked his stirrup, and said before all that he cared no more for it than he did for that." The Council had begun to give up hope of any English help, and the Dean of Saint-André had been heard to say that if the enemy came to Bordeaux and the English sent a thousand men, they must abide by the stronger. At last Hull arrived with his small detachment of men and a " letter of comfort " from the King. More encouraging even than the letter was a successful skirmish led by Hull and Roos against the enemy on the outskirts of Bordeaux ; the French were forced to beat a retreat from Saint-Loubés, and a little later from Langon. The feeling against the French in the neighbourhood of Bordeaux was evidently very strong, for even the women of the country are said to have aided in their capture. Charles VII himself nearly came to a disastrous end at the close of this campaign, for his lodging in the town of La Réole was set on fire—whether by accident or design is unknown—and he only managed to escape in his nightshirt, along a mine which had been constructed for purposes of the siege. In the end the weather fought for the English, for the hardness of the winter and the freezing of the river made it difficult for the French to undertake the attack on Bordeaux ; whether on this account, or because he needed more of a fleet before undertaking an attack on the main stronghold of the English, Charles VII gave up the attempt early in 1443, retiring to Poitiers and ending one of the most serious of the campaigns yet undertaken. Several places fell back into English hands ; Dax itself was regained, as also the Castle of Orthe ; in 1444 a truce was made with France by the peace party in England, and the King, who had long abandoned his Armagnac plans, was married to Margaret of Anjou.

In 1449 the struggle in the south was once more resumed. The first action which heralded the breach of the truce was an attack on Labourd by Gaston, Count of Foix, Lieutenant of Charles VII in the south, who claimed to have done it at the royal command. He first besieged the English in Mauléon, which was supposed to be under the protection of the King of Navarre. The protection was of very little value. The King (John II of Aragon who had become King of Navarre by marriage in 1425) did remonstrate with the Count and beg him to raise the siege, but on his refusal he took no steps to defend the town. The Captain of Mauléon, Louis de Beaumont the Constable of Navarre, yielded up the town in September, possibly by the command of his sovereign, who was in difficulties of his own, and did not wish to alienate his powerful neighbour the Count of Foix. The English were allowed to save their lives, but not their goods, but each one was given *un grand blanc* to provide himself with drink on the retreat. After Mauléon the Count turned his attention to Guiche, about fifteen miles from Bayonne, which he captured by a night attack, and which rendered the position of Bayonne very unsafe ; but Gaston was fighting more for his own hand than for the victory of the French, and he made a triumphant entry into Orthez, his capital town, instead of pursuing his conquests farther.

Charles VII was at the time engaged in the conquest of Normandy, but he determined to follow up the successes of his Lieutenant, and he sent a force under the Count of Périgord which took Bergerac, while the young Albret, the Sire d'Orval, attacked Bazas. The burgesses of Bordeaux, furious at seeing the French once more within the borders of English Bordelais, rushed to arms with more haste than reflection, and whether warriors or no they prepared to advance against an enemy of whose numbers they were completely ignorant. This time their efforts met with a terrible reverse. They had Pey Berland to encourage them in the background, but they had no good leader in the field to direct their undisciplined efforts. Shorthose the Mayor was not only feeble, but cowardly. The result was a rout known as " La Male Journade," and the capture or death of nearly all the combatants. Their effort had been a total fiasco, and Pey Berland was plunged into the deepest grief : "inconsolable du malheur et de la mort de ses concitoyens il passa deux jours et deux nuits presque en entier dans la solitude et la prière." The Sire d'Orval boasted that English Gascony was an easy conquest, but Charles VII knew better than to take risks. He collected a very large army and placed it under the command of Dunois the bastard Orleans, renowned as the greatest captain of his age.

The campaign of 1451 was prepared with the greatest care : Dunois was far too good a commander to underestimate the enemy, and the whole military system of France had been improved in every way during the reign of Charles VII. Also Dunois evidently had in his mind the recovery of the province, not the punishment of his adversary ; thus the strictest regulations were published to the soldiery as to their behaviour during the campaign : they were to take nothing without payment (a list of prices was drawn up), never to injure the ploughing oxen, and so forth ; very severe penalties were laid down for any breach of these rules. Similarly Dunois endeavoured to obtain the surrender of the places he besieged and as far as possible to avoid their destruction, whilst the terms he offered were always fair, and often generous. Four different lines of attack were planned. Dunois himself was to begin his operations on the borders of Saintonge by the siege of Montguyon ; the Count of Armagnac was to attack Rions ; the Count of Périgord to lead his forces to the assault of Castillon on the Dordogne, while Dax was to be besieged for the second time by the Count of Foix. Gascony was ill-prepared to meet this formidable expedition. In England the quarrels of the great lords and the threatenings of the Wars of the Roses were preventing any active steps being taken in support of the royal rights, which the King himself was too feeble or too ill to defend. Sir Robert Roos was dead, Sir Edward Hull had returned to England, Richard Woodville, appointed Seneschal in 1450, seems to have left little trace of decided action ; the chief defenders of Aquitaine were the Gascons themselves, especially the Captal de Buch and the two Mont-

ferrants; there were a certain number of English officials
and garrisons, but no large force to resist invasion.

The danger chiefly threatened Bordeaux from the north.
Dunois entered easily by Montguyon, and then laid siege
to Blaye, the key of Gascony; here he was joined by the
forces from Castillon, the capture of which seemed less
important than the concentrated effort on so important
a place as Blaye. Blaye was bravely defended, but it was
so strongly besieged, and so carefully blocked by a French
fleet in the Garonne, that despite the efforts of ships from
Bordeaux to come to aid the inhabitants by river, no help
was able to reach them, and they hoped in vain for adequate
assistance from England; even the strong fortifications of
Blaye could not withstand the French artillery under the
able direction of Jean Bureau. On 23 May the town capitu-
lated and received fairly generous terms from Dunois. The
capture of Blaye was all-important, and the fall or surrender
of other places followed so rapidly that it was evident that
the attacked had little hope of holding their own. Bourg
submitted after a few days of siege; Libourne and Saint-
Émilion opened their gates *sans coup férir*; Fronsac, though
well victualled and of great strength, agreed almost at once
to treat. The name of Dunois was a name to strike terror
into all hearts, and the English help did not come, whilst
the King of France was waiting at Saintes with fresh troops
ready to come up and complete their destruction. Perhaps
there is some truth in the tradition that resistance was
weakened because the time of vintage was drawing near,
and the failure to harvest the vintage would have meant
something very like economic ruin.

Bordeaux, after all it had dared in the past, might have
been expected to make some sort of stand; the Captal de
Buch, who had done great deeds in 1442, was in command,
and although he was getting an old man, he was not too
old to fight. But the situation seemed so hopeless, and
the lack of help from England gave such a feeling of abandonment and neglect that even the Archbishop counselled
negotiations and the making of the best terms possible.

The three Estates met, representatives were chosen to treat with Dunois, the Captal was sent to gain the goodwill of his nephew the Count of Foix, and instead of war the town saw the French enter to hold debates and conferences.

On 12 June a treaty was signed, and ratified by Charles VII on the 20th. The Bordelais were still hoping against hope that they need not "become French," and they were given until 23 June before they need surrender : but if English help did not come by that date they agreed to submit, and to swear allegiance to the King of France. The terms which they obtained were extremely liberal. Their privileges were to be safeguarded, a delay of six months was given before the inhabitants need take the oath to Charles, and at the end of that time those who still did not wish to submit were free to go where they would and to purchase a safe-conduct from the King for one golden crown. A general amnesty was promised, goods might be kept, and the clergy were not to lose their benefices. No new taxes were to be levied, no new tolls exacted, and Bordeaux was still to possess a high court of appeal with sovereign powers. Military service was not to be forced on the burgesses, and those who did fight were always to be paid. New French money was to be coined in the town, but the old coinage was to pass current for the two coming years. The Archbishop's name was first amongst the signatories to this agreement, and his influence was doubtless a help in gaining such extraordinarily good conditions.

On 30 June the French made their solemn entry into Bordeaux, and the fleurs-de-lis replaced the banners of England. The clergy and nobles of Bordeaux met the procession, and the townsmen must have been impressed by the magnificence and the ceremonial of the invading host. The Marshals and Captains of France led the way, followed by the Counts of Nevers and Armagnac, and the lords of the King's Great Council accompanied by trumpets and heralds. The Royal Seal in a little casket was borne on the back of a white horse and was followed by the Chancellor of France, Juvenal des Ursins. Dunois himself rode alone in the centre of the procession, dressed all in white and mounted on a charger with blue velvet trappings. After him came the main body of the army. At the cathedral the Lieutenant took the oath in the name of the King to observe the customs and liberties of the commune, and then the Archbishops and lords took their oath of fealty to the King of France. The Captal de Buch was not prepared to break his allegiance to England, and he was allowed a year to decide whether or no he would become a French vassal. Olivier de Coëtivy was appointed Seneschal of Guienne for Charles VII, Joachim Rouhault Constable, and Jean Bureau Mayor ; the Count of Clermont was left as Captain and Governor of Bordeaux. For a fortnight Dunois stayed in the conquered town, keeping the strictest order, and a French soldier, who was found guilty of theft from the inhabitants, was hanged on the new gibbet set up as a warning to malefactors.

Meanwhile the English possessions in the south were being one by one wrested from them. The Count of Foix had been successful at Dax, and on 6 August turned his army against Bayonne, and there Dunois joined him when he had settled the affairs of Bordeaux. The usual preparations were made for what was expected to be a difficult siege : the French dug trenches and cast up *taudeys*, behind which they could advance to attack the walls. Very speedily the Count took possession of one of the *faubourgs* and prevented the English from setting fire to it before they took refuge within the inner walls. The discomfiture of the town was completed by its blocking on the sea side by Spanish ships, and provisions began to run very low. At the end of a fortnight the inhabitants were ready to treat, and bought their lives and goods in return for a large sum of money. On 20 August the appearance of what all the chroniclers describe as a great white cross in the sky seemed to witness to the favour of Heaven on the capitulation, and did much to encourage the simple folk in the belief that the French cause was that which God supported. Once more Dunois made a magnificent entry, doubtless to convince the conquered people of the splendour of France, and the joy that they should feel in becoming a part of so rich and glorious a kingdom. French officials were appointed, and garrisons were left in the principal fortresses, after which the army retired under the impression that Gascony was finally secured.

But meanwhile all was not well in Bordeaux. The new rulers were not always so observant as they should have been of the old liberties and customs, the French colony in the town became increasingly unpopular, and furious anger was roused at the levy of taxes despite the promises which had been made to the contrary. The castle of Rokeley in the Seigneurie of Lesparre was still waving the English flag; some of the burgesses were secretly in correspondence with the English King. Henry VI—or his Council—seems to have thought that the best way to act was to ignore the French conquest; the Gascon Rolls of 1451 and 1452 show English officials still being appointed and grants being made to the Gascon nobles. The Bordelais had been too long under the English and too independent under the old rule to submit willingly to the new: " La plupart étaient si fors Anglois (et encores sont)," says a Chronicler writing of this time in 1487, " qu'il ne savoient aymer les François, car il y avait bien trois cents ans que continuellement avoient esté Anglois." Eventually the discontent came to a head in September 1452, and Pierre of Montferrant with other Gascon nobles set out secretly for England to make one more bid for English help. Pey Berland took no part in this final struggle, he would not break the oath he had taken, however unwillingly, to the French overlord. The nobles had a case, however, for Charles had not kept faithfully to the Treaty of 1451, and they argued that they were no longer bound to keep their part of the compact. The English Council was summoned to consider the request of the Gascon delegates, and it was decided to send over a force under the veteran John Talbot, Earl of Shrewsbury, already widely renowned for his warlike feats in France. Talbot was a man of eighty years of age, but still full of fire and energy; perhaps no better choice could have been made at the time, nor anyone sent out more fitted to lead a forlorn hope.

On 21 October Talbot landed with a small army in the Médoc and advanced at once to Bordeaux. Here the citizens were discussing what they should do with the French garrison, whether they should be taken in their beds, or whether they should be allowed to escape. The alarm got about and some of the French certainly effected their escape, and when the gates were opened and Talbot entered he proclaimed that none who had taken the oath to the French King should presume to lay hands on Frenchmen or their goods. Despite his order Coëtivy, the French Seneschal, was found hiding in a garden and taken prisoner with two others, and they were sent off to England, though their captors had the expected ransom confiscated as a punishment for their disobedience. Talbot was given the fullest powers as the representative of the King, and the people overjoyed at his arrival were prepared to yield him enthusiastic obedience : " Le Roi Talbot," as he was called, had at first successes everywhere. Libourne, Cadillac, Rions and Castillon-sur-Dordogne at once sent in their submission, La Réole and Fronsac were captured. Early in 1453 more men arrived under Talbot's son, the Viscount of Lisle, and English ships brought much needed provisions into Bordeaux. But Charles VII was not going to submit tamely to such a breach of allegiance. He began at once to collect a very large army, which was ready to take the field by June 1453. The French policy now was very different from that of Dunois in 1451, it was war to the knife, and the conquered could no longer hope for favourable terms ; the English were sometimes allowed to keep their lives and leave the country, but the Gascon rebels received little mercy from their enraged sovereign. Slowly but surely the enemy from three directions began to close in on Bordeaux. The King took Chalais on the Charente, Clermont captured Gensac on the Gironde, and the Marshals advancing on the Dordogne laid siege to Castillon. Jean Bureau advised the concentration of forces on the little town to give the King a hold on the river and to deprive Bordeaux of a large source of supplies. The siege was undertaken very seriously and with large forces (19 July

1453). Jean Bureau, again in command of the artillery, enclosed a great field as his park, and surrounded it with ditches and fortifications. An abbey outside the walls formed a fortress for the rest of the French army. News came to the old leader in Bordeaux, and he is said to have hesitated, realizing the strength of the French and anxious to get up reinforcements. One of the chroniclers tells us how the people twitted him for his delay and reminded him that he had promised to drive off the French even with only 10,000 fighting men. Perhaps Talbot felt that he must not allow any to think that his great age made him a slack leader ; in any case he collected what men he could, marched to Libourne at once and sent messages to Castillon bidding the garrison be of good courage for help was at hand.

On 17 July the English and Gascon force attacked the abbey and won a momentary success, which made them feel that the task was an easy one. Talbot was just about to hear mass, which he had been too hurried to do before leaving Bordeaux, when a rumour reached him that the French were preparing to escape from the enclosed park, and that if he delayed he might lose a great chance of striking a decisive blow, and destroying an already intimidated enemy. This was the fatal mistake. Talbot swore that never would he hear mass again if he did not drive the French before him. One, wiser than the rest, warned him that the rumour was untrue and that he could do nothing against the French, entrenched as they were, and begged him at least to wait until his foot soldiers came up ; for the whole force had not yet had time to collect. Talbot was furious at the suggestion, and some say struck the counsellor across the face ; in any case, he ordered the advance and set out himself on horseback on account of his great age, but the rest of his men on foot. The English threw themselves boldly against the fortifications of the park, and despite a perfect hail of bullets very nearly effected an entrance. Forming a wedge under their shields they struggled on under their intrepid commander, who continued to urge them to the battle though half blinded by a wound in the face. The day was

still doubtful, when the French were reinforced by a small
body of Bretons which had been stationed on a neighbouring
height ; attacked suddenly on their flank the English broke
in confusion, leaving Talbot and his son, Sir Edward Hull
and many others, Gascon and English, dead on the field.
The French scarcely realized at first how much they had
gained, for they were still uncertain of the fate of "le roi
Talbot." On the morrow the herald of the Earl came to
seek his master, hoping to find him amongst the prisoners.
He was shown the body of an old man disfigured by a wound
on the face and scarcely recognizable ; he knew his master,
however, by the loss of a tooth, and falling on his knees beside
him, he exclaimed : " Monseigneur mon maître, monseigneur
mon maître ce estes vous ! Je prie à Dieu qui vous pardoinst
vos meffais. J'ay esté votre officier d'armes XI ans au plus,
il est temps que je le vous rende," and weeping sadly he
covered the fallen warrior with his coat of arms.

The death of Talbot was a very serious blow to the cause.
Pierre of Montferrant had escaped and returned to Bordeaux, and the English Seneschal Roger of Camoys was
in the city, but the heart had been taken out of the defence,
and it was now only a question of time when the end would
come.

Castillon fell almost immediately after the battle ; Saint-
Émilion, Libourne and Fronsac submitted ; Clermont wasted
the country of Médoc and took Castelnau and Lesparre.
Cadillac and Blanquefort held out bravely, but when they
fell Bordeaux lost heart completely. The siege, nevertheless,
lasted from 1 August to 18 October. Charles VII established
himself at Lormont, on the opposite side of the river, behind
strong defences. Clermont conducted the land attack ;
vessels of war skirmished continuously in the river and
blocked supplies. The Seneschal Roger of Camoys commanded the defence, helped by Henry Retford, the English
Mayor, Pierre of Montferrant and the Captal. At last famine
and despair did their work, and the garrison in Bordeaux
began to treat for peace. The debates were long, for at
first the King demanded the lives of twenty leaders and

the besieged could not permit such a sacrifice. At last the sentence was changed to one of banishment, and on those terms the surrender was made ; but Bordeaux had also to renounce all her old privileges and to pay the heavy sum of 100,000 crowns. The English were allowed to leave the town and were escorted to the coast by heralds and men-at-arms ; several of the burgesses begged to accompany them and left their native land to settle in England. The gates were opened to the French on 19 October, and the banners of France for the second time floated from the fortifications and from the Castle of the Ombrière.

When Bordeaux fell the little towns of Bénauges and Rions gave up the resistance which they were still maintaining. The period of English dominion was finally over. One more attempt was made to renew the vain struggle. Of the banished leaders, the Captal de Buch retired to Aragon where he had a little property, but most of them took refuge in England. Amongst them came the restless Sire de Lesparre, Pierre of Montferrant, and it was he who in 1454 came back secretly to stir up enmity to the French ; but this time he was to have no mercy, and his discovery and capture ended in his execution. The country was subdued, Bordeaux was reduced to comparative insignificance, and for long the burgesses looked back to the golden days of English rule. In 1457 the King of France wrote to the King of Scotland :

" As for the country of Guienne everyone knows it has been English for 300 years, and the people of the district are at heart entirely inclined to the English party ; wherefore it is more necessary to be watchful over than any other of our lands."

CHAPTER VII

GOVERNMENT AND ADMINISTRATION

A T the risk of a certain amount of repetition it may be of use to put together the conclusions which can be gathered as to the method of government adopted in the Duchy. Only a short sketch is possible here [1] and one or two general facts should be noticed. In Gascony—or in the larger Aquitaine—the system of central government and the procedure of the royal courts only represent a very small section of what was really happening. Here, as in all feudal countries, there was a great chaos of jurisdiction and a vast number of courts. The lords all had at least low justice in their own estates, and most of them claimed more than that, and whether they claimed it or no they exercised it : to some, rights of high justice were definitely granted by the King. The great Churchmen had their own seignorial jurisdiction as well as their own ecclesiastical jurisdiction, and it is not always easy to distinguish the cases which fall under one or the other. Above all, in Gascony there were numerous municipal courts : from those in which, as at Bordeaux, the Mayor and jurats exercised rights of the most ample description, to courts in the small bastides, where cases were tried according to the customs of that bastide, and where rights of jurisdiction were often shared between lords and *voisins*. The great communes again had governing bodies, which made them almost republics in all but name, and in some of the small valley communities meetings were held in which the *beziau* (the collection of all the *bezis* or *voisins*) decided

[1] The writer is hoping to work out this subject in far greater detail in the near future.

questions of war and peace as well as of bye-laws and pasture rights.

Central government can, however, be considered to some extent apart from the chaos of feudal courts. The royal Dukes of Aquitaine governed their country not merely as a feudal holding, but as a dependency over which they were sovereign lords, and in which they could introduce something of the centralized organization which they were building up in England. From the reign of Edward I, at least, Gascony had a very definitely formed administration, official rather than feudal in character, but influenced in its form by the conditions of the country itself, by its distance from England, by the fact of its strong municipal life and the need for maintaining it, and by the ever-present danger of the French claims of overlordship. The broad outlines of this system of government remained the same until the loss of the province, and can be described more or less as a whole ; but there are three periods in the course of this history which present some distinctive features of their own. These periods are the reign of Edward I, the time of the Black Prince's rule over the Principality of Aquitaine, and the fifteenth century after the Treaty of Troyes. Edward I's reign is important as that in which a regular system of Gascon administration was introduced and its machinery developed. After 1360, when the centre of government was shifted to the Principality, a few administrative changes were made and an independent court of justice for appeal was established. After the Treaty of Troyes, when the English King was recognized as Regent and heir to the French throne, Gascony became theoretically a French province under the supremacy of the King of France.

Even during the Black Prince's rule, however, with the exception of the new court of justice, no really-drastic changes were introduced in the machinery of government ; and it will be clearer, therefore, to consider briefly the nature and functions of the different officials and courts in turn, and as far as possible throughout the whole period of English dominion.

In periods of special stress and danger, generally when war

was threatening or the nobles revolting, and when the sovereign was unable to go himself, it was usual to send over a Lieutenant or Vicegerent with the very fullest powers, practically equal to those of the Duke himself. This office being of such great dignity and responsibility was generally bestowed on some very important noble or member of the Royal Family. Simon de Montfort, though called Seneschal, was really a Vicegerent, for he was given a completely free hand to conduct operations as he would. Sometimes these Lieutenants were more particularly leaders in war, and their authority was not so great and was less fully defined. Thus in 1337 we find Oliver of Ingham and Bernard d'Albret both called Lieutenants of the King, but chiefly taking military command. Henry, Earl of Derby, was the King's Lieutenant in 1345, and in 1355 the Black Prince was sent out, his powers being almost as complete as those which were bestowed upon him as ruler of the country after the Treaty of Brétigny. When he returned home to die in 1373, John of Lancaster was appointed Captain-General. Later we find (to enumerate only a few of them) such men as John Beaufort, Marquis of Dorset, in 1398; Thomas of Clarence in 1412; John, Earl of Huntingdon, 1438, and finally John Talbot, the Earl of Shrewsbury, in 1452. The Lieutenant took complete control during his term of office, and was the superior of all the permanent royal officials, but he was only the King's representative, and had to account for his acts to his royal master. The powers granted to the Black Prince after his appointment as Lieutenant in 1356 were the control of justice high and low, the summoning of the army, the punishing and pardoning of rebels, the granting out of lands in reward for service rendered, the levy of taxes and the making of truces with the enemy. The sole appointments which the King never granted away to his Lieutenants were those of the Seneschal, the Constable and the Mayor of Bordeaux. The actual carrying out of those powers and the independence or otherwise of the King's representative depended a good deal on the vigour of the King and the character of the Lieutenant, but the general custom was practically to hand over full control for the time being.

The permanent head of the government, however, was the Seneschal. His was an office which brought with it powers almost as great as those of the Lieutenant, but for the ever-present danger of dismissal should the King's anger be incurred. When neither King nor Vicegerent was in the Duchy the Seneschal was practically supreme and had a very great amount of business in his hands ; he was not essentially a military official, although he often had to fight, but he was the administrative head of the Duchy. The office in Gascony dates from the/twelfth century and was originally merely an honourable post in the Duke's household. The Seneschal was generally a knight, not a clerk, but not, as a rule, a noble of the first rank whose authority might have rendered him a serious danger, when he became the head of the government under the Duke. Edward I made a usual practice of choosing strangers to the Duchy for his Seneschals, doubtless to put them above local rivalries and intrigues : thus, in his reign, besides Englishmen such as Luke de Thanny, William Middleton and John Havering, we find Otto of Grandison, a Swiss (1278), Jean de Grailly from the Pays de Gex (1278–86), and John of Brittany (1294–5), a younger son of the Count of Brittany. The later Kings almost always chose Englishmen as Seneschals ; one Gascon, Gaillard de Durfort, Lord of Duras, held the office in the reign of Henry IV, but this was very unusual. The appointment was made at the good pleasure of the King, and there is great variety in the length of its tenure. Under Edward II the changes of Seneschal were constant, one year or two years seem to have been the usual period of office ; under later Kings some officers kept to their task much longer and were many of them very able men, such as Oliver of Ingham, Sir John Chandos and Sir Thomas Felton. The duties connected with the office were sometimes defined for special occasions, but as a rule the Seneschal had to be prepared to take the lead in everything, and to be ready for whatever might turn up. He might have to negotiate with the King of France and neighbouring Princes as well as with the Gascon vassals of the King. He had to be prepared to go to Paris to represent the King and guard his interests, should his overlord

of France receive petitions and try cases against him ; he was
generally given power to appoint the officials under him,
though not the Constable of Bordeaux, nor the Chancellor of
the Duchy, who were also special royal officers ; he presided
over the King's Council in Gascony, and the Court of Gascony
for judicial business, which met at first in the four different
centres of Bordeaux, Dax, Bazas and Saint-Sever.   He was in
fact the King's chief minister and responsible for all but
financial business, though the spending of the money was
largely in his hands ; that meant in the days when there was
little division in the functions of government that he was at
the head of military matters, justice and administration.
Constantly he was put on special commissions, or sent on
embassies and entrusted with exceptional powers, such as the
construction of bastides, the pardon of offenders, the putting
out of custom duties to farm.   The personal character of the
man really very much determined his authority.   The Gascons
were always ready to appeal to the King if they disliked the
Seneschal or had any grudge against him, and the King could
always dismiss a man whose judgment he could not trust, or
who seemed to be rousing too much opposition.   On the other
hand, the Seneschal could not always be sending over to England for advice, and often had to take important decisions on
his own responsibility.   We find an illustration of this in the
case of Oliver of Ingham, who put down troubles in the Landes
on his own authority in 1341, and had his action confirmed by
the King in the following year.   For his very arduous duties
the Seneschal was paid at the rate of £2,000 a year, but only
in money of Tours or Bordeaux, which was worth about a
quarter of the sterling money of England.   He had besides
something over and above that for expenses ; in 1317, £5,000,
and in 1318 his expenses and a gift of £5,000 into the bargain.
He had, however, to account to the Exchequer in England for
his expenditure, and was liable to get into trouble if the King
thought he had been either unnecessarily extravagant or oppressive to the people.   It is a little uncertain, also, how much he
was expected to do with this salary.   In 1289 John Havering,
who was paid £2,000 in the money of Bordeaux, was told that

he was not responsible for the wages of the under-Seneschals. Some servants he had, however, especially to help him and he probably paid some of them.   In 1317 an ordinance, drawn up with the consent of the Council at Bordeaux, decreed that there were to be twelve serjeants to help the Seneschal in the Duchy, who were to be nominated by him and only to be changed and replaced with his consent ; they seem to have been especially employed for putting in force his judicial sentences and helping at the assizes ; and a few years later Amaury de Craon ordained that the Seneschal should have a Chancellor to settle small cases which were purely formal, and to affix the seal to the decrees of the court of Gascony.   The judicial work of the Seneschal brings up the whole question of the different courts, and can best be considered under that heading.

The official next in importance to the Seneschal was the Constable of Bordeaux.   The usual duties of a Constable were military ;   he was at the head of a *connétablie* or troop of men-at-arms ;   but from Henry III's reign onwards the duties of this special Constable became financial and his office was the *comptablerie* ;   this became important and carefully organized under Edward I.   The Constable, unlike the Seneschal, was almost always a clerk, and as such better fitted to carry out the sort of duties attached to his office.   In the fifteenth century, however, this practice of employing clerks seems to have been sometimes abandoned, and several knights were appointed ;   for example, Sir William de Faryngdon and Sir William de Clifford in 1413, Sir John Ratcliffe (who afterwards became Seneschal) in 1419, and Sir Edward Hull in 1433.   It is not nearly so unusual, as in the case of the Seneschal, to find Gascons appointed to this office, although the majority of the Constables were English.   The appointment was in the King's hands, and the finance was carefully supervised by the Exchequer, but the Constable had a good deal of authority as the holder of the purse-strings, and no one in Gascony was allowed to interfere with him in his official duties. In 1445 the Gascon Council had tried to step in and prevent any expenditure without their consent, but Sir Edward Hull seems to have had the King on his side in his plea that he was responsible only to the Exchequer at home. The Constable paid out the salaries of most of the officials in Gascony; he received their accounts or appointed men under him to act as "receivers," and he did occasionally have Lieutenants, or sub-constables, probably to take his place when absent, for the Constable like the Seneschal might be put up on all sorts of special commissions, or sent up as a proctor of the King to represent his interests in Paris. The payment of the Constable in the thirteenth century is given as 20s. a day, Bordeaux money, and he was to have £70 with which to purchase robes for himself and his servant, a very much smaller salary than that allotted to the Seneschal. The whole cost of his office was, however, very heavy, for he had various officials to help him: his own clerk and his own serjeants; a controller to look after the rolls and papers at 10s. a day and £25 for his robes; and a number of collectors of taxes, treasurers, receivers and so forth. By degrees the Constable seems to have got the whole finance of the Duchy into his hands. At first when the King was present in person he might bring with him his own "travelling Treasury," the Wardrobe. Professor Tout has made this clear in his *Chapters in Mediaeval Administrative History*. From 1286 to 1289 when Edward I was administering the Duchy he had with him his Wardrobe and his Wardrobe officials, headed by William Louth as Keeper of the Wardrobe or Treasurer, and the accounts of officials were audited there and the very heavy expenditure financed. As a rule, however, the Constables are commanded to send their accounts straight to the Exchequer in England.

In the same way the King might at first take with him the English Chancellor. Thus in 1286 Edward I was accompanied by Robert Burnell and half his Chancery. But in the fourteenth century there seems always to have been a special Chancellor for Gascony, who is mentioned amongst the officials in the ordinance for reform of the government in 1322. He is, says the ordinance, to be a sufficient man, appointed with the approval of the Seneschal, Constable and members of the Council, he is to be guardian of the seal of the Duchy, and to receive as salary the emoluments of the seal.

In 1373 an ordinance of the Council at Bordeaux drew up a table of the exact sums which ought to be paid for the sealing of different writs, and from this we learn that at that time there was also a keeper of the little seal. The work during the rule of the Black Prince being more concentrated in Gascony itself doubtless became heavier and more organized, and there were more officials. From his time dates also the Judge of Gascony or Aquitaine, an official occasionally mentioned with the Seneschal and Constable when formal letters are sent out from England. He was at the head of the Court of Gascony ; but neither Judge nor Chancellor ever took the same important position as the two original officials, who were supreme under King or Lieutenant for administration and finance.

Besides the chief Seneschal for the whole Duchy there were under-Seneschals over the different districts, their numbers varying according to the extent of the country in English hands at the time. The main divisions under these subordinate Seneschals were the Landes, Saintonge, the three provinces of Périgord, Limoges and Quercy, and Agenais. The Agenais was organized with very special care by Edward I after its acquisition and had a good deal of separate organization of its own, almost as though he wished it to have a modified form of home rule ; it was, however, nominally under the Seneschal of Gascony and the central courts. On occasion there was also a Seneschal of the Isle of Oléron (1289), of Bigorre (1304) and during the rule of the Black Prince, of Poitou and Rouergue.

By the Ordinance of 1323 we find that the Seneschal of the Landes was to be paid £700, of Agen £600, of Périgord £500, and Saintonge £400. All were to have their commissions under the Seal of Gascony. These sub-Seneschals were frequently Gascons ; this was particularly the case during the rule of Edward I, but other Kings also often made use of the loyal nobles of the country to fill subordinate offices, a practice which was rather markedly abandoned by the Black Prince, who liked to fill all offices possible with his own English friends. Below the Seneschals were hosts of minor officials, provosts, bailiffs, constables or guardians of castles. Provosts as a general rule were over towns, and bailiffs or reeves over districts, but that is not by any means a universal rule ; the divisions were more often known as *baillages* in the Agenais, and *prévôtés* in the south, but on the other hand there were sometimes bailiffs in Labourd and Gosse and Seignans (divisions of the Landes), and provosts in Entre-deux-Mers. The difference of title does not seem to imply any special difference of function, and the office could be filled either by Knights or burgesses, Gascons or English. The most important Provost in the Duchy was a royal official, the Provost of the King's Castle of the Ombrière in Bordeaux, quite distinct from the Provost of the town of Bordeaux, who was a municipal agent. This officer was chiefly responsible for safeguarding the King's rights of justice in Bordeaux, where he divided authority with the Mayor and jurats. The Castle of the Ombrière had a certain district round it, where the King's men were subject to royal jurisdiction exercised by the Provost, and he was responsible for all strangers coming to the town or for offences committed on the river ; over all foreigners he had rights of high as well as of low justice, and possessed his own gallows. In 1314 the Seneschal Amaury de Craon arbitrated in a dispute between the municipality and the Provost, and drew up a careful division of their powers ; and in 1373 the King's Council laid down a table of fees due to the Provost and his clerk for certain necessary transactions. Besides justice he was supposed to report generally on the affairs of the town, especially in regard to military defence and war material.

Besides these main posts there were all sorts of offices, generally of a more or less lucrative nature, which could be given in reward for service by the King or by the Seneschal (apart from the strictly judicial offices which will be considered under the system of justice). There were secretaries, notaries or registrars and serjeants attached to all the great officials, or to the courts over which they presided, and there were besides gaugers of wine, whose business it was to see that casks were the right size and properly sealed, *bourdenagii* who supervised the making of barrels, collectors of *guidagium*, or payment due for the passage of cows to the different pastures ; criers who made known events and royal commands in the larger towns ; porters of castles, especially of the Ombrière, and many others.   The moneyers of Guienne were very important owing to the special coinage made there, and in 1289 an agreement was drawn up with them, fixing the special allowance granted to them for minting the different coins.   In the fourteenth century we find that they were under the jurisdiction of a special official of their own, the *Prévôt des Monnaies*, and they and their families were given special safeguards and were exempt from all taxation.

The government of the Duchy was thus partly controlled from England, partly organized on the spot, and the Gascon officials worked through certain recognized bodies, which varied in importance and independence, according to the character of the home government.

The King's Council in Gascony was regularly established, at least from the time of Edward I, and although it showed traces of feudal character since some of the great tenants-in-chief of the crown were always members of it, he organized it as far as possible as an official body, to which members were regularly appointed, and for attendance at which most of them were paid a definite salary.   This salary at first might vary very considerably, from £20 to £100, according to the ordinance of 1323, where it is also stated that in Périgord, the Abbot of Cadouin and the Provost of Pannac, " who are wise and rich, are to be Councillors without pay."   Evidently there was an old feudal element and a newer official element.   Unless the King was present, the Council was presided over by the Seneschal ; at first, meetings could be held wherever it was convenient ; in 1289 Edward I summoned a Council to Condom, but by degrees its official seat came to be the King's castle in Bordeaux.   The Council was to some extent a check on the power of the Seneschal, for most of his acts, the appointment of officials and so forth, were to be done with the consent of the Council.   It was the Council which was asked in 1313 to consider injuries inflicted on the country by French officials, and in 1326 to decide about losses claimed as due to the war.   It was the Council in 1378 which drew up ordinances fixing the salaries and fees of the various royal officials, and " the discreet men of the Council " considered the state of Dax in 1427 and allowed special tolls and perquisites for the repair of the forti-fications.   In Gascony, as elsewhere, administration and justice were never very distinct, and the Council had certain judicial powers especially over treason and the offences of nobles ; in 1445 it was reproved by the King for slackness in not bringing to justice a certain Bertrand de Gramont, said to be guilty of many evil deeds : and it was the Council which had to judge in a quarrel which the Captal de Buch and his son were having with the burgesses of Bordeaux in the fifteenth century.   Dur-ing the rule of the Black Prince the Council became known as the Great Council, and when Seneschals failed in doing justice or compelling payment of rents he would send out to summon the guilty parties before " les gens de notre grant conseil," but beyond the name it is difficult to see much difference in the body itself.

As for the composition of this body, it would appear that certain important Gascons were generally members of it, the Archbishop of Bordeaux, for example, and other leading ecclesi-astics of the city, the Dean of Saint-Seurin and Canons of Saint-André, and the chief nobles who were supporting the English.   Thus, for example, when Amanieu d'Albret died in 1324 his son Bernard was put in his place.   On the other hand, people were invited to be Councillors and could be dismissed if unsatisfactory.   Thus the Bishop of Saintes was added in 1423, the Bishop of Dax in 1433, and in 1424 the King threat-ened to remove Councillors who were not good men and who were receiving payments to the danger of the country.   Not only were the Councillors paid wages, and bound by oath, they were expected to be present when once they were appointed. Thus in 1423, when the Bishop of Dax was made a Councillor, it was to be for as long as the King wished, the salary was to be 100 marks annually, and if he were ever absent during the time that the Council was sitting, he must prove that he had a special excuse from the King himself, or that he was on royal business elsewhere.   The official character of the

Council is shown by the fact that men were appointed clearly not of noble rank. Thus in the fourteenth century we find mentioned as King's Councillors, Robert Gast and Gerald de Meuta ; in the fifteenth, William Boisset armiger, George Swythington, and Bernard de Garos, a burgess of Bordeaux. In 1433 the Council sent a deputation to England about certain grievances, and in his reply the King lays down the rule very firmly that the Councillors are only to be paid by himself, and to take their oath to him. Any receiving payments from local magnates should at once lose office. They were told that it was in their power to examine all letters patent sent out to Gascony, to complain on any matters, and that they should be under special protection as well as receiving a salary ; but in their turn they must defend the royal rights throughout the Duchy and be diligent in putting down anything to the prejudice of their sovereign lord. The Council by this time, at least, was clearly an official body with special oath and special duties, no feudal assembly of the great tenants-in-chief of the crown by virtue of their tenure.

Besides the royal officials and courts, the people of Gascony had certain powers, and at least the opportunity of making grievances known by means of the Provincial Estates. These are said to date from very early days, but they seem to become more active in the fourteenth and fifteenth centuries, and were chiefly of use in voicing the wishes of the people and in sending up complaints to the Seneschal, or to the English Government. They did, however, evidently claim to have some sort of control over taxation, for it was a meeting of prelates, nobles and commons at Angoulême in 1368 which granted to the Black Prince that *fouage* of ten shillings on each hearth, which was eventually to cost him so dear. This grant was made in return for redress of grievances which they themselves drew up. It is, however, fairly evident that the nobles took the lead on this occasion, for one request was that no taxation was to be levied on the subjects of the seigneurs without the consent of the seigneurs ; and no cases were to be removed from the rightful seignorial courts.

In 1394 the three Estates met to obtain concessions from

John of Lancaster, and here again the nobles were in considerable numbers, whilst the third estate chiefly represented Bordeaux and Bayonne. They gained practically all they asked, and it is interesting that John sent his reply not only to the body as a whole, but to each Estate separately. In 1414 the three estates at Bordeaux " ajustatz ensemble en parlement " in Saint-André sent an urgent request to the Seneschal that new money should be made ; and in 1447 the King sent an official notice concerning grants of land made to the Earl of Kendal, not only to the Seneschal, Constable and Judge, but also to the men of the Three Estates of Aquitaine. Despite the obvious importance of this body, there is nothing to indicate that it met at all regularly, or that it had much definitely recognized power beyond that of proffering requests and calling attention to grievances.

The remaining central bodies and government officials were mainly concerned with the administration of justice, and appointed directly for that purpose. At first the Seneschal held what were practically feudal courts of justice, at four centres, as a rule, Bordeaux, Bazas, Saint-Sever and Dax. These Courts existed in the time of Simon de Montfort, and nobles were summoned to answer at one or other of them, largely on land questions, but also on criminal matters. Apparently these courts were not always in the same towns, for in 1276 we read of the King's Court of Bazas at Saint-Macaire trying a complaint of the Lord of Bergerac against royal officials : and in the same year Arnaud Bernard de Lados was summoned to the Court of Gascony at Langon to answer before the Seneschal for a murder of which he was accused, and after three defaults had a fresh summons to appear at Bordeaux. There seems to have been no fixed composition of this court, but the number and importance of the members varied according to the nature of the case. By the fourteenth century, however, the Court of Gascony had become a permanent tribunal at Bordeaux, either under the Seneschal or the Judge of Gascony, who acted as his Lieutenant in judicial matters. The Court of Gascony was superior to the other courts in the country ; it could hear appeals even from the municipal court of Mayor and jurats, and could deal with disputes between secular and ecclesiastical jurisdictions. Professional judges were appointed to it : either ordinary judges or judges of appeal for both civil and criminal cases. Men learned in the law were appointed, and we find both Englishmen and Gascons amongst its members. In the fifteenth century the King appointed also a special " procurator fiscal." This office was often a stepping stone to that of Judge, and presumably included the presentation of criminals to the court. In 1430 one of these procurators was granted in reward for his good services houses and lands bringing in a revenue of about £10 a year. In 1320 it was decreed by the Seneschal Amaury de Craon that whilst his private Chancellor could settle small non-contentious cases, anything complicated must go up to the Court of Gascony, and its decrees were to be issued under its own special seal. There were judges in the different districts as well as in the central courts, and the Seneschal is said to hold assizes through the country, but the Court of Gascony was superior to them all. It did not, however, make the final decision. The Kings of England were always prepared to hear appeals themselves, and in Parliament special triers were appointed to hear Gascon petitions, many of which petitions were for the reconsideration of some decision given in the Courts of the Duchy. Till 1360, however, the real weakness of the royal position lay in the fact that as Gascony was held as a fief from the King of France, it was the King of France who really had the right of final jurisdiction, and Gascons could always appeal against the English royal Courts to the Parliament of Paris. The King of France was only too glad to press this right of superiority, and there are instances of his attempts to extend his right still further, as in 1317 when the men of Bayonne complained that burgesses were summoned to Paris in the first instance, when the French King only ought to have exercised jurisdiction if they had appealed. It was, however, a good method of expressing disapproval of the English overlord and his officials, and English proctors had to be kept constantly in Paris to deal with cases which occurred there. In Edward I's reign such cases were numerous. In 1277 the Archbishop of Bordeaux and the

Dean of Saint-Seurin complained that the Seneschal was encroaching upon ecclesiastical courts and interfering with Church rights : that the Provost of Barsac had hanged a clerk and arrested a crusader. The French King in this case sent arbitrators to try the case on the spot, and heavy compensation was imposed on the officials who had offended. In 1289 certain Gascon nobles appealed to the French overlord about the doings of English officials ; a little later a merchant claimed that he was unable to get redress from the court of the Seneschal, although a certain man from Condom had actually confessed that he had been hired to murder him. In the fourteenth century the same sort of thing was going on, and any noble who felt aggrieved by the decision of the Seneschal could render himself obnoxious to him by carrying his case up to Paris. This grievance was met at last by the Treaty of Brétigny : Aquitaine was to be held independently of France, and that meant an end to the supreme justice of Paris. At first King Edward kept the power of hearing appeals in his own hands, but it was clearly a great difficulty for subjects to come to England, and in 1365 he commissioned the Prince to give the final decision in his own Principality. There seems to have been a temporary court at first for this purpose, known as the *Curia Magnorum Dierum*, and in 1366 judgment was given before it in a dispute as to the rival jurisdiction of Mayor and Seneschal, the decision being in favour of the Mayor. At last in 1370 a Sovereign Court, *Curia Superioritatis*, was instituted, which was to be the final court of appeal in all disputes from all courts, and which continued to function until the first conquest of Bordeaux in 1451. This court was largely composed of Gascons and chiefly of clerks with only a few lay nobles. It met at first at Saintes, but when all that part of the country was overrun by the French it went in its turn to Bordeaux. Here we find it recognized under Henry IV, who increased its legal element, and its members were evidently salaried officials, paid by the Constable of Bordeaux. The members of this High Court of Justice were renewed from time to time : one or two of the chief nobles were generally members (e.g. in 1378 the Captal de Buch, the Lords of Lesparre and Duras) and some of the leading Bishops and Abbots, and generally the Constable of Bordeaux ; power was put into the hands of a quorum, three generally being considered sufficient, and they were commanded to give their decisions in accordance with the customs of the country.   The Chancellor of the Duchy was sometimes the president of the court.   In 1414 John de Bordil was given the seal of the Supreme Court, and also appointed Chancellor.   As usual division of justice was vague, and there was no definite enforcement of the rule that appeal must finally go up to this *Cour Supérieure*, with the result that there is often some confusion between this court, the King's Council and the Court of Gascony, which still continued to sit.   The fact that members of one were often members of the others makes this confusion more marked, but they were nevertheless three quite distinct bodies.

Despite all these various methods of securing justice, the practice of sending out special commissions from England to hear certain cases, and the appointment of arbiters *ad hoc* was very usual, and continued even after the establishment of the High Court ; indeed it would appear on the whole as if the method of arbitration was the most popular and attended by the best results.

The mere enumeration of courts and officials gives little idea of the real history of judicial procedure in Gascony.   The complication of many courts and many jurisdictions meant that almost as many trials were held for deciding the competence of courts, as for settling civil or criminal cases.   In Bordeaux there were not only the courts of Mayor and jurats with authority over the burgesses to dispute with the court of the Provost of the Ombrière with authority over foreigners, but there were also the courts of the Archbishop of Bordeaux and of the Dean of Saint-Seurin, both of whom had parts of the town under their special justice ; and in the fifteenth century, at least, there was a Military Court held there, under constables and marshals, in which cases were tried by wager of battle. There were also disputes as to the trial of clerks and the extent of benefit of clergy.   In Bayonne the town had two courts, one for noble and one for non-noble, and here also there were disputes between Municipality and Bishop ; and in the smaller towns and bastides justice was frequently divided between lord and King or lord and town.   Whenever possible the King tried to keep in his own hands the control of high justice, but many seigneurs exercised it, sometimes as the result of a royal grant, but still more frequently without.   For procedure and punishment also it was necessary to follow the customs or *fors* of the town and district ; in some places the customs of Bordeaux, in some the customs of Bazas ; justice in Agen had different rules from those which prevailed in Labourd and so forth.   All this makes the study of justice in Gascony complicated and lengthy.   One feature, however, stands out clearly from the reign of Edward I onwards, and that is the effort of the ruler to centralize the system of justice as far as possible without antagonizing the nobles and towns.   Thus we find the Seneschal holding assizes through the country, lawyers and judges constantly sent out from England to assist him, and the attempt to establish a strong central court, culminating in the Sovereign Court of Appeal in 1370.   Although this court was never very popular nor much used, Bordeaux felt it to be an additional grievance against France, when she ceased to be the seat of final jurisdiction after 1453.

CHAPTER VIII

THE COMMUNES OF GASCONY

GASCONY contains much of interest for the student of communal development in France. The chief towns were midway between the *Communes jurées* of the north and the *Consulates* of the south. They were greatly privileged and very powerful, but not wholly independent, and they can be closely compared to Rouen, another great centre of early English rule. They show, therefore, distinct signs of English influence and of the policy of English Kings, but they also illustrate the fact that French towns very largely worked out their own salvation, for they generally won for themselves the powers and independence which were later confirmed to them by royal charter, and even though under some degree of royal control, they were the most important of vassals and had to be conciliated rather than coerced. Gascony also furnishes illustrations of the affiliation of towns and of the influence one great privileged centre could have on others ; and we find here a wonderful body of municipal law, for each great town had its own customary code of rules and procedure, which was added to later by the statutes issued by the governing body. The effort to maintain these old *fors* or customs, which were looked upon by the inhabitants as a charter of liberties, helped to bind the townsmen together, and thus played a part in the formation of the Commune very similar to that so often ascribed to the Merchant Gild in the northern towns. The Gascon towns do not appear to have had actual Merchant Gilds ; trade regulations were inserted in the customs, or were given by charter to the burgesses or to the governing body of the town, not to a special trading community. Even craft gilds

152

were rare. At Bayonne, in John's reign, an important society of navigators was formed with its own officials and its own regulations ; but the other *corps de métiers* had their rules laid down in the *établissements* ; whilst at Bordeaux separate trading associations were not at all encouraged by the municipality. A few small crafts, such as those of the goldsmiths and the barbers, existed in English Bordeaux, but no other trade societies were formed there before the latter half of the fifteenth century, in the reign of Louis XI. Up till 1453 the *Jurade* itself was all-important. Another special feature of Gascon towns was chiefly due to historical events and to the long effort made by the English to maintain their rule in the southwest. In the fourteenth century, when other towns in France were tending to decline and to lose their independence before the centralizing policy of the monarchy, the towns in Gascony were gaining new privileges and new strength. Their support —and especially that of Bordeaux—was vitally important to Edward III in the Hundred Years' War, and to the House of Lancaster in its final effort to retain the French possessions. Hence the towns were constantly favoured and were able to occupy a position which it was impossible for them to maintain when once united to France.

The fortunes of the country were obviously swayed by the three chief towns—Bordeaux, Bayonne, and Dax ; and on the loyalty of these three towns largely depended the fate of English rule.

Bordeaux was early bound to England by strong trading interests. The centre of a rich wine-growing district, and the main port of that district, she looked to England for her chief market. The English demand for wine was constant, and the perils of the sea passage were no greater than those of land transport through the most turbulent part of France. The French could drink other wines, and had perhaps less money to spend on purchases than had the English, whilst trading privileges were early granted as inducements to the merchants of Bordeaux to give England the preference in her treasured export. Every English King grasped the essential need for binding Bordeaux to the English cause. But Bordeaux was not only important on account of her own wealth, her own trading value and her own strong military position, but because her attitude decided the attitude of the surrounding country. Commanding as she did the great waterway of the Garonne, she commanded also the welfare of the little towns along its banks, which were practically bound to conduct their trade with whatever ruler Bordeaux favoured. Saint-Macaire, La Réole and Bazas all used the river for transporting their goods to the sea and they could scarcely venture to dispute the mastery of Bordeaux. Saint-Émilion and other towns on the Dordogne were rather less dependent geographically on Bordeaux, and therefore rather more doubtful in their allegiance to England, but the Gironde, formed by the junction of the Garonne and Dordogne, was much under Bordelais control, and the river Dordogne, therefore, could not wholly shake off the influence of Bordeaux.

Bayonne seems in some ways to have been less dependent on the connection with England than was Bordeaux. She could send her goods fairly easily to Spain, and she could trade on her own account instead of through Bordeaux as did the smaller towns. But the welfare of Bayonne depended not so much on her trade as on her shipbuilding ; Bordeaux largely made use of her ships, and here again, therefore, the final word was in favour of the English connection.

Dax on the upper reaches of the Adour, though able to carry on some inland trade, was inevitably affected by the influence of Bayonne which stood at the mouth of the river.

As has been already stated, the English Kings early grasped the essential value of town support and, with very few exceptions, adopted a policy of conciliation and generosity, of granting privileges and of treating turbulence with as little severity as might be.

Bordeaux had not yet gained her municipal organization when she came into the hands of Henry II, but she was already a town of considerable prominence and importance. There was a royal palace there in which Eleanor of Aquitaine had stayed with her first husband Louis VII, and in which she later spent Christmas with her second husband, Henry Plan-

tagenet ; and there also Richard Cœur de Lion was proclaimed
Duke in 1169. The royal Duke and his Provost were still,
however, the chief authorities in the town ; but the growth
of municipal liberties and self-government was not long in
beginning. Bordeaux, important as she was commercially,
could not fail to desire political powers, but it was not till
John's reign that she can be called a Commune, and not till
that of Henry III that she was formally recognized as such.
The royal charter of 1224 ratifies an already accomplished fact,
when the King states that he grants " a commune and an
elective mayor." Some proofs are available that this was
the culminating point of a gradual development. In 1200 a
royal letter is addressed to the jurats and burgesses of Bordeaux ; in 1205 the faithful *prud'hommes* are let off a *maltolte*,
and in 1206 a Mayor is mentioned for the first time. The King
writes humbly to the " Mayor, jurats and faithful men of Bordeaux " to ask if they will accept the Seneschal whom he has
appointed. There was very good reason why John should
acquiesce in the communal government which Bordeaux had
established. Gascony, at this date, was being threatened by
Alfonzo VIII of Castille. He had married a daughter of Henry
II in 1169, and in 1204 he claimed Gascony as a dowry and
crossed over the Pyrenees to assert his right. There were
always Gascon nobles ready to support any pretender against
the *de facto* government, and after an interview with the
Viscount of Béarn and the Count of Armagnac, Alfonzo took
the title of Seigneur of Gascony. In 1206 he had captured
Blaye and Bourg, and was threatening Bordeaux herself.
This explains very readily John's acceptance of the independent
action of a town whose loyalty to himself it was essential to
maintain.

It has long been a questionable point how far the constitution of Bordeaux was influenced by the constitution of
Rouen, favoured by the English Kings because not too independent. This form of constitution had already been extended
to some of the towns of Aquitaine, notably La Rochelle,
Saintes, and Poitiers, and was evidently the model for the
municipalities of Bayonne and Saint-Émilion. But the con-

stitution of Bordeaux was no exact imitation. At Rouen the
Mayor was chosen by the King from a list of three ; there
was a body of *échevins*, twelve in number, and a body of twelve
Councillors, these twenty-four elected by the *cent pairs*, the
special characteristic of the Rouen *Établissements*. Bordeaux,
on the contrary, had a Mayor elected by the body of jurats,
who were fifty in number and who also chose their successors
when they left office at the end of a year. Mayor and jurats
together chose thirty Councillors for advice and assistance,
and a large elective body of three hundred was responsible for
the good order of the town. The whole body of burgesses—
the commune itself—was also called together on occasion ;
to them the jurats had to swear to exercise their functions
justly, and to them they had to prove their innocence if accused
of revealing the secrets of the municipality. Though the
government tended to become oligarchical, the burgesses as a
whole took considerable part in the life of the city.

Clearly the town had made for itself a more independent
constitution than that of Rouen, but there are details of the
organization, form of oaths, and so forth, which imply that the
Établissements were not unknown to the framers of the municipal government of Bordeaux, that a certain number of the
regulations were adopted as they stood, but that others were
modified to suit the circumstances of the more independent
town, at a time when it was able to assert its wishes with good
expectation of success. The Mayor and jurats had both civil
and criminal jurisdiction in their hands, but royal authority
was maintained by the King's official, the Provost of the
Château of the Ombrière, who had jurisdiction over officials
and inhabitants of the castle and its immediate surroundings,
and over any stranger coming to the town. But the power of
the municipality was very great. Mayor and jurats could
make rules and add to town statutes, although this had to be
done subject to royal approval, and with possibility of appeal
to King or Seneschal against them : they could collect taxes,
could call the people to arms and could even make treaties and
alliances with neighbouring towns. Bordeaux was a Commune, a vassal of the English King, a *Seigneurie collective*.

Its authority was shown by its belfry (attached to the Church of Saint-Éloi) to summon its own dependents, and its common unity by its seal and by its power of owning corporate property. The wisdom of the Kings in allowing Bordeaux to keep this independent constitution was shown by the loyalty of the town when the royal charter was granted in 1224. The French were invading Gascony, Saint-Émilion, Saint-Macaire and Langon were ready to open their gates to them, but " nothing, neither prayers nor money, could turn the Bordelais from their fidelity." This early constitution did not stay intact. It was altered both by royal interference and by municipal regulations. The most important change was that introduced by Edward I, when in 1261 he took the *Mairie* into his own hands (see page 52) and saw to it that he nominated, as Mayors of Bordeaux, men who would be loyal to him and who were not concerned with town rivalries. For a time in Edward's reign the town regained its right of election (from 1277 to 1288), but this was soon lost in consequence of an unwise appeal sent up to the King of France by some of the jurats, and the control of the King remained until 1343, when Edward III was anxiously striving for all the support he could get, and allowed the jurats once more to elect the Mayor. The number of jurats was also changed from time to time ; they were reduced to twenty-four in 1241, and to twelve in 1375. The qualifications for this office at that date were fairly high. A jurat must be born in Bordeaux, free and independent, a householder residing in the town and possessing at least £1,000 in Bordeaux money, or £200 of annual rent.[1] The thirty Councillors were paid a salary and did not need to show a special property qualification : the 300 were only summoned on special occasions, and scarcely can be said to form part of the actual municipal government.

In the fourteenth century, Edward III's policy towards Bordeaux is shown by his constant grants of increased trading privileges ; Richard II endeavoured to put the Bordelais on exactly the same footing as English merchants ; Henry IV had to do what he could to gain over a town whose sympathies

---

[1] On the value of Bordeaux money see p. 205.

were strongly in favour of the fallen Richard of Bordeaux (son of the Black Prince and born in Bordeaux). In the fifteenth century not only was the town itself more influential than ever, but the burgesses seem to have won for themselves rather more democratic influence within the town itself, for general meetings of all the burgesses were held more frequently than before. In 1408, for example, the people were summoned to choose a Lieutenant to take the place of the Mayor whilst he was absent in England; in 1410 a general meeting actually drew up rules for the municipality: and in 1415 the general assembly was held on three occasions, to hear news of the French wars, to make complaints against certain officials, and to say farewell to the Mayor before his departure to England. Apparently the general body had to be summoned when special subsidies were required by the King, before the consent of the townsmen to such taxation could be secured. It was no wonder that Bordeaux was anxious not to risk her unusual independence in the fifteenth century, nor her commercial prosperity: and the French had a hard struggle to conquer her in 1453. Charles VII took into his own hands the appointment not only of the Mayor, but also of the jurats and town clerk: heavy tolls were imposed, and it was long before Bordeaux recovered her early prosperity and ceased to regret her English connection.

Bordeaux had always been important for her influence over the neighbouring towns on the Dordogne and Garonne: it was, however, during the Hundred Years' War that the influence she had so long exercised through trade was turned into a definite alliance, and Bordeaux became the centre of a confederation of smaller towns known as *filleules*, which imitated her privileges, looked to her for protection and were bound with her as vassals of the English King, their immediate overlord. Some of these smaller towns had been for long in possession of municipal organization, though in times of war they were not strong enough to defend their right alone. Saint-Émilion had a charter dating from John's reign, and a constitution in which the influence of Rouen is clearly seen; Libourne had been created by Edward I near the royal castle of Condat ; Bourg-sur-Mer claimed to be more free than the Lombard cities, it owed military service to the King, but under the banner of Bordeaux ; La Réole, a town which had given much trouble in the past owing to its strong position and its fortifications, was now under the direct safeguard of Bordeaux ; the others were all privileged, though not completely independent. Bazas, Saint-Macaire, Rions, Langon, Meilhan, and a few others, complete the number of *filleules*. They were all important for military reasons and for trade. Fortified and strongly situated, they were also centres of the main wine-growing district of Gascony, from which England bought so largely. Bordeaux and its *filleules* remained to England when so much was lost at the close of Edward III's reign, and in the fifteenth century formed the last bulwark of her falling fortunes.

Bayonne, the town second in importance to Bordeaux, had never quite as much independence in its constitution, although it could act independently enough on occasion and was the scene of many a turbulent uproar. Bayonne won her way gradually to communal existence through the stage known as that of a *ville de bourgeoisie*. Economic progress, as ever, gave rise to a desire for political advance, and by a charter of Richard I it acquired some measure of jurisdiction and various communal privileges. A court of burgesses was formed, though as yet not under a town magistrate, but under a royal Provost. The charter speaks, however, of the Council of Bayonne and the whole community. In the early thirteenth century the town was working towards more independent powers, for a Society of Mariners was formed in 1213 " by the will and consent of all the Bayonnais people," without any mention of royal approval. The communal government, which was apparently formed by the town before the consent of the King confirmed and established it, was in 1215 almost exactly like that of Rouen. A body of *cent pairs* elected twelve *échevins* and twelve councillors, and sent up a list of three names to the King, out of which he nominated the Mayor, and all the inhabitants took oath to form the new association. But Bayonne was constantly giving trouble, and in 1243 Henry III not only nominated the Mayor, but all the hundred peers, and when Edward took over the government he forced the men of Bayonne to swear that they would obey the Mayor he should appoint, and never bind themselves together in leagues and confederations. Bayonne did, however, acquire a good deal of communal power ; the municipality was allowed to make its own statutes, so long as they were neither against old custom nor royal right, and there was a municipal court of justice under the *échevins*, as well as a royal court under the Provost, and an ecclesiastical court under the *official* ; but the communal court did not have criminal justice over life and limb, and it was the royal Provost who collected the King's taxes, not the town officers. In the fourteenth century, however, the *cent pairs* did, for a time at least, elect the Mayor, and there were meetings of inhabitants or *voisins*, who occasionally even sat with the peers. Treaties of peace were made between Bayonne and Biarritz, between Bayonne and Saint-Sebastian, and between Bayonne and the Lord of Gramont : the formula runs " by the Mayor, jurats and *cent pairs* of Bayonne in the name of the whole city of Bayonne." Thus Bayonne showed development similar to that of Bordeaux, though not the same. Its powers depended a good deal on its behaviour, for at times the Kings had to take more control than at other, when loyalty was rewarded by fresh privileges : the power of the town increased on the whole in the fourteenth century, and the *voisins* played a considerable part in town life, not only for police and militia work, but for assent to regulations and for occasional conferences.

Dax was a very early commune under an official known as a *capdel* and twenty jurors : up till the reign of Henry III, the English Kings granted chiefly trading privileges to the town, but in 1243 it was given the right of having a Mayor, though the Mayor was to be chosen by the King or his Seneschal from a list of those presented to them by the people. The powers of jurisdiction were never wholly communal, profits were shared between the King and the commune, and the same division was to take place if any citizen forfeited his goods by reason of offending against the rules of the town. In the fourteenth century Dax also seems to have gained some further rights. All burgesses, and even the inhabitants of the suburbs were to be under the jurisdiction of the Mayor and jurats, whilst the King's court was confined to cases concerning nobles, royal officials and strangers ; at times treaties were made with other towns, but chiefly on trade questions.   On the whole, it would appear that the importance of Dax was chiefly commercial, and it was bound to the English crown by the grant of trading privileges and freedom from tolls.

Smaller towns, all with some degree of municipal organization, have been mentioned amongst the *filleules* of Bordeaux ; others, such as Agen, Blaye, Lectoure, and Saint-Sever, had their own customs from old times and their own privileges from royal grant, but they are not on quite the same footing as these three larger places.   At the same time the little walled town of Lectoure must have felt full of importance when their consuls issued a declaration in 1274 that they would desist from pursuing the King and his Seneschal Luke de Thanny any longer on account of their evil deeds, since they recognized that full satisfaction had now been received for them.

Some of these smaller towns, and also the bastides (see Chapter IX), adopted the southern name for their town officials, and instead of *échevins* or jurats we find consuls forming the municipal government : but both forms are found scattered throughout Gascony, there is no invariable rule as to nomenclature.

The old customs and the later statutes or *établissements* of the *Jurades* throw considerable light on town life and habits in these early days.   The customs generally represented very ancient customary law handed down by tradition, and only drawn up in writing at a much later date, often about the thirteenth century.   Sometimes these were in force beyond the actual town itself.   Thus the customs of Bordeaux prevailed throughout the diocese of Bordeaux ; and those of Bayonne were observed by several of the surrounding towns.

All these town customs were largely made up of judicial regulations, such as the amount of the fines to be levied for certain offences, the punishment to be imposed and the method

of procedure to be adopted.   From those also can be learnt
the special rules as to succession to property, which often varied
from place to place, and any conditions affecting prosperity in
any one town or the industries which were practised there.   To
these were added by degrees trading privileges granted by
charter, rules as to town administration, election of officials,
and sometimes strict sumptuary laws imposed by the municipality.   Punishments and fines were very similar in different
places, although the sums exacted varied somewhat and the
tendency to commute penalties for money payments was fairly
constant everywhere.

The customs of Bordeaux are fairly typical.   They represent
for the most part primitive customary law, codified little by
little after Bordeaux had become a Commune, and with some
very slight traces of the influence of Roman law.   Recourse
to actual Roman law, according to a fourteenth-century decree,
was only to be made if Bordelais customs, similar customs of
the neighbourhood and general principles of local law had all
been tried and proved insufficient ; a proof that local law was
distinct from Roman and superior to it in the eyes of the
populace.   The decrees of different Mayors, grants from the
English overlord, and occasionally decisions of the Parliament
of Paris when appeal had been made to it, were added by
degrees to the original material, and thus was built up a whole
body of rules for judicial and other cases.

In Bordeaux fines varied from five shillings for trespass in
a garden or vineyard to as much as 300 shillings for inflicting
the most serious injuries.   Crimes committed at night were
always fined double those of the day, but no money penalty
was allowed to exceed 300 shillings.   Sixty-five shillings was
a very usual fine and was imposed for a great variety of misdeeds : for taking the grapes of other people, for dirtying
the public fountain, for throwing dirty water out of window,
or rubbish into the stream running through the town, or even
for leaving a pig on the paved pathway.   One very interesting
feature of the rules made by the magistracy of Bordeaux is the
fact that officials were punished more severely for their offences
than were the ordinary townsmen.   The reputation of the

members of the Jurade was high and they meant to maintain it. Thus in the *établissement* drawn up in the thirteenth century we find that a Mayor who broke the rules of the town must pay four times what an ordinary citizen would pay, and a jurat must pay double ; a very heavy fine was imposed if a jurat should so far demean himself as to strike one of his fellows. On the other hand, a jurat could clear himself from accusation by a simple oath which must be believed, but if he could not swear that he had not betrayed town secrets, he might never again be elected to his high position.

For some offences definite punishments were decreed by the customary law, although it seems probable that many such punishments were commuted for money, as the money equivalent is often added in the regulations. Some of the penalties imposed by primitive law were very horrible ; the customs in Bordeaux and elsewhere decreed that a murderer should be buried alive below his victim. Hanging and burning were also employed as death penalties ; hanging for so terrible an offence as mutilating a child for purposes of begging, and also for digging up corpses to be used in sorcery ; burning for bringing about the death of an enemy through sorcery. For the first offence a thief was to be put in the pillory, for the second he had to lose an ear, and for the third to be hanged. Certain misdeeds obliged a man to forfeit his burgess-ship altogether, such, for example, as killing the Prince, counterfeiting his money or seal, stealing from the Treasury, or becoming a heretic. On the other hand, officers of the King or of any other lord were to be punished severely for any miscarriage of justice, for execution without due cause, for killing by torture or by starvation, for keeping anyone in prison in order to get hold of his wife or his lands.

In the fourteenth century a good many regulations were laid down for the conduct of ordinary life. Marriages were only allowed to be made in the daytime, and the newly married couple were not to be persecuted by their friends : there was to be no dancing nor reception outside the house of the parents ; and at funerals also expenditure was to be reduced, only candles of a special size and quality might be burned and only two grave-cloths used.

The town itself of Bordeaux was gradually growing. The original wall enclosed a very small space in the centre of the present town : the rampart of 1200 one slightly larger, and still a third fortification surrounding that was begun at the close of the thirteenth century. It was ordained that anyone climbing over the fortifications into the town, unless he did so to escape some danger to his life, must be condemned to lose a foot. Incidental notices throw light on the nature of the town dwellings in the thirteenth and fourteenth centuries. The nobles and important burgesses had stone houses, and it was a sign of importance to have a little turret at the side of such a dwelling ; simple burgesses might live in wooden houses, and the poorest classes of all in poor little hovels. The house covering in the town was generally of tile ; thatch was not common in Bordelais even in the country. The only castle in Bordeaux under the English was the King's palace of Ombrière, the seat of the magistracy was in the neighbourhood of Saint-Éloi, and it was the tower of that church which was used as the municipal belfry. A man's house was very much his castle, and the house of a citizen of Bordeaux might never be destroyed for misdeeds or debt, but the doors could be carried off or the place occupied until satisfaction was made. Edward I had once pulled down a house in error and was obliged to give back the property to its possessor. So privileged was Bordeaux that residence in it for a month and day would confer freedom, instead of the usual year and a day which is common to most towns.

In Bayonne the town court had less authority than that of Bordeaux : the old customs are largely made up of family rules showing the characteristic which prevailed throughout the Basque country, in which the family had practically community of goods. The later rules made by the municipality show how much attention had to be given to keeping the town even comparatively peaceful, and they also point to a popular tendency towards extravagance and luxury in dress, for the sumptuary laws were very detailed and severe. In 1290 an order to roof houses in the town with tiles seems to indicate that thatch had been used here in the past. There are records of fires taking place in Bayonne, and this was probably an attempt to obviate such a danger. At the same time it was made a serious offence to carry arms about the town, to shield malefactors, or even to share houses, as that was said to have given rise to too many disputes. A little later special guards were appointed for the streets and country roads, and no one was allowed to be out after the *couvre-feu* had sounded ; anyone stretching cords across the streets after dark was to be fined 100 shillings. Despite such laws, riots in Bayonne were of constant occurrence.

The sumptuary laws were, as in Bordeaux, partly aimed at the expense caused by funerals and weddings. Criers were not to be hired for funerals and women might only wear the special black mantle, which was the sign of mourning, for specified periods. At weddings only a few guests might be invited, and each guest was ordered to pay 12*d.* for his supper, so that the invitations cannot have been accepted with much alacrity in any case. For a long time only three men and six women were allowed to be present, and a bride was not supposed to give to her husband a present of more than two shirts. Women were not to possess more than one dress lined with silk and three head coverings, one of which alone was to have a silk lining. Coverings and ornaments on beds were also carefully defined, and such coverings were never to be adorned with gold or silver fringes.

Swearing and gambling were offences which evidently required drastic treatment. Games of chance were forbidden on pain of a fine of ten shillings ; blasphemy incurred a fine of twenty shillings, as did also the swearing by God or the passion of God, the Holy Virgin and the Saints. Bribery and corruption were also dealt with severely, for officials and those anxious to obtain positions were not above illicit methods of obtaining posts and power. In 1327 the magistrates state that money and presents had been offered the Seneschal by those anxious to become Mayor, and this was strictly forbidden for the future ; whilst no one in a municipal office was to be allowed to receive more than £100 as salary.

The general behaviour of the inhabitants was certainly kept under close supervision by the governing body and it did its best to avoid the disorders for which Bayonne had become sadly notorious at one time. Special oaths were taken by all the leading inhabitants. Doctors had to swear to visit sick people at a reasonable charge, and to go to the poor for less payment than the rich, to use good drugs in their medicines, not those weakened by age, and never to intrigue with the apothecary. Apothecaries had to promise to follow the doctors' prescriptions faithfully and not to use bad materials. Lawyers, traders, taverners, manufacturers of all sorts had their special oaths, and experts were appointed to supervise shipbuilding, barrel-making, fish-curing, and so forth. Shipping and fish naturally obtained rather special attention in Bayonne.

At Dax, where members of all the different trades had to take a similar oath, the butchers objected and wished to make their own oath that they would form no league for the sale of meat, instead of the form laid down by the *établissements*. The matter was sufficiently important to go up from the Court of Dax to the Court of Gascony at Bordeaux, and the butchers had to give way.

At Bazas the customs were largely concerned with rural matters. Punishments were imposed on those who did not cultivate their vineyards properly, and what fruit they did produce had to be forfeited in whole or part. Here the lord might take away the door of a house for non-payment of rent ; or if the door was shut he could put a nail on it, and then the tenant was not allowed to enter until he had made up his arrears and also paid a fine as punishment. Theft at night in Bazas involved hanging, and so did the third offence of a thief ; no one under fourteen, however, could be condemned to death for any crime, but had to be whipped through the town. There were exact regulations for the trespass of beasts. If a cow strayed into the field of another master, 4d. for each of the beast's feet could be charged ; for a donkey the due was 3d. a foot if it were shod, 2d. otherwise, and for a sheep or a dog *2d.* a foot was the sum. Here also we seem to find a trace of the primitive custom which once prevailed in the Pyrenees of punishing the animals, for a beast might have its tongue cut if it did damage in a vine already worked, and a goose trampling in the corn could have its beak pulled off. It was lawful to set traps in your garden to catch the straying chickens of your neighbour.

It is impossible to enumerate all the usual town regulations. It would appear that in every case where a body of customs has been preserved that these represent very primitive rules, closely resembling one another throughout the country, and very similar to old Germanic and Scandinavian customs free from much intermixture with Roman law. To those were gradually added regulations which arose from the local characteristics of the different districts, with an occasional trace of Roman law as studied by the jurists of the time. There was evidently strong local feeling and considerable local variety in details and in development. This is shown in the varying rules as to the position of nobles in the towns. In some cases they might be received as burgesses, but more frequently this could only be done with special leave (after 1261 in Bordeaux only with consent of the King). The burgesses of a great town, however, were practically equal to the nobles in importance and superior to many of them in wealth and power. Some were climbing up to the position of great seigneurs. Whilst still burgesses with town property they could acquire noble lands without the walls, and so we find Gaillard Delsoler also becoming Seigneur of Belin. It was a real honour and an advantage to become a burgess. Edward III constantly rewarded knights and nobles for the help they had given him in his wars by conferring on them the privilege of burgess-ship in Bordeaux. There are frequent instances of the daughters of burgesses marrying nobles, and they must have often brought considerable accession of wealth to their husbands, for the nobles of Gascony were conspicuous for poverty as well as for pride.

In 1289 Jean Colom gave his daughter in marriage to the son of the Seigneur of Langoiran, and bestowed upon her not only three robes lined with vair and a palfrey and harness worth £100, but £1,000 down in money and the promise of an annual sum of £50 for the future. Bordeaux merchants were not unlike the great merchant princes of Italy in their wealth and power, and their constant loans to King and government gave them a hold over the public administration of Gascony, as well as over the affairs of their own town and its management.

No account of towns or town-life would be complete without some description of the trade which was the great source of their wealth and which did so much to bind them to England. The whole history of Gascony was influenced by the fact that its soil was pre-eminently suited to the culture of the vine. This is especially true of Northern Gascony, but to some extent of the whole country, except the waste Landes and the wild mountains. The result was that vineyards were increasingly planted at the expense of other crops, and far more wine was made than the country itself needed, whilst other produce was often lacking. Thus commercial exchange became early an urgent necessity, and Gascony looked for it to those countries where the demand for wine would be greatest and where supplies of corn and wool could be procured for home consumption. Naturally it was Bordeaux, with its excellent position for foreign trade, which became the chief centre of the wine export ; Bayonne and Dax, as has been already seen, were also mercantile towns, although shipbuilding was the main industry of the Bayonnais burgess. The growing of vines became more and more the prevailing form of agriculture, above all in the Bordelais district. Townsmen of Bordeaux had their own vineyards both within and without the walls, and most of the great landed proprietors produced wine for sale as well as for their own consumption, and were quite ready to earn an honest penny by trade. The Archbishop of Bordeaux, with his extensive property in the very heart of the wine-growing district, was one of the chief of these private traders, and the whole management of his estate reflects the influence of this early bent to commerce, so rare a characteristic as a rule in feudal times.

The trade of Bordeaux dates from very early days. At first it was chiefly conducted by road to places in France, but after the connection with England was formed there is no doubt that the town soon found there her best market. At the time of Domesday Book, it is true that we read occasionally of vines in England, but they can have been of but little value, and in the twelfth and thirteenth centuries the King and all the great men of the country became extensive purchasers of foreign wine. Considerable salt-trade was also carried on with England and elsewhere, for valuable salt-mines existed in Northern Gascony; resin was exported from the extensive pine-forests, and occasionally steel and leather; but more and more wine began to usurp the place of other goods as a trading commodity, whilst Gascony needed increasingly in return corn in considerable quantity, wool, cloth, and articles of clothing of all sorts, spices, pepper, and dried fish. Gascon merchants are found elsewhere than in England. To Flanders they went, to Spain, to Italy, and in France their chief connection was with Normandy and Brittany; but more and more they concentrated their chief trade with England. From England they could get corn, wool and cloth, and dried fish from Cornwall; at one time the Archbishop of Bordeaux even bought cheeses in England. They are found constantly carrying their wine, not only to London, but to Bristol and Southampton, to Plymouth and to Hull. Sometimes their ships went direct to Scotland and Ireland; but as a rule the goods seem to have gone to English ports. The demand for wine was extraordinarily great, the King's purchases alone were constant and extensive: when any fighting was going forward, wine was ordered in still larger quantities, presumably because the troops had to be kept well provided on active service. A war with Scotland, Wales or Ireland always involved special purchases from the Gascon merchants.

From the first the English Kings saw the value of this trade connection as well as the importance of conciliating the towns, and from John's reign onwards there are constant grants of privileges to the merchants. Sometimes to the whole body, more often to inhabitants of Bordeaux or some other town, frequently also to individual burgesses as a reward for services done, or as a guarantee of future loyalty. Thus in 1205 John granted to the inhabitants of Bordeaux that they should be quit of toll on wine and other goods in the town and on the Gironde, and he encouraged merchants of Poitou, Périgord and Gascony to trade with England. In Henry III's reign trade was active and his own purchases vast, although it was largely left to his son to make payments for them ; the Bishop of Agen in that reign was allowed freedom of trade on the Garonne. Edward I in 1302 made a special agreement with the wine merchants of Gascony. He gave up himself his rights of prisage, the taking, that is, of two casks of wine from every ship unloading in England, promised to purchase no goods except at current prices, and allowed Gascon merchants to lodge where they wished in England, not in the special quarters of the town often put aside for foreigners in London and the ports. In return they were to grant him an increase on the ordinary custom on wine, to allow their casks to be examined by experts, and to pay a due for the making of them by the special official known as the *jaugeur*. Edward's successors continued the same policy. In 1301 the merchants of Bordeaux in England were only to pay on goods they actually sold, not on things unloaded and left on their hands or carried elsewhere, and they were to be allowed to take out unlimited quantity of corn, so long as the due customs were paid, and provided that they did not deliver it to the enemies of England. Richard II confirmed all old privileges, declared that none but old dues should be exacted, made repeated promises as to freedom from toll, and ordered all English merchants who carried corn out to Gascony to return to England with money or with goods from Bordeaux and not to make their purchases elsewhere.

Despite the constant grant of privileges, trade in the Middle Ages was burdened by many restrictions, and the Gascon wine-trade was no exception. It was freed from many tolls, but some had always to be paid before even the home port was left, and the price of goods must have been almost doubled to the consumer when all was told. A ship leaving Bordeaux, for example, had to purchase papers from the Constable to allow it to sail ; a special sailing due known as the *coutume de Royan* was also required and a branch of cypress had to be bought from the Provost of the Ombrière and fastened to the mast, whilst still further payment was demanded towards the upkeep of the lighthouse at the mouth of the Gironde. On arrival in England some custom duties were always paid, although royal charters forbade any undue and increased demands, and there were inevitable expenses for the housing of wares and for having them inspected.

Besides the expense of trading, there were real dangers connected with it ; ships were small and misadventures could readily occur in the ten days which were generally spent in getting from the mouth of the Gironde to the mouth of the Thames. Storms were serious perils, and there still existed men who wrecked ships for their own advantage. Laws against this show that it was a real menace, but penalties were severe ; any lord found so doing was ordered to be tied to a stake on his own land and burned to death. If the ships escaped storms there were still pirates to be feared, and there might even be danger of hostility on arriving at the English port. In 1293 some Bayonnais merchants suffered very great ill-treatment in the Isle of Wight, because the Englishmen thought that they were Spaniards, and had an old grudge to pay off on Spanish traders ; and that was only one of many instances of private war amongst the merchants ; sometimes even goods were seized to make up for losses due to storms, or debts owed by the country to which the merchant vessel belonged.

So great were the perils of the sea-crossing that ships had to go in a body and pay for an escort to guard them as a general rule. Edward I made a regulation in 1301 that masters of ships sailing to Gascony, or to any port in France, should always keep their vessels in the form of a fleet and in such a depth of water and so gathered together that none could be suddenly taken or aggrieved by an enemy : and he sent out the same order to Bayonne. This order was repeated in the fourteenth century, and English ships had to collect in Plymouth and take out a special escort : a practice which meant that trade had to be restricted to certain times, and generally ships were only able to collect and go out in spring and in the autumn at the time of vintage. Of course such restrictions were very hampering to trade, and it all added greatly to the cost of the goods and to the demands of the merchants. On the whole it was always the burgesses of Bordeaux who were the most favoured of Gascon merchants, and though the smaller towns had some concessions made to them, their traders generally had some duty to pay in addition to those owed by their richer and more favoured neighbours.

The Kings were anxious, for political reasons, to put their Gascon towns on the same footing as their English towns, and to free the trade as far as possible in order that wine might not be sold at too exorbitant a price ; but here they were met by grave difficulties in the shape of the jealousy of the English towns roused by this policy and sometimes the open defiance of their commands, especially by the Londoners. London's jealousy of foreigners was stronger than her realization of the gain to her of being an open port, and London was at daggers drawn with Bordeaux. Again and again, despite the promises made to them, the Gascon merchants complain that they are not allowed to stay where or for as long as they wish in London ; that they have to pay wrongfully as though for sales on goods which were being carried to a market elsewhere, or that their ships were actually pillaged by their rivals.

The Londoners, on their side, declared in Edward II's reign, that the promises made by Edward I were temporary and now obsolete ; that it was an established custom in London to forbid any foreign merchant to sell to any other merchant, but only to allow them to trade with great magnates for their own use ; and that any infringement of this justified them in seizing the wine. Sometimes Gascon merchants paid large sums that they might be admitted to the citizenship of London and so avoid these foreign disabilities, but a great uproar followed such a case in 1312 ending in the death of a Gascon merchant and consequent complaints. The Gascons naturally harboured grudges against the men of London, and the Londoners complained that they were charged dues wrongfully in Bordeaux, when it was well known that they had freedom to trade through all the ports of the sea.

Despite these constant bickerings and infringements of rules, the trade was profitable enough to continue actively and to flourish despite difficulties. Both sides really needed each other's produce: quarrels generally ended in some sort of reconciliation. When war or internal need caused the Kings to restrict export of English corn, an exception was frequently made for Gascony; and in 1364 Vintners of London were allowed actually to take £2,000 out of the country wherewith to purchase Gascon wine, although the fear of losing bullion was one of the reasons for constant restrictions on imported goods. Prices were so high at this time that it was found necessary bit by bit to relax the rules for hindering freedom of trade. Plymouth first was allowed to export cloth in order to purchase wine, and this permission was extended to Hull, Ipswich, Colchester, Fowey, Plymouth, and Mousehole. Later restrictions were still further removed, because the Black Prince complained that the English policy of protection was reducing his customs and was leaving wine on hand unsold. Till the very last, however, London remained ready to pick a quarrel on any opportunity, and in 1446 the Mayor and Aldermen wrote to the commune of Bordeaux, reminding them of the privilege by which London merchants could take their goods freely throughout all the King's dominions, and complaining that the Bordelais had demanded dues wrongfully from two English merchants. Should this grievance not be at once removed, an indemnity would be taken from Bordelais ships at that time in London. At almost the same date, however, the Londoners consented to pay certain dues in Bayonne, in regard to the long fidelity of that city, and promised to do all they could " to further the welfare of our sister Bayonne." Common foes were enough at any time, however, to draw closer together the proud cities of London and Bordeaux, and at one time they both joined in a common petition to the King of England against the Flemings who have " robbed them feloniously on sea and land."

Despite these difficulties trade did tend to bring the two countries closer together, and there are frequent instances of Gascons living in England, and Englishmen in Gascony. Not only was Henry de Galeys Mayor of London in 1274 and Mayor of Bordeaux in 1275, but there are records of Englishmen who were citizens of Bordeaux, and of others who were given land in the forest outside, or land elsewhere in the country ; while Gascons noble and simple came over to help the Kings in their wars against Scotland, Ireland, and elsewhere, and some at least settled down in the country and made it their home. In 1392 a Londoner who was anxious to get rid of an enemy hired a Gascon to do the deed for him.

The wine trade certainly occupied a great number of townsmen in Bordeaux and elsewhere, for apart from the actual growing of vines, making of wine and conveying it to its destination, there were officials to taste the wine and to fix its price, to test the casks and pass them for use, to inspect taverns and to see that regulations were carried out, to say nothing of the industry of making casks and hoops, tubs and vats, and all the necessary articles required in viticulture and the vintage.

The townsmen, therefore, were many of them connected with the wine industry in some way or another, but artisans of various kinds were of course needed for all the usual occupations, and everywhere we find carpenters, masons, tilers and thatchers, all of whom gained a good wage rather higher than that of the agricultural labourers or vintagers, when they worked for money. Bordeaux had at one time a considerable reputation for the making of armour and weapons, an industry which gave occupation to some of the burgesses, and the goldsmiths there were numerous enough to form themselves into a regular guild in the fourteenth century, with elected *prud' hommes* and certain privileges conferred by charter. Shipbuilding was an industry almost entirely confined to Bayonne, for at Bordeaux only river boats were built, not the bigger vessels for foreign trade. All towns, however, even the largest and richest, had still a good deal of rural life. Many of the inhabitants were agricultural labourers, who worked on the estates which some of the burgesses held outside the city. There were professional men, too : lawyers, notaries, doctors, and occasionally schoolmasters, but education was chiefly in the hands of the religious houses, and schoolmasters only appear rarely and seem to have been very poorly paid.

In town and country alike most of the inhabitants were fully occupied in providing the material necessities of life, in buying and selling, in building and repairing, and above all in defending their property against enemies and marauders. The country was seldom at peace, strongholds and fortifications needed constant attention. The military character of Gascon history can still be seen in the numberless castles, the little walled towns and the fortified churches, often the last refuge of the people in case of a siege.

CHAPTER IX

BASTIDES AND RURAL COMMUNITIES

THE bastides of Gascony were more like walled villages than walled towns, but small as they were their inhabitants were townsmen or *voisins*, and privileged as such. The name bastide comes from a word meaning fortress, and fortifications were the main feature of all these little strongholds. Each was built at one time and for a definite purpose by King or lord, who granted it from the first a charter of privileges, so that people came willingly from the open country to enjoy the protection and advantages offered by the new town. These southern bastides date very much from the same period and were all built on a very definite and very regular plan, which aimed at defence and equality. They differed, therefore, from communes, which were generally the result of very gradual growth and the grafting bit by bit of new privileges upon ancient rights, and they never attained to the same degree of independence as the communes, for formed as they were from above, the great man or men who created them was not likely to reduce his own powers more than was necessary and always kept the supreme control. The typical bastide, many examples of which can still be seen in modern Gascony, consists of a walled enclosure, very frequently on a hill-top, or in some place where natural features offer good possibilities of defence, and built in a way to furnish the strongest security to the inhabitants. The form is as nearly as possible rectangular, and in each of the four walls, gates are placed with straight streets leading through them ; where these streets intersect the market-place is formed, and round the market-place covered arcades with arches, known locally as *cornières*, are a very special feature. In some cases the lord's castle may form part of the fortifications, but more frequently the bastides are built near rather than round the lord's dwelling, and the church is strongly fortified and pre-pared to shelter the inhabitants in time of danger. Off the main streets run lanes so small and narrow that a number of houses can be built close together in a very small space, and the entrance to these lanes can be easily defended.

This form had of course to be modified according to the lie of the land. In some bastides, such as Monpazier, there are two gates in each of the side walls and the two main streets run parallel to one another and go through each side of the wide market-place. In others the market-place is not in the centre, but to one side of the town, because for some reason it is impossible to place the gates in the centre of the walls ; other towns, again, may have to be curved in shape, as for example Sauveterre-en-Guienne, while in some cases so steep is the hill on one side that no gates lead out in that direction since no roads can be made (Domme). But on the whole there is very great similarity and obvious indication of definite plan-ning. The straight streets, the strong defences and the forti-fied gateways are universal, as are also the arcaded markets and the narrow side streets.

In many of the market-places the town hall is found, gener-ally built on arches to act as a market on its lower floor ; but the distribution of buildings varies from place to place. Some-times a ditch surrounds the town walls, but this again depends on the nature of the country : and in some towns watch-towers are placed on the top of the fortifications to guard against unexpected attacks on a dangerous front. The bastides were constantly formed by treaties between two lords : perhaps between the King and an Abbey or the King and a lay lord ; but also between two lay lords or between a layman and a religious house. One of the lords would supply the land, while the others would build the fortifications, and the profits of the undertaking were then to be shared between them. The land once taken over was planned out according to the nature of the locality, and inside it was staked out into building lots, each lot of a certain size, enough for a small house and garden, and these were let at very low rents to inhabitants, attracted by the chance of protection and privilege, who were themselves responsible for the building of the house ; so that here there was possibility of showing individual taste, even though all were alike in actual size. As time went on inequality arose, since some greater *voisin* might acquire two building sites ; but the equality of the first distribution is very usual. At Saint-Osbert, and in many other places, the new-comer was bound to put up at least one-third of the building in the first year, another third in the second year, and after that to finish when he could. At Monpazier the King had to interfere because the buildings were not completed so soon as was desired. The walls were, as a rule, erected by the lord, but the inhabitants had then the duty of the upkeep, for which material was allowed to be taken free of charge from the forest and waste of the lord. Occasionally special collections or special grants had to be made for this purpose, and the inhabitants were generally given help if the walls had actually been destroyed in the bad fortune of war. Most of the dwellers in these towns were rural cultivators, and lands were allotted to them outside the walls, whilst some arrangement for pasture on the lord's waste was always made. In this way little centres of population were formed throughout the country, and the peasants were given some measure of freedom and some responsibility for town administration, although they had not shaken off dependence on their seigneur.

As has been already stated (see Chapter III), the policy of Edward I led to the creation of a great number of the Gascon bastides. Several were built round Bordeaux, probably with a view to diminishing to some extent its undue monopoly of influence, and a great many were created in the Agenais after that province came into the King's hands in 1279. Forty-nine at least can be dated from Edward's reign, and great men were occasionally rewarded by him with permission to create bastides for their own people. The bastide of Baa (Bath) recalls the name of Robert Burnell, Bishop of Bath and Wells ; John de Grailly the Seneschal, in 1280, was given power to build bastides and to grant them charters, whilst some were created by the Gascon lords themselves on their own lands. But although so many bastides owe their existence to Edward or to his direct instigation and example, he was not an originator in this any more than in his other policy. Some *bourgades* or *sauvetés* were founded by Abbeys as early as the eleventh century, and in the south, Saint Louis and his brother, Alphonse of Poitiers, built many little walled towns in the thirteenth, although many of these lay outside the English dominions— they were very numerous in *Gascon Toulousain*—some still existed in the lands taken over by Edward from the French King, and he had plenty of examples to follow in Toulouse, Rouergue, Quercy, and Agenais. Domme, erected under Philippe le Hardi to guard the frontier of Quercy against the English, is one of the best specimens left of these strong hill fortresses. The names of these towns often recall their character, their new creation, their freedom or their security. Thus we find numerous Villeneuves, Villefranches and Sauveterres in all parts of the country.

The nobles, on the whole, were favourable to the formation of bastides, for if they joined with the King by a treaty of *pariage*, and gave him land for the erection, they gained by the attraction of population to the stronghold and could always secure their own profit with a little care. They could—and generally did—stipulate that their own *serfs questaux* (villeins) should not gain freedom by residence there, and if the serfs of neighbouring lords acquired freedom within their walls, so much the better for them. Occasionally it is true that complaints were made to the King by lords in the neighbourhood, who felt injured in some way, and Edward frequently had to promise not to admit their serfs at all, or if their jurisdiction was injured by the new town to inquire into the matter, and to see that recompense was made and their rights restored : thus both King and lords were satisfied and the movement was peaceful and profitable. The peasants were attracted by the charters and were content with a dependence which gave them a considerable amount of security ; even when serfs did not gain freedom by residence they shared in some of the advantages and lived more safely behind the strong walls than in the open country.

The Gascon Rolls of Edward I's reign give good examples of the various ways in which bastides might be created. Some were purely royal bastides ; the King alone commanded their construction and granted their charters, a royal bailiff was put in charge, or they were farmed out on occasion to royal governors. Among these purely royal bastides were Beaulieu (Dordogne), in which the burgesses bought their right for an annual rent : Lalinde on the river Dordogne, Monpazier, Villefranche-du-Queyran, Villeréal, and many others. Arouille the King formed by a treaty of *pariage* with Arnaud Guillaume de Mauvezin, and the rights of justice were divided between them ; Boulogne-sur-Gesse was the result of a *pariage* with the Dean of Le Paradis, who gave the land and retained some free places in it in return ; Fleurance, a bastide taken over by Edward, had already gained some rights whilst in the hands of the King of France before 1279 ; Montfaucon-du-Lot was constructed after an agreement made by Edward with the lords of a neighbouring castle. Thus it will be seen that these towns did not invariably enjoy exactly the same origin, although the influence of the King himself is prominent in most of the creations of Edward I's reign, and a considerable number were formed by the treaties of *pariage*. Edward II followed the example of his father, and granted liberties to Créon, an important bastide in Entre-deux-Mers, by a treaty in conjunction with the Seneschal Amaury de Craon. Sauveterre-en-Guienne is a good example of a royal bastide. It was built on land acquired by the King from three noble proprietors —the Abbot of Saint-Ferme, the Lady Attalens, and Jordan de Percy, who said that they possessed it in free allod and could therefore bestow it freely. There was, however, a good deal of trouble about this property, since none of the three seigneurs was very clear as to the exact extent of their territory or nature of their rights, and the Lord of Pommiers tried to claim that they were granting away what was really held in fief from him. The case, however, must have gone in favour of the grantors, for in 1283 the King issued a charter to his " beloved and faith-

ful burgesses of Sauveterre and their successors present and to
come." This charter to Sauveterre was almost word for word
the same as that granted to Saint-Osbert in 1276, and shows
the sort of privileges and constitutions usually given to the
more important of these royal creations. Sauveterre was to
be a real community possessing a common seal and with a
body of twelve jurors elected every year by the outgoing
officials ; but at the head of the jurors was a royal bailiff instead of a mayor, without whose consent no document could
be sealed, and therefore no important action could be taken.
Each burgess was to have a space for his house and garden four
stadia by nine, that is about 24 feet by 54 [1] ; for this he was
to pay a rent of 12 denarii and *esporle* of the same at change of
lord. Two-thirds of his house must be built in two years'
time. Besides his property in the town he could have land
for cultivation outside the walls, but for this he was to pay
an annual rent of three shillings for each *concate*, and two
shillings for the same amount of woodland. Should a burgess
die without an heir, he could leave his property as he wished,
so long as the new tenant held at the same rent and the same
esporle. All men could be received in the town who wished to
live there, unless of bad reputation, and at Sauveterre (not at
Saint-Osbert) the charter specially added " except *serfs questaux* of lords who were burgesses or who lived in the neighbourhood " ; every new-comer was free from all military service
for seven years and was under royal protection. Knights and
damoiseaux who were burgesses were to be free from all services
except to repair bridges, walls, roads, and fortifications, and the
first fortification was to be erected by the King ; whilst this
was being done, however, the knights were to keep guard
night and day, and they were always to be responsible for
watch and ward in the town and the extirpation of malefactors.
Burgesses were allowed to retain lands they held before coming to Sauveterre, except those which they had held by *questal*
services ; they were allowed to take freely all the wood neces-

[1] This size was not always the same. At Monségur, for example,
the house space was to be 24 feet by 72. The main streets here were
to be 24 feet wide.

sary for building purposes; they could hold a market every Thursday, and a fair four times a year, while throughout the district they enjoyed freedom from toll and could sell without restriction wine, salt, and baked foods. Burgesses were not to be drawn out of the town to other courts, and must be tried according to the customs of the town ; neither King nor bailiff could take from them for pledge or debt, bed-clothes, wearing apparel, or weapons, the corn that they were carrying to the mill, or the wine which they had for their own consumption.

This charter, or variants of it, was granted to several other bastides and shows the nature of the privileges which were likely to attract inhabitants from the open country. Defence within the walls, security for property, certain rights over their lands and goods, and freedom from some of the tolls and conditions so burdensome on the would-be traders were advantages not to be despised, and the authority of the royal bailiff does not seem to have caused discontent amongst burgesses, who had acquired so much by royal grant.

There were considerable differences amongst the various charters, but the sort of privileges most desired by countrymen occur again and again, they were naturally those which distinguished burgesses most definitely from *questaux*. Thus we find that rights over property are generally stated. Freedom to alienate—as a rule the stipulation is made that it shall not be to nobles or churchmen—freedom to come and go ; the suppression of arbitrary *quêtes, tailles* and *aubergades*—i.e. duty of hospitality to the lord and his followers. As a rule contributions of some kind of military service are obligatory, but new inhabitants are excused for their first years, while they were naturally busy building their houses and bringing their new land under cultivation ; very often limitations are expressly put on purveyance : thus at Gontaud neither the King nor his officers are allowed to take corn, wine, straw, garden produce, or beasts. Sometimes the inhabitants are allowed to have their own mills and ovens, whereas serfs were always obliged to use those of their lord ; sometimes this permission is accompanied with conditions upon those who baked bread to sell, and the lord as a rule had some profit in that case ;

even dovecots are occasionally allowed to the *voisins* (Gontaud), a right, as a rule, reserved for the seigneurs alone. So clearly were such privileges those of the ordinary free men, that it was no wonder that Edward I had to be careful not to offend the lords of the neighbourhood, who might lose considerably if their dependent cultivators took to seeking safety from their exactions within the walls of these numerous little towns. The difficulty was met, as we have seen at Sauveterre, either by the exclusion of serfs of the neighbouring lords, or by keeping certain houses in the bastide for *questaux*, who were able to enjoy the security offered by the fortifications, but who did not thereby rise into the condition of free men and shake off the servile duties they owed to the seigneur. In other cases the lords may have learnt that in the long run they gained as much from the services and dues of men who were free in status, and the usual regulation that *questaux* could not be received without the consent of the lords may still have enabled a good many of them to come. That lords did not object to the creation of bastides is shown by one of the petitions which was sent up from a number of lords to ask the King to build a bastide on their land, half the profits of which should go to them. They were most condescending and encouraging to him about it, and pointed out that they were offering him one of the most beautiful sites in the Agenais, on a fine river and surrounded with fertile fields and meadows.

The inhabitants also had to be satisfied as well as the lords. Thus at Labastide d'Armagnac fresh privileges had to be granted in 1283, as the growth of the place had been retarded by lack of liberty, and there are frequently petitions for increased money help or better pasture rights. All the bastides, and indeed many communes, were very rural, and the charters often contain special regulations concerning agriculture and pasture. At Marmande there was to be a common guardian for the sheep and pigs of the place, but no one man, it was stated, ought to have more than forty pigs or sixty sheep to look after ; beasts were not to be grazed in the fields from which the corn had been carried until at least a day had elapsed so that the gleaners might have their chance : it was also forbidden to give workmen drink, except at harvest time, as they would then only give their services where they knew that they would get the best wine.

The administration of the bastides was always presided over by a royal official, or in the cases where the King shared rights with a lord or abbey, each party had a bailiff. But below the bailiffs the burgesses had the right as a rule to elect officials ; in some towns jurats as in the chief Gascon communes, in others consuls after the pattern of many towns of the south. These jurats or consuls varied in number from place to place, and in some instances they were nominated from amongst the people by the bailiff, not elected by the inhabitants at all. At Villeréal there were six consuls chosen by the King's bailiff from a list of twelve presented by the outgoing consuls. At Saint-Pastour the six consuls were nominated and had to swear to serve the King faithfully, but they did their work with the council of twenty-four burgesses elected by the people themselves.

A rather curious ceremony is noted in the customs of Gontaud for the reception of a new burgess : not only did he have to take the oath which was always demanded, but he had to put a penny on the altar of the church and pay as much as twelve shillings to the bailiff. After that he was, however, free of contributions for a year and a month. The King generally had to stipulate for a good many dues as well as the small rents that were paid, for a good deal of expense was incurred in the building of the walls and in compensation very often to the lord whose land was being used. These dues were generally judicial fines and dues on sales of land and goods. At Gontaud, again, a purchaser of shoes always had to pay a tax, unless he carried them away on his own feet. In Monségur there were strict rules for innkeepers, who were not allowed to sell wine on credit ; any man who should beat the innkeeper because he refused him wine had to pay sixty-five shillings, or be banished from the town for a year and a day.

The general character of these little rural fortresses is easily gathered from the charters : they were evidently of great benefit to those peasants who could afford the initial expense of entering and who could pay the rent demanded, since conditions were certainly made as easy and attractive for them as possible.   The King had a whole network of little strongholds throughout the country; almost certainly loyal to him and not at all unprofitable.   He could, if he wished, farm them out for fixed sums, or collect the profits through his own officers.   The result on the country was to promote the advance of serfs towards freedom and to make life a little more secure in times of turbulence and civil wars.   Incidentally, it trained up more people ready for military service, for whilst this was not—in theory, at least—demanded from the *questaux*—it was always owed by the heads of the households or by some quota of the inhabitants in a bastide.

The bastides created by the seigneurs were not very different in character from the royal bastides, but as a rule their charters were rather more restricted and freedom was limited.   Valence-sur-Baïse is a good example of one of the most important of these ; it owed its origin to a contract of *pariage* between the Count of Armagnac and the Abbot of Flaran (1272), whilst the Agenais was still in French hands.   It was in a splendid position for defence, and its solid walls, straight streets with four gates and a guard tower, the fortified church and castle are all exactly made to the approved plan.   Fumel was created by agreement between three lords, who put a common bailiff to supervise the administration, with a council under him, two members of which were nobles and four burgesses.   It had an unusually liberal charter, for all the inhabitants were declared to be free, the lords gave up all their rights to *quête, taille, fouage*, and *aubergade*, except when the army had to be sent out under the Seigneur of Agenais ; and to this army Fumel only seems to have owed the service of one knight, who was to be paid for his services by the council of the town.   Contributions to town expenses were taken from burgesses, but freedom from these was granted for a year and a month to knights, squires, and new inhabitants, after this time every head of a house " eating his bread and drinking his wine " was to pay his share.   One regulation seems to point to great generosity on the part of the founder, for should the lord strike an inhabitant he was to pay as much as £5 in fine. Some seignorial towns were much less free than this ; for in some the inhabitants had to perform labour services as well as pay rents, and dues were owed to the lord for buying and selling, for all beasts kept beyond the two plough oxen, for hunting rights, and so forth. But, nevertheless, there were always considerable advantages. The obligations of the inhabitants were fixed, and they had security, as well as other conditions usually characteristic of the lesser free tenants.

Besides the real bastides, Gascony had a great many little groups of dwellings more or less privileged gathering round the castles of the King and the great nobles. These were not necessarily walled, though occasionally they are so, but they were to some extent protected by the castle which stood in the midst, and inhabitants were often attracted by grants and charters. Many remains of these little *castra* or *castella* are still to be seen ; the houses clustering thickly on the sides of the hill on which the fortress of the lord was situated, often with a strongly walled enclosure into which the peasants could flock in case of attack. These little villages often had charters not unlike those of the bastides, but they were generally less full and less liberal. They are not planned out and built at one time on one model, as were the bastides, but present all the features of places gradually formed round some definite nucleus. When fortifications are made, it is generally by a grant to inhabitants already there. Thus in 1308, at Terraube, the people were collected in the church to form themselves into a community, and the lord granted them permission to enclose the place with good stone walls, at the expense of the whole body : there were to be three gates surmounted by towers of a special form. There was no necessity for the inhabitants of these *castra* to be freed : more frequently many of them were serfs, but privileged and protected. They still had, as a rule, to take corn to the lord's mill and bread to bake in his oven ; they gave to the lord dues in kind, or they did him labour services ; but there are many variations in these respects. Some were entirely free from *taille*, others paid at a fixed amount, and others, again, on special occasions ; some charters gave free pasture, but frequently the number of beasts that could be sent on to it was specified, or in other cases small payments were made. All had to take oaths of obedience to the lord and to pay something to him, more frequently in kind than in money, and only occasionally did they have officials of their own to take part in the administration of the place.   In any case, the benefit of security and certainty was again of real advantage to the inhabitants.   Little by little the serfs with their arbitrary payments are changing into tenants whose duties are fixed not only by custom but by contract, and though not theoretically free, they possess some important elements of freedom.   If the lord of the castle carried out his part of the contract fairly and gave real protection to the lives and property of his dependents, the services rendered by the inhabitants of these *castella* were not really excessive, and their lot was preferable to that of ordinary villagers and servile tenants.

The creation of bastides did not cease with the reign of Edward I, but there were fewer new towns made during the later period, and the privileges of the fourteenth and fifteenth centuries were often confirmations of older rights, which had perhaps grown up but never been recognized before, or that needed re-confirmation by some new ruler.   Lords often found it profitable to grant some privileges to their tenants, even when they were not allowing much actual independence or self-government.   A good example of this is in the customs and privileges of Lormont, confirmed by Archbishop Pey Berland of Bordeaux in 1445.   The inhabitants had to take an oath promising obedience to their ecclesiastical overlord and the payment of dues to him.   Almost all transactions involved some profit to the Archbishop.   Thus whilst all men of Lormont might have ovens to bake their own bread, they were bound to pay twopence a week if they baked for sale ; anyone selling wine must also pay two *deniers* to the Archbishop, and no taverner might sell wine at all in his inn without licence from the lord.   Sellers of beasts also were taxed at a certain rate ; one penny for selling an ox or cow ; threepence for thirteen sheep : twopence for a pig if sold alive, and so forth.   When meat was sold, the Archbishop was to have some of it : and the same for salt and other goods. If anyone brought mussels or oysters into the port a basketful must be brought up to the palace. Judicial fines all went to the Archbishop, and he made stringent regulations for the well-being of his town and its inhabitants : to throw dirty water out of windows involved a penalty of four shillings, and to strike a man in the road 300 shillings. Certainly these customs were more concerned with the rights of the seigneur than with the rights of his tenants, but the men of Lormont gained a few advantages in return for their promises. No merchant might be arrested for a debt before trial ; if a man was punished for murder, his heirs were to be properly provided for, vassals of a neighbouring place might be summoned to help with building fortifications or guarding the Archbishop's palace, and if a serjeant of the court had to be chosen, he was elected by the people themselves. But Lormont is clearly a community of dependents, not a body of free and privileged tenants.

Besides communes, bastides, *castella*, and privileged groups of dependents, Gascony had many rural communities of a most interesting character which show signs of very early freedom. Sometimes a village or group of villages would gain some sort of community feeling through the possession of common pasture lands, and they might join together to acquire some joint privileges from the lord, by means of some common payment, or in return for some special services. In 1291 three lords agreed to grant customs to the Seigneurie of Graulhet, to the castle and its surroundings and to two or three neighbouring hamlets. All the inhabitants were promised freedom from dues, *quêtes*, labour services and various payments in kind, in return for fixed rents in money, and all were to have free pasture and the right of leaving their land by will ; and the whole group had consuls of its own, with the supervision of roads, lanes and waterways. The rest of the customs are mostly concerned with fixing the prices of various tools, and the rate of fines for misdeeds, such as poaching. One or two of the clauses are rather original. For example, all poplar trees in the district were to be divided between the lord and the man on whose land they grew ; and in case of non-payment of rent for three years, instead of the loss of the property, the rent was to be doubled for the future.   Here and in other similar communities the privileges are granted to both men and women—*bezis* and *bezias*—that is *voisons* and *voisines.*

These rural communities are found most frequently in the region of the Pyrenees, where the inhabitants were naturally independent, and where much allodial property existed even amongst the poorer peasantry.   Tradition claimed that this freedom was natural and of ancient right.   The *Fors* (customs) of Soule, for example, declare that all the inhabitants are " free and of free status without any stain of servitude."   In Labourd every parish had its own separate common pasture and the parishioners were allowed to meet for common business whenever they wished.   In Béarn tradition tells of the stabbing of the lord who refused to take the oath to observe the customs of the country.   In Bigorre even serfs were allowed legally to resist the lord were he to burn their houses or seize their beasts. How much this freedom really meant depended a good deal on the character of the individual rulers, for it was one thing for a peasant to have the right to resist, it was a very different matter to exercise such right against a powerful overlord.   In Béarn independence was perhaps greater theoretically than in any other state, but an inquest into the position of the Béarnain serfs in the thirteenth century shows the existence of much poverty and distress, despite the traces of some unusual privileges ; and in the fifteenth century under Gaston Phébus the peasants suffered terrible things at his hands.

Really independent communities did, however, exist in many of the Pyrenean valleys, where natural frontiers took the place of artificial fortifications, and where the lords had little to gain by interference or by assertion of rights which could have brought them very little profit.   The mountaineers were poor and proud, they were protected in their rocky fortresses and they were united by their common interests and their common pastures.

In Comminges, Bigorre, Béarn, and the Pays Basque, as well as on the Spanish side of the Pyrenees, there were valleys in the mountains which were almost little republics in virtue of their independence and self-government. They were really seigneuries, for all had lords above them, generally the counts or viscounts of the whole district, but they were left very much to control their own affairs, and they made wars and treaties with the neighbouring valleys with no mention of permission on the part of the overlord. Just as Andorra in the Eastern Pyrenees, at the present day, is strictly a seigneurie and not a republic, for it pays tribute half the year to France and half the year to Spain, but has its own council, its own parliament, and its own court of justice, so these valleys of the Western Pyrenees in the Middle Ages had their meetings of the whole *beziau* to manage their own affairs and to treat if necessary with the seigneur on almost equal terms. The valley of Aspe indeed declared, when it was disputing with Gaston Phébus, Viscount of Béarn, that " la vallée d'Aspe était avant seigneur et que le seigneur n'a que ce qu'ils lui ont donnée." These valleys were composed of hamlets, each with their court and little meeting, while general meetings of the whole *beziau* were held for public business, and in these the women, as a rule, had full rights with the men. At Cauterets the record of a meeting to decide as to some change in the situation of the baths, preserves the fact that one woman opposed the decision. The inhabitants of the valley shared the mountain pastures or *ports*, and if any profits were made they were divided amongst the community, they generally had common regulations for the use of wood and water for the passage of the beasts ; each valley had its old customs, reduced to writing and confirmed by the lord in the fourteenth or fifteenth century. Nearly all had their own special rules of succession ; frequently, and always in the Pays Basque, there was a tendency towards primogeniture either male or female, in order to maintain the little properties intact, for it was difficult enough to get a living out of them even without excessive subdivision, and it would have been impossible to divide these pastoral estates as was done in the case of arable land and vineyards.

The younger children either lived at home and shared in the family work on the family property possessed by the eldest, or they went out to seek their fortunes elsewhere. So strong was the feeling for the maintenance of the family that a younger son marrying an heiress would be expected to take her name, in order that the family holding might be continued.

The most important of these valleys were those of Ossau and Aspe in Béarn, Lavedan, Barèges, Azun, Saint-Savin, Cauterets in Bigorre, and Luchon in Comminges, for in these provinces the mountains were highest, and the valleys most enclosed and independent. In the Vallée d'Aspe, which is very long and narrow, and important because it leads to one of the few good passes into Spain, there were two assemblies, for the upper valley held at Cette and for the lower valley in the Church of Accous. The Vallée d'Azun had a regular meeting at Guiserix, and elected its own bailiff as well as three consuls; not only did the inhabitants have rights of war and peace, of justice and of police, but they could arrange their own taxation and their own legislation.

The business done in these valley assemblies was largely rural in character, and so were the treaties with other villages, which naturally concerned pasture rights very frequently, since disputes were certain to occur on the high unenclosed slopes of the mountains. When later the Pyrenees became the boundary between France and Spain, these rural agreements between valleys on opposite sides became regular international treaties and were known as *lies* and *passeries*. Some of them established ceremonies which lasted on until the close of the eighteenth century, as, for example, the following. There was a great quarrel over certain fountains on the hills, between the valley of Barétous on the French side and the valley of Roncal on the Spanish side, and the struggle, which involved serious fighting, was ended by a peace and a tribute of cows from Barétous to Roncal. Representatives of each valley were to meet on the tops of the pass, place their hands on crossed lances and declare *Pazavant*, i.e. " Paix d'orénavant." The three cows, all alike and decked with ribbons, were led over the pass to the Spaniards, and a joint meeting was held to settle any outstanding difficulties between the two little communities. The exact origin of the ceremony, whether, as the Roncalais said, it was in compensation for the fountains which were really theirs, or, as the Barétous said, in compensation for the murder of adversaries they had killed in the war, it is impossible to determine.

Besides actual treaties of peace, the *beziaus* met to make peaceful arrangements one with another, or to come to some agreement with the lord, sometimes on the subject of military service, for the mountaineers generally bore arms as free men and fought when required, although as a rule on quite restricted conditions ; often not more than nine or ten days could be demanded from them.   The men of the Vallée d'Aspe were privileged to form a special bodyguard for their lord, the Viscount of Béarn, to lodge near him and to fight before him in the battle ; a proud position which they claimed to be their right from old custom.

The freedom and rights of these mountain people show the importance that geographical characteristics play in social life. They point also to relics of old free conditions and to the survival of many old customs, despite the universal development of feudal overlordship.   Here where the country was rough and poor, the ruling lords came but seldom, whilst those whose little castles were in the mountains were poor enough themselves, and not so widely removed from the free mountaineers amongst whom they lived.   There were some so-called *questaux* in these valleys, not all the inhabitants were nominally free, but there seems to have been much less distinction between free and servile than in those parts of the country where feudal control was more firmly established and legal conditions more defined. In the mountain valleys, the peasants who held by *quête* and not by *cens* shared in the general life of the community : they could bear arms with the others, and were even members of the governing body.   At Cauterets in 1316 the heads of all houses were summoned to meet, male and female, *questaux* and *censitaires* (*bezis e bezias, cessaous e questaous*).

CHAPTER X

NOBLES, BURGESSES, FREEMEN

GASCONY was a land with great traditions of freedom: traditions which lingered on through the Middle Ages despite the increasing dependence of the people on the feudal nobles; whole districts laid claim to free privileges, and simple peasants asserted their rights to the title of *francau*. There was, therefore, a very large class of free landholders, a class very varied and very vaguely defined, so that the smaller freemen are difficult to distinguish from their neighbours, the servile cultivators; whilst the great burgesses, on the other hand, are not always easily divided from the old nobility. This must be remembered in any description which treats of noble and non-noble, free and unfree. Divisions are never absolutely distinct, no definitions can really be exact, and it is only possible to give some idea of typical nobles, typical free men and typical serfs.

In Gascony there were a few very great lords holding extensive properties and exercising almost independent powers: and there were a vast number of smaller seigneurs, with little to rule but their own castles and the immediate dependents, but who were nevertheless proud, privileged, and dangerous as enemies. The largest estates were in the hands of great ecclesiastical overlords, such as the Archbishop of Bordeaux and the Abbot of La Grande Sauve, or of the chief of the lay lords, such as the Counts of Armagnac and Fezensac, the Viscounts of Fronsac and Bigorre, and the Lords of Albret. These great men were tenants-in-chief of the Duke of the country, King of England, or King of France, as the case

might be, and their allegiance was all-important to the suzerain. Most of the lesser lords were tenants-in-chief also,
and so were a number of knights and *domicelli*, though many
were tenants of the Gascon nobles and owed homage to them,
and fought under their banners. The word *domicellus* or
damoisel seems to have meant little more than a young noble
who had not yet taken up the rank of knighthood. He
could hold just as much land as a knight and frequently
on exactly the same terms, so that the difference was not
tenurial, and any young seigneur might be called a *damoisel*.
The name may, however, in some cases have been given
to less important nobles. A similar class of *domengers* in
Béarn were paid less for their services than the knights and
were under their jurisdiction ; but as a general rule age
was implied rather than rank, and as far as landholding
is concerned knights and *damoiseaux* can be considered
together.

Although society was very feudal, and the nobles displayed
most of those characteristics which are usually associated
with feudalism, ordinary feudal landholding did not wholly
prevail in Gascony. A very interesting feature of Gascon
property is the prevalence and long continuance of the allod.
Land, rents, tithes, even men, could be possessed allodially.
It has been claimed that originally all Gascon property was
allodial and that the maxim held good there of *nul seigneur
sans titre*. Such a statement cannot really be supported as
far as the period of English rule is concerned ; but that there
were many so-called allods, that the extent of such property
was one of the things Edward I wished to discover in his
inquest of 1273, and that he did find a great deal then exist-
ing is certainly true. What then was the " allod " as it is
found in Gascony ? In its fullest and most complete sense
it was land owned, not held from any lord at all, and therefore free from service, rent, homage, or fealty. The Archbishop of Bordeaux could claim that his property was free
and allodial and bound him in no way either to the Kings
of France or the Kings of England. But there were other
conditions which came to be associated with allodial pro-

perty, and these conditions little by little tended to modify the fullest sense of the word. Even in the case of the great ecclesiastical seigneurs, who certainly had property more fully their own than that of any other lords, it was usual to find that they said prayers and masses for the ruler of the land or for the donor of the property, and in fact, if not in name, their estate became similar to land held in frankalmoign, very free and unburdened no doubt, but still with some characteristics of tenure about it. In any case, most ecclesiastics added some other possessions to their allods, and might hold land in return for duties of hospitality, or even of military services. In the case of lay lords, even the greatest, their property was never wholly allodial, though as a rule some of it was, and it became increasingly difficult to draw the line between what was allod and what was fief. One thing was clear. An allod could be handed down from father to son, or given at will with no consent sought or granted. Thus the hereditary character of allodial property became prominent. Then again its relation to the King or suzerain of the whole country was very close—should an allodial owner die intestate and without heirs, an allod would escheat to the King, a fief only to the overlord—thus the special characteristic of close connection with the King was emphasized. This was shown in many other ways : an allodial proprietor, having no lord, must seek justice in the King's courts, and as a good subject must aid the King with arms in case of need ; and something very like a holding by military service was beginning to appear, although the service and jurisdiction were personal and not territorial and the allod was still land owned and paying no feudal dues, whereas the fief was land held on definite feudal conditions. By the time of Edward I's inquest in 1273 it is obvious that the exact distinctions between allod and fief were often very obscure, and that their possessors had themselves very little idea of the actual character of the property, or in many cases whether they owned it at all. Some answer proudly enough that for their allods they owe nothing, or even that they are not bound to answer any questions about them, not even to the King; but others are very vague on the subject, and ask for delay that they may go home and find out what they really possess; or they think they have allods, but are not sure. Most of them agree, however, that the distinguishing feature of such property is the absence of feudal obligations; but they owe personally to the State the essential duties of every good citizen of the time, military service, suit of court and the maintenance of fortifications. The customs of Bordeaux, which claim that most of the property of the burgesses is free and allodial, say that the rights of the King over it involve rights of justice, escheat and forfeiture.

On the whole allodial property was free and hereditary, although its owner was a subject of the King and all the more closely bound to him, since no immediate landlord intervened between them; but there was a tendency for the allod to approximate to the fief, and in many cases to be definitely changed into it, in order to gain the protection which an overlord could give. Allodial property therefore was gradually on the decrease. The value of an overlord was considerable in troublous times, the duties for a fief need not be onerous and the difference between owning and holding freely not so very great. By degrees we find the term allod used occasionally in a vague way for land held by very light service, or for land paying rent rather than service; whilst a small piece of allodial land possessed side by side with other property would very easily be confused with the rest and tend to take on the general condition of the tenure, whatever that might be.

Whilst, however, among the nobles the allod was tending to disappear before the fief, new allods were at the same time being created amongst the peasantry. It was a very great object of ambition to possess a real bit of private property subject to no burdensome dues and exactions, peasants would often pinch and squeeze that they might have money to buy a portion, however small, of their very own, and it is by no means unusual to find a serf, the chief part of whose possessions are still held by base service, having also a little piece of allodial property, acquired by gift, by marriage, or by purchase, for which he owes nothing of any kind.

Most of the nobles, however, were tending to hold fiefs. The word is not only used in Gascony for noble property; the rent-paying tenements of the simple freemen might also be called fiefs, but there were noble fiefs held by noble services, which can be first considered. The great lords possessed many fiefs, which they sublet to their own vassals; the small seigneurs had few fiefs; the knights and *domicelli* had one or more knights' fees, but these also would be held as a fief or fiefs, and all in return for some sort of feudal service to the overlord, whoever he might be. • For all fiefs homage was due and *esporle* had to be paid.

Homage could be one of three kinds: *hommage lige*, *hommage franc*, or *hommage plein*. Liege homage was the most important and formed the most binding connection: it involved unconditional allegiance to the seigneur, it was rendered by the vassal on bended knee, clad in a simple tunic without belt or sword, his folded hands placed between those of his overlord, who kissed him on the mouth and received him as his man. Free homage was similar, but less formal, and appears but rarely. Full homage implied a less unlimited vassaldom, a less complete surrender; the vassal might perform the ceremony standing with his hands joined.

Esporle or *accapte*, which was paid to every new lord, was really a recognition of overlordship rather than a payment for the use of the land; it corresponded very closely to the relief. Such *esporle* might be paid in actual money, but for noble fiefs, as a rule, some fancy article was offered by the noble tenant. Such articles were usually gloves, spurs, or lances, but other things were sometimes rendered: hawks, full-fledged or straight from the nest, horseshoes, and gold coins; occasionally very exceptional gifts appear amongst the *esporles*, such, for example, as a bow with a green silk cord, a piece of cloth, and an overtunic. These gifts were sometimes commuted for money, and some nobles did definitely hold at a money *esporle*, which might vary from a few pence up to the considerable sum of a hundred shillings.

The *esporle* and the duty of *esporler* or *monstrer*, i.e. of describing a property and its duties when summoned to do so by the lord, were the special characteristics apparently of a noble fief (without *esporle* there is no fief, according to the customs of Bordeaux), and hence comes the occasional refusal of an allodial owner to make such *monstrée* of his property.

Added to homage and *esporle*, the nobles, knights and *damoiseaux* might also be bound to military services in return for their fiefs. The greater the noble, however, the less were his services apparently, and Counts and Viscounts owed rarely anything but homage, except that they were bound to be under the jurisdiction of their royal overlord. But even when military service is definitely required, such service is extraordinarily light and extraordinarily little proportioned to the amount of the property. Fief and knight's fee alike, when held by service of arms, seldom owed more than one knight ; it is not even impossible to hold two knights' fees for the service of one knight, and the amount of land which could be included in the term *militia*, or for which that service was due, varied to almost any extent. It is very rare to find more service from any landholder, however wealthy, but there are occasional exceptions. Otto de Lomagne, who owed fealty, but was not sure about homage, owed one knight for his fief and another knight for his rights of justice. Rostand de Landiras, *damoisel*, held two fiefs and separate services for each of one knight and *esporle*. But clearly the usual tenure was for a man to give his own services, and no exact estimate had been made as to the proportion of land which that implied. If an extra estate was acquired, the duty of extra service might also be necessitated. Very rarely was any stipulation made as to the length of service owed by these knights, though occasionally special equipment is mentioned, and two or three men-at-arms have to be substituted if a knight is not sent, or another knight if the tenant does not go in person. The personal obligation, however, is practically always re-

corded, and it seems as though such tenure was a survival
of the old allodial conditions of individual service to the
King later affixed to the soil and appearing as a territorial
duty.

Clearly Gascon military service was less in value than
English military service, and the King did not dare, and
perhaps did not wish, to enforce it any more strictly upon
the nobles. The nobles were ready enough to fight, as a
rule, when opportunity arose, either for their overlord or
against him, and their tenants had to follow them to war,
whether they wished it or not, in many instances. But when
the English Kings raised a Gascon army, they asked for it
rather than demanded it ; they begged the nobles to bring
all the men they could, they did not demand the service
due from an estate, and both nobles and followers were
paid, it would appear, for the service thus rendered.

By no means all the noble fiefs were held by military service ; quite a number of knights and seigneurs paid rent
for their land. Under the circumstances money payments
must often have been of more value to the overlord than
rather uncertain service, and even the tenants-in-chief of
the crown could hold in return for money. The Castle of
Blanquefort in the fourteenth century paid an annual rent
of £70.

Besides military service there was also tenure by serjeanty,
the performance of some personal service or the giving of
some small token, much of the same nature as those due
for *esporle*. John de Grailly, Captal de Buch, for each of
his fiefs paid to Henry IV a pair of golden spurs. Sometimes a kiss or a rose would be accepted as rent, or a torch
of wax twisted round a lance, whilst a few nobles were
pledged to provide a feast if required. Arnaud d'Estang
in 1273 declared that he owed a fatted cow according to
old custom and bread and wine to eat with it, and in the
neighbourhood of Aire several men had to provide food for
the King's huntsmen and dogs and to accompany them if
required. These services, as a rule, depended on the locality.
All round the castle of Puyguilhem the knights owed a

month's castle guard in lieu of other service, and along the Dordogne the duty of ferrying across the King and his household, and keeping the boat covered with fresh straw or reeds, was enjoined on a number of small but apparently noble tenants. Occasionally these serjeanties are amusing and seem to have no purpose but that of giving the King a little variety. One tenant in return for his so-called knight's fee was bound to join the King whenever he travelled through his neighbourhood, go with him to a certain oak, taking with him a cartload of faggots drawn by two tailless oxen. Here he was to set fire to the tree and let all be burnt unless the oxen could escape. The family of Pommiers had to supply a meal for the King and ten knights, comprising beef and pork, chickens and cauliflowers, and to wait at table in person: those of them who were knights wearing red shoes and golden spurs, those not of knightly rank in white shoes and silver spurs only. Evidently service for land was not valuable, but appears more as a sort of recognition that such land was held as a fief than anything else. The real value of the fiefs depended on other dues, on wardship, marriage payments, judicial profits, and so forth. The King certainly got more money from his towns than from his noble vassals.

A natural result of the comparatively small value of the duties owed by the nobles, and in the case of the tenants-in-chief the constant absence of the King which rendered personal services of little interest to him, was a growing tendency to let out fiefs for *cens* or to commute the services by which they were held for money. There were various other circumstances in favour of this, apart from the fact that the money connection came altogether rather early in Gascony, owing to the commercial element in the country and the increasing need for buying and selling. For the lord it was obviously an advantage, and even for the tenant in some cases, for it simplified his landholding to some extent: the extraordinary amount of subdivision and co-partnership in regard to lands, rights, castles, and even houses, rendered the reckoning of any form of service exceedingly difficult. Sometimes two brothers would hold a property and either one or the other would perform the service for it, or they would do it in turns ; but very often three, four or more lords combined to hold some small territory, and rather than divide the service amongst them it was easier to have it changed into a money payment, or to take up the land frankly at a money rent. In a record of homages in Agenais and Condomois, where most of the holdings did not exceed one knight's fee, and many were only half, there occurs the declaration of a noble who with his partners held the sixteenth part of a castle, for which they owed to the King the sixteenth part of one knight ; and in Bordeaux one noble tenant speaks of holding the fourth part of a stone house. Sometimes these tiny bits of property were in different localities ; most lords had scattered fragments of land, and it was difficult for them to collect their own dues, as well as difficult for their seigneurs to get from them what was owing. With one or two tenants in one village, tithes due from another, the fourth part of the right of collecting a tithe shared with another man elsewhere, a *cens* due from the fourth part of a house in one town ; with certain tenants providing cartloads of wood, which it was the duty of a separate batch of villeins to convey to their destination, a seigneur can have had no clear idea of his own revenue, and may be excused if he were equally hazy as to the duties which he in turn owed to his feudal superior. Certainly this sharing of tiny properties points to the prevalence of considerable poverty throughout the country : a poverty which affected the nobles as well as the small freemen, and which has been accepted as a Gascon characteristic in tradition and literature.

These Gascon lords seem to have had rather less regularity in their estates than we find in the English manors, though those were varied enough. Home farms cultivated by labour services certainly existed, but, on the whole, the lords tended to get food rather than labour from peasants, and generally demanded hospitality as they rode about their scattered estates (*aubergade*). This was sometimes due by customary right, but only too often they were a law to themselves and took what they wanted without much regard to legality. But on the other hand they protected their dependents from other lords, and the little villages tended to group themselves round the castle of the seigneur, whilst the lands which the inhabitants cultivated lay outside in the open country. It was the lord's interest as well as his duty to see that his peasants had enough to live on and sufficient pasture for their beasts, a need which it was easy to supply from the wide stretches of waste land and forest which existed over most of the land. Wars were too constant for the country to be really prosperous, but the fertile soil, the great demand for the fruits of viticulture, the existence of good rivers and trading towns, enabled more wealth to be produced than would have been otherwise possible, although the greater share of it went to the towns themselves.

The revenue of the nobles came not only from the ordinary dues, rents and services of their tenants, but largely from the tolls, which hampered the free transport of goods throughout the country. Most of the seigneurs received payment for any goods brought into their estates, or on boats passing up the river, should the property lie on a great waterway. A lord had dues on sales made to his tenants, on sales in the market or on the country produce sent out from his estate to other parts. His serfs brought him nuts when they went nutting, or fish when they went fishing ; his mill had to be used by his dependents, and in return he was to receive corn or payment in return ; his tenants' bread was brought to his oven to bake and he would have loaves in plenty for his own use. Besides such sources of livelihood every landlord would hope for profits from his courts of justice, and from the fines for which punishments were almost always commuted. The greatest seigneurs, such, for example, as the Archbishop of Bordeaux, had high, middle and low justice on their estates, they could try great lords as well as simple vassals, and mete out punishment for the most serious crimes. Low justice, i.e. usual manorial jurisdiction, comprised civil justice and the trial of small offences and misdemeanours.

Middle justice was criminal, and included the power of inflicting the punishment of mutilation ; high justice gave authority
over life and death and what amounted practically to royal
power, though appeal could still be made to the Ducal Court
of Gascony, or even to the supreme suzerain the King of
France and the Parliament of Paris. The English Kings,
as at home, tried to limit the possessor of high justice, or
at least to claim that it could not be exercised without royal
grant, but there was a great deal of unlicensed jurisdiction
and most of the chief landholders acted as though supreme
over life and limb. Free tenants were often protected by
the customs of the town or district to which they belonged
and which the lords had sworn to obey, but serfs were very
much at the mercy of their landlord, whatever theory might
have to say as to their protection in life and limb. Nevertheless serfs could be brave enough to oppose their lord on
occasion ; trials between seigneur and peasants were by
no means rare, and on one occasion at least the *hommes questaux* sent proctors to England to assert their rights in the
court of the overlord himself.

The life of the Gascon noble was chiefly made up of hunting and fighting. When no big war was waging private
quarrels constantly occasioned the resort to arms. Their
castles were military strongholds of the most uncompromising
nature, built for defence and with little regard to the ameni-
ties of life. Some of the great counts had large castles,
with living-rooms and great halls and enclosed gardens, in
addition to the main tower of defence, but the seigneurs
seem, as a rule, to have built many castles throughout their
estates, in which they would stay as they travelled from
place to place, and it is rare to find them settling down in
any one fixed spot.

The lesser lords might have but one dwelling-place and
that was sternly built as strongly and impregnably as possible. Quantities of these strongholds have left their ruins
throughout the land and they present very much the same
features of strong towers, tiny windows and surrounding
walls. Some of the nobles lived in the great towns, either

as burgesses or without the burgageship, where it was not allowed unless by special leave. Here also their houses were fortified ; but the King's consent had to be asked for this as well as for the building of a castle, and this consent is generally accompanied by the condition that house or castle must be handed over to the royal Seneschal whenever required.

Next in the rank of freemen came the burgesses. The Gascon towns had one very striking feature and that was their military character. The Kings looked to them not only for money but also for soldiers ; but this service was personal rather than territorial, and did not mean that townsmen held their houses and lands by military service. The service was always limited in time and generally to some special district, unless the King was willing to take over the whole expense.

In 1273 the leading communes sent representatives and made recognitions to Edward I in their corporate capacity. The declaration made by Bordeaux is characteristic of the proud position taken up by that commune even after the King's control had been secured in 1261. The Mayor and twelve *prud'hommes* came for the ceremony to the Cathedral of Saint-André. First the King and Seneschal had to swear to observe the customs of the town, and then, and not till then, the burgesses took their own oath of fealty. The town was said to hold no fief properly so-called from the King, though it held from him its use of the public ways, empty places, walls and ditches ; most of the houses and vineyards were claimed to be allods, over which, however, the King could exercise justice and receive escheat and forfeiture. The town owed to the King the guard of the city and military service for forty days in the year throughout the diocese of Bordeaux, for which the head of each household was responsible ; should the King himself be present with the army the burgesses must fight in person, but in other cases a substitute might be sent. In most towns similarly at least one man from each house had to be provided to the King's army.

Individual burgesses are often found holding noble fiefs

and performing noble services. They might hold land by homage and military service, just as a noble, on the other hand, might hold land by money rent, but for town property and for townsmen the usual condition was the payment of money rent and money *esporle*. In the bastides, where the sites were all of equal size, each inhabitant paid the same amount in return for his holding, but elsewhere rents could vary to almost any extent, and they are very difficult to compare and estimate owing to the uncertainty of money values and the great variety of coins which were used in the actual payment of them. The usual method, however, was to reckon in money of account, i.e. in pounds, shillings and pence (*livres, sous* and *deniers*), of which twelve pence went to the shilling and twenty shillings to the pound. But in that case the value depends on whether the reckoning is made in the money of Bordeaux, the money of Tours, or the sterling money of England. As a rule in Gascony accounts were kept in the money of Bordeaux, but in Agenais a special money known as *arnaudins* was also used : as these moneys also varied in value from period to period any sort of comparison can only be approximate. A pound of Bordeaux money was less than a pound sterling, more than a pound Tournois ; in the fourteenth century a, Bordeaux pound was roughly about a quarter of the pound sterling. This means that the real value of rents and *esporle* is difficult to calculate. Sometimes rents were purely nominal. In 1400 a knight in Bordeaux, for example, paid only one penny a year to the Archbishop for a house, and clerks in the town at that time often paid extraordinarily small sums : a halfpenny, a penny, fourpence, and so on ; at the same date, however, a stone house in Bordeaux was costing as much as £5 14s. a year, although the average house-rents seem to have varied from about 2s. 6d. to 15s.

Esporles in Bordeaux were generally low. A very usual rate is twopence : so usual that it has been thought to be universal for that neighbourhood, but this is a mistake, for there are some instances when the *esporle* rises as high as the rent. The class of townsmen was a large one, spreading into the rank of the nobles on one hand, and very little distinguished from the small peasant freeholders on the other. The more important burgesses were distinguished from their neighbours in the town by the turret on their houses which witnessed to their social status. The *voisins* of the bastides, who had built their own little dwellings, were rural freeholders with some town privileges.

Fixed rent, whether in town or country, was known as *cens*, and the free but non-military lands were *censives* held by *censitaires*. The small free men, peasants free in status, or sometimes the inhabitants of bastides and *castella*, usually paid their *cens* in kind, or partly in money and partly in produce ; or they might pay a fixed proportion of their crops known as *agrières*. A tenant of Saint-Seurin of Bordeaux gave yearly to the Dean and Canons twelve loaves of bread, a load of the best wine and 2s. 6d. for his vineyards ; the tenants of Saint-Jean de Sorde paid for their rent, loaves, wine, barley, a pig and a cow. The *Censiers* of Bigorre are full of the records of rent in corn of all sorts and cheese, but above all of eggs and chickens, and occasionally of lambs. Bread and wine were perhaps the most usual commodities used for rent, but there were great varieties : cows and horses, cartloads of wood, or wax when for a religious house, are all found repeatedly. Free tenants might also be asked to give work in return for their holdings as well as food rents, but as a rule such labour was fairly light, only a few times a year or at special seasons. Very often these extra labourers were only needed at the time of vintage or when vineyards required some special attention. The rendering of labour did not in itself imply serfdom, although regular week work was generally only demanded from the *questaux*.

Some very small rents owned by free tenants were called *oublies*. The word originally was used for an offering of rolls or cakes, made by the tenant on certain festivals, but gradually it came to be applied to any very small payment. Round Saint-Macaire in especial this expression for small rents was in general use, and even some of Edward I's tenants-in-chief held land from him by *oublies*.

There was often little to distinguish the small rural *censitaire* from the servile cultivator; but however humble his services he was, in theory, free; he could move from place to place (occasionally by contract with the lord this liberty was given up), could buy and sell as he wished, could marry his daughters and send his sons to school without asking his lord's permission, and above all his *cens*, whatever it might be, was fixed and certain: he was not a tenant holding at the arbitrary will of the lord.

The tenure by payment of part of the produce was a very usual one, and led directly to the métayer system of modern days. Only very occasionally was as much as half the produce given, sometimes it was as little as one-sixth. When new lands were to be brought under cultivation or forests to be cleared, a tenant could often be found to do the work if he could have the land free of rent for the first few years, and when once it was tilled and doing well the payment of part of the fruit was a very fair rent. By the fourteenth century the system of the stock and land lease was also spreading. The lord would arrange to let out to tenant, not only the soil, but the seed and the necessary beasts of labour, for three years, six years, or nine years, as the case might be; and in return the tenant would promise to pay a share of the produce, to cultivate the land well and to restore it in good condition at the end of the term. Sometimes the terms of conveyance of an ordinary *censive* included the requirements of good work on the land, and a renewable lease differed very slightly from the tenure of a *censitaire*, except that the payment of *esporle* was not required and that the lord generally appointed a guard to supervise the harvest, and the leaseholder had to feed and sometimes to lodge him. The class of rent-paying tenants was a large and increasingly growing one, for it comprised those nobles and knights who had ceased to hold land by military service, burgesses of all kinds from great merchants to humble inhabitants of bastides, small free rural cultivators, and the serfs who had gained freedom and changed their arbitrary *quête* into a fixed *cens*.

Besides these freeholders there were groups of men called *francaus*, who claimed to be specially privileged and specially protected and to hold their lands directly from the King himself. The freemen of Entre-deux-Mers were the best known of these free tenants, but there were groups of them also at Barsac and Bazas in the north ; in the districts of Soule and Labourd in the south. The distinguishing feature of these groups of free men seems to be that they made a special payment as a body to the King, each member of the group contributing his quota to the sum, and in return for it demanding from the King, and whoever his representative official was in that region, protection and justice. In some cases these free men held their little plots directly from the King, but in other cases it appears almost as though they were personally bound to the King and that their lands were really allodial. Their holdings are not true fiefs, for as a rule there is no mention of *esporle*, and sometimes a portion of the sum due is contributed by a man who states that he holds nothing. Some sort of military service was also due from these free men, either individually or one man at least from each house, though it might be for as little as one day at their own expense.

To give a few illustrations in more detail : In certain hamlets round Bazas a lump sum of £20 was due. This sum was divided amongst the villages, and allotted in each village to the individual households, which paid contributions varying from 3*d*. to 4*s*. 6*d*. The inhabitants were under the jurisdiction and attended the court of the reeve of Bazas, to whom also they contributed some food in the year, and before whom they took the oath of fealty, whilst he in his turn vowed to defend them. There are some slight varieties of condition from village to village, but the one thing constant is the quota of the £20 and military service. It is evidently the lump sum for protection which binds the different villages and their inhabitants together.

In Soule and Labourd there was no joint payment, but the inhabitants claimed special rights of freedom and did military service to the King. They all held directly of the

King, paid 3*s*. a house, and had rights of free pasture. The Barsac group was only formed in 1243, when the King took it over under his special protection, after having thrice summoned Gerard de Montremblanc to defend his claim to the district. The freemen of Barsac claimed to hold their bodies of the King and their common property such as water and pasture. They were to fight under the reeve of Barsac and to take the oath of fealty to him.

The freemen of Entre-deux-Mers looked back to very early days for their privileges. It was their claim that Charlemagne had especially rewarded the vigour of their assistance against the Saracens by giving them all their possessions freely, on condition that they should still owe military service for the protection of the land which they had already defended so well. These men paid a royal *questa* or *captenhe* of £40, though this they said was imposed on them after the time of Charles the Great, who had burdened them with no such payment. By the thirteenth century, in any case, the freemen of Entre-deux-Mers contributed by hamlets or by families to this joint payment in the same way as did the men of Bazas, and their other conditions were very similar. The reeve of Entre-deux-Mers was placed there by the King for their defence, and his two servants were to help him guard the two divisions of Upper and Lower Entre-deux-Mers. The hamlets provided hospitality and food for the reeve and his servants when they journeyed through the country, and some made an annual payment of a penny to him, very much resembling the English Sheriff's aid. Military service in this district was to be limited " according to what the lesser men can do " ; and the freemen were always ready to complain if they found their privileges in any way infringed. As late as the seventeenth century the Chapter of Saint-Seurin had a hard struggle to assert its rights to a tenement in Ambarès, one of these independent hamlets, although it claimed to have held it for 400 years. The claim was resented on the ground that the King of England had right of *quête* over the whole of Entre-deux-Mers, and was *seul seigneur direct universel*.

As far as can be judged from the evidence, these freemen seem to have represented old peasant *allodarii*, who were given special privileges when the King took their districts into his demesne, and who were protected by him from most of the usual encroachments and oppressions of the feudal overlords.   They are one of the many instances of the amount of freedom which survived in Gascony right through the feudal period, and which make the social conditions under English rule so well worthy of special study.

CHAPTER XI

SERFDOM IN THE PLAINS

IN treating the question of the Gascon serfs or *hommes questaux*, it is necessary to divide the subject in order to get any clear idea of the general conditions, for considerable variety existed in different parts of the country. This was partly due to different stages of development, partly to geographical and social causes. The inhabitants on prosperous estates were more advanced than those on small and poor properties ; peasants in the country round the trading towns where vines were grown largely differed from those on pastoral lands where life was simpler and commerce unknown ; and those parts of Gascony where equal division amongst the children was the usual custom had conditions other than those which prevailed in the places where primogeniture was practised amongst the peasants as well as amongst the freemen. Roughly, however, these differences can be said to be most clearly marked between the inhabitants of the plain and the inhabitants of the mountains. In Northern Gascony conditions tended to approximate to those of the Bordelais district, where land was fertile and the practice of equal division prevailed. In the Pyrenean countries—Bigorre, Béarn and the Pays Basque—where primogeniture was usual, and where the inhabitants lived mostly on the profits of their flocks and herds, life was different and the serf had his own special characteristics and peculiarities.

Throughout Gascony the lands of lay and ecclesiastical lords were let out and cultivated by dependents free and unfree. These unfree tenants came to be called very generally *hommes questaux*. Leaving out of account, for the time being,

Pyrenean Gascony, let us consider the usual conditions which prevailed amongst these *hommes questaux,* and what were the essential features of their class. Despite much that was similar, they differed to some extent from the English villeins of the same period, owing to the differences in the land system. There was nothing that corresponded exactly to the English manorial system, with its regular organization, its equal strips and its three-field system. Manors of a sort existed, but owing to the custom of equal division amongst the children lands were very much subdivided. Dues, services, landholding and everything else were split up into innumerable fragments and almost hopelessly confused. A good deal of land also was in the hands of small free tenants or allodial owners ; even on the larger estates of great lords, whether lay or ecclesiastical, there was much indefiniteness about the position of the tenant. The consequence was that labour dues divided amongst families and co-partners were so useless and so difficult to allot that it was to the interest of lord and tenant alike to commute services as much as possible into money or payment in kind ; the large amount of coin, meat and food of all sorts which the lords thus received from the peasants tended to diminish the necessity for the possession of a large home farm cultivated by villein labour, so that among the *questaux* we find rather less regular work on the lord's own demesne than in England : there were more payments in money and less in labour.

The name *questau* did not come into general use before the close of the thirteenth century, although it begins to appear occasionally as early as 1220. Before this the great variety of names used to signify men of servile condition points to a considerable variety in their conditions. In the twelfth and thirteenth centuries the terms *villani, rustici, decimarii, homines ligii, vectigales, pagenses, casali, tributarii* are all applied at one time or another to the unfree peasants, although some of the terms could equally be used in speaking of the free. This vagueness in terms implied a vagueness in actual status, and no fixed rules existed as to serfdom ; no certain name existed for the serf—free and unfree were very loosely divided. In the thirteenth century, as the theory of serfdom became more defined, this abundance of nomenclature gradually gave place to uniformity, and by the fourteenth century the term *questau* was used for a tenant holding by base services, the character and conditions of which were more or less universally recognized in legal theory. To say this, however, does not mean that serfdom in actual practice was the same all over the country. Variety still existed, and there was uncertainty, even amongst contemporaries, as to the essential conditions that rendered a man a serf. To draw an exact line between free and unfree in the Middle Ages is not easy in any country, and Gascony is by no means an exception. There are many lesser freemen whose duties and payments are practically indistinguishable from those of the serfs ; there are *questaux* who have certain attributes of freedom and who are certainly better off materially than many a tenant nominally above them. There is the usual complication as to status and tenure : the same man may possess both a *questave* and a *censive*, even indeed an allod—to what rank does he belong ? and what is it that fixes his condition ? All through the fourteenth and fifteenth centuries also, although the theory of serfdom has become more definite, perhaps indeed because of this very definiteness, there is a distinct tendency to struggle against these conditions, to break free bit by bit from the most galling disabilities and burdens, and to rise to a position of modified servitude, or in some instances to actual freedom.

But though the border line between free and unfree must inevitably be indistinct, and some men must remain unclassified, it is possible to form an idea of a typical *questau*, and to enumerate those services which bear a specially servile character. Clearly the adoption of the name of *homme questau* for a serf implied some universal characteristic, and without doubt it was the payment of an arbitrary *questa* or *quête* which distinguished him from the free rent paying *censitaire* whose obligation was fixed. The serf was the man " quêtable et taillable à merci." The word *quête* had two meanings. It could be used in reference to fixed payments to the sovereign, a sort of tribute to the Prince as a mark of sovereignty and return for the protection he granted to all his subjects ; but its ordinary meaning was that of a seigneurial due representing the right of patronage over tenants of servile condition. This seigneurial *quête* or *taille*, by the fourteenth century at least, was a personal tax paid by the man himself, and above all arbitrary, regulated entirely by the will of lord. Earlier the word was used more vaguely, and may have merely meant any payment sought rather than bought ; but more and more the arbitrary *quête* came to be contrasted with the fixed *cens* as a sign of serfdom. A villein given to Saint-Seurin was to pay *quête* according to his power and at the will of the canons ; in 1347 the Seneschal declares certain inhabitants of Caudeyran, Bouscat and Villeneuve to belong to this same ecclesiastical body, which was to hold them with full power of taking *quête* from them according to its will. When as a special favour this *questa* was made into a fixed payment, a privilege frequently granted to inhabitants of bastides, it appears to have been often equivalent to enfranchisement, and is certainly a condition which constantly accompanies enfranchisements.

There were, however, other essential characteristics which distinguish the typical *homme questau*, very similar to those which were legally incumbent on English villeins. In 1322 a grant of servile land was made on the following conditions. The new tenant was to hold as a serf *a questa, a talha e a merce*, he was to promise personal residence, not to quit his holding, not to seek a new lord, nor to obtain freedom by residence in a chartered town, nor in any other way ; should he break these promises and free the land, his lord might bring him back, wherever he might be. In 1371 similar conditions were laid down in another conveyance of servile land, and in addition it was stated that the tenant must always be ready to obey his lord's summons to work, he must not send his male children to school, nor allow them to enter a religious house without leave, his daughters were not to be married without permission (which meant, of course, not without payment also—the *merchet*), and the land was not to be alienated. Probably the servile condition next in importance to that of the arbitrary *quête* was this close connection of the serf with the soil. Gifts of land implied gifts of the serfs upon it, and no *questau* could ever leave his holding without his lord's consent : the lord had the right to bring him back, as was stated above.

The servile *reconnaissances* vary, however, very considerably and so do the conditions laid down in the conveyances of land. One man might be burdened by some of the conditions, another man by others, a few by all. The more severe the conditions the lower the stage of serfdom. In the most complete form of serfdom there is generally some kind of labour to be performed for the lord, and to be performed when and where the lord may wish. The *homme questau* at his lowest was completely at the mercy of his lord and could do nothing without his leave. He was debarred from all judicial privileges, he could make no contracts nor wills ; his holding was not only inalienable, but he was bound to cultivate it exactly in the manner ordained by his lord, his beasts might be seized and his fields might be ravaged to supply his master's table and he would have no redress. Besides these services and disabilities the serf was also liable to a vast number of dues and payments which made up the income of the lord and which strictly speaking were arbitrary when demanded from the unfree tenant. He might have to pay dues on his own marriage, dues on the birth of his children, dues on the death of his parents ; he could be called from his fields at the busiest moment in his own harvest to work on the lord's land ; he was often forced to carry the best of his corn, the ripest of his fruit and the fattest of his flock to the feudal castle ; he was liable to lose the contents of his poultry yard in one day to feed a party of his lord's friends ; he could be made to spend days in carting wood to supply the castle kitchen, or in labouring to repair the castle walls, and his nights in keeping watch in the castle towers.

But to picture the life of the serf as hopelessly burdened by such conditions, and all the *questaux* as overworked and unfairly treated, would be a libel on the man of the Middle

Ages.   Many of the seigneurs were good landlords and looked
after the material well-being of their tenants.   Dues were
numerous, but so were the serfs, and not every payment was
exacted from the same man ; services were divided amongst
the tenants and did not fall invariably on the same individual.
It was by no means universal for the serf to be " corvéable à
merci."   The amount of labour services was generally fixed,
though the time and nature of them were subject to the lord's
will, a very usual condition at any time in the case of farm
work.   That a serf had no judicial privileges meant rather
that he was not able to act himself as assessor in a local court
than that he had no trial granted him, or it may have ex-
pressed his exclusion from royal courts, a regulation frequently
laid down.   Despite its many disabilities, also, serfdom brought
with it certain advantages.   A lord was some protection in
time of war, he was as a rule responsible for his serf's fines,
and the dues of a serf, when fined, were generally at a lower
figure than those of a freeman (e.g. in Barsac in 1307 free
tenants paid 4 sous and 1 denier for *albergada* or *aubergade*
(i.e. forced hospitality), the *questaux* 3 sous 6 deniers) ; their
land was practically hereditary, divided as a matter of course
among the male children, and no *esporle* was due as from free
tenements.   The real hardship was no doubt the uncertainty.
To do a few days' work for the lord was not excessive, if only
the labourers had known when and how much ; a heavy rent
was better than an arbitrary *quête* ; and it was on these lines
—the fixing of services and dues—that advance had first to
be made.

There are, however, other points to note in considering the
position of the serf.   The typical *questau* was indeed burdened
by many disabilities, he was almost rightless against his lord ;
had to bear arbitrary exactions and labour services unfixed
in amount, besides having constantly to provide food for the
lord and his retinue, and to ask his permission for almost
all he did.   But if this was the theory it was not necessarily
the universal practice.   Quite a number of *questaux* were only
under a certain number of the servile conditions ; or in other
cases the vagueness of the custom had led to the dropping of

some of the worst disabilities ; constantly the fixing of services, or even of rents, was more advantageous to the lord, and materially a serf might be quite well off and have most substantial possessions. In 1384 a *questau* who wanted to purchase his freedom gave up his " houses, vineyards, lands, beasts, great and small, woods, pastures, meadows, streams, rivers, mills, and other goods, movable and immovable " ; the mention of mills makes this long list particularly noteworthy, since it was usual to find all dependents obliged to make use of the lord's mill for grinding their corn. Besides their *questaves* they frequently held pieces of land at *cens* and *esporle*, the usual tenure of non-military freeholders ; and not only this, but they appear to have owned allods fairly frequently, and it must have added greatly to their general welfare to have a piece of land free from burdens. The Terrier of Comprian (Gironde) is full of entries of these villein allods, some of which were the result of purchase, some of gifts, some of unlicensed appropriation, while others were given as dowry with a wife. There were frequent marriages between serf and free ; in one case a royal serf, having married the daughter of a burgess of Bordeaux, petitions the King for leave to share all the liberties of burgageship which his wife's family had enjoyed for generations. Serfs are occasionally found receiving legacies over which they may exercise considerable powers, and which they can sell again if they wish, although for them the lord's licence is sometimes required. Thus in 1377 some serfs belonging to Bernard d'Albret received house and lands from an uncle who was a priest, and they sold it again on the presentation of a guarantee from the lord that their *questalitat* should not invalidate the transaction in any way. Some serfs were better off than others, even according to legal conditions, those, for example, on the royal demesne, where payments were generally very reasonable, and where protection in the King's court was possible. A good many *questaux* made attempts to claim this position, or to demand the survival of privileges when royal demesne had been alienated.

Besides this great discrepancy between theory and practice,

there was a constant confusion between tenure and status which complicates the study of servile conditions, and which produced difficulties at the time. Was it only the land which was *questal*, or was serfdom a matter of birth and inherent in the person ? That services were based on land and that a freeman could hold a *questave* is incontestable, but there were certainly serfs by birth as well as by tenure. Generally in a *reconnaissance* both reasons for servitude are given, viz. : that a *questau* " holds for his body and his lands and that he is a serf as his ancestors have been and as his children shall be." This hereditary character of serfdom is strongly marked : in disputes as to a man's rank a constant argument brought forward is as to his birth—was he or was he not the son of free parents ? Evidently there were two classes : (1) Those whose serfdom was the result of birth, who were descendants of a long line of servile ancestors, and in all probability still working on the old servile holdings of the family, mere appendages of the soil, given and sold with it. (Some instances are even forthcoming of the giving away of a serf as an actual chattel, apart from the land.) (2) Those who through the possession of *questal* land took up temporarily the duties of the *hommes questaux*, but who, on getting rid of the land, would return again to their condition of freedom. In some instances this latter state would degenerate into the former, and a man who remained all his life the holder of a servile estate might leave behind him a family of serfs, whose position would be little distinguishable from those whose servitude was of more ancient origin.

The indefinite position of the *questaux*, and the fact that many peasants had no idea what their actual status was, is shown by the frequent cases which come between lords and tenants on the subject. Tenants often claimed to be free when their lords wished to treat them as serfs, and the arguments sometimes brought up in defence of their contentions show a very hazy idea of what disabilities were really inherent in the status of a serf. The courage with which the peasants maintained their claims points to a good deal of boldness and independence amongst the country people, and shows that judicial disabilities were not very exactly defined, although in the majority of instances they lost their case. An interesting dispute of this sort ending in a victory for the peasants on the main question took place in 1366 between Élie de Pommiers, Lord of Civrac, and certain men and women of Portets and Arbanatz who claimed to be free from all charges of *questalitat*. The case was tried in the castle of the Ombrière before arbitrators chosen by each party. Élie chose a canon of Saint-André and Saint-Seurin, the peasants chose a doctor of laws. Élie's contention was that these peasants were *questaux* in body and goods at *questa, talha e merce*. They, on the other hand, claimed that they could not be forced to pay more than certain annual sums and that his bailiff and officers had burdened them with other dues and services to their great prejudice. The arguments brought forward by both sides are instructive and show more clarity of ideas than usual, doubtless owing to the fact that the peasants had an expert to help them and were not acting alone. Their statement was that they and their ancestors had been free (a claim of *personal* freedom), and that they owed jointly each year to the lord a fixed sum of £200, and also individual *cens* for what they held in fief ; that if they possessed hens they must give one at Christmas time, but no one without poultry was forced to procure one for the purpose ; that from certain meadows they paid a fifth of the produce, and that each of them only did one labour service a year, on which occasion he was to be given meat and drink ; that they gave the bailiff six quarters of corn, that no bailiff could be chosen without their consent, that should any of their beasts commit trespass they paid fixed fines according to the custom of Bordeaux, and their property could go, not only to the heirs of their body, but to the next nearest relation should such heirs not exist. The lord objected to each of these statements. He did not deny the joint £200 payment, but insisted that it was *questa*, paid by reason of *questalitat* (evidently a claim that fixing of the *quête* by consent did not mean enfranchisement), that all men must pay hens at Christmas, that they must give more than a fifth of the fruit from their meadows, the

labour services wherever required and without food, and that
he had certainly the power to appoint any bailiff he wished.
That for any trespass of beasts they must pay for damage done,
not only the fine settled by the Custom of Bordeaux, and that
in case of failure of direct heirs the land must always go to
the lord himself. Unfortunately the reasons for the final
award in this case are not given in the record. In similar
cases, as a rule, witnesses were called up from the locality
and the case was judged more or less according to precedent.
In this instance the arbitrators decided that the men and
women were free without trace of servitude, and could not
be made to do *questal* services ; but on some of the detailed
points they allowed the lord his way and so arrived at some
sort of compromise. Six *corvées* a year, not only one, were
to be done by the peasants, but the lord must provide them
with food ; hens must be given at Christmas by all the tenants,
whether they kept them themselves or no ; and the men
and women had to pay large sums of money towards the cost
of the inquiry. Probably the fear of expense must have
prevented peasants from facing such actions even when the
lords were exceeding their powers, and those cases which
do take place are more often caused by a group of men acting
together than by individual claimants. The men of Caudeyran, Bouscat and Villeneuve, tenants of the Chapter of Saint-
André of Bordeaux, made frequent attempts to throw off
their serfdom. In the end they were declared to be *questales*,
but privileged. One curious case took place in 1376, when
the Abbot of Sainte-Croix tried to force *questal* services on
Pierre deu Carrost, clerk and burgess of Bordeaux, on the
ground that his father and grandfather had been *questaux*
and that therefore the son must be the same and submit
to servile conditions. Pierre not only denied that he came
of servile parentage, but urged very pertinently that he had
been a clerk and burgess of Bordeaux for more than thirty
years, and had never payed *quête* or *taille* in his life, and that
he did not even hold the same land as his father had done
in the past. Apparently the dispute had arisen because Pierre
was trying to recover his father's lands from the Abbey, pos-

sibly his death had only just occurred. A Chapter was summoned at sound of bell, and it was decided, in order to avoid the expense of a trial, to give Pierre the lands of his father as a new fief, and to be held freely for forty sous of *cens* and three sous of *esporle* ; he was also to pay for the right of entry £30 and a pipe of good wine. Pierre consented to this and promised loyal obedience " as a free man should do to his lord."

To sum up, therefore, a serf or *homme questau* was an unfree tenant who suffered under disabilities which could be legally enforced, and of which the most characteristic and the most burdensome was uncertainty. By the end of the thirteenth century the legal conditions of serfdom were generally recognized, and a class of peasants existed whose conditions approximated more or less closely to these legal theories. But the very fact of defining and hardening conditions brought about an opposite movement. No sooner did a regular class of *questaux* appear than resistance to these disabilities began, and there was a tendency for the serf to rise and to shake off some at least of these *questal* burdens. Thus the very fact of defining servile disabilities was a step in the direction of freedom. From the certainty of knowing that they were uncertain came the attempt to define them still more accurately ; and in the fourteenth century an upward movement can be traced which ameliorated the condition of the serf, until it is difficult to be sure when he has or has not reached the position of a free man.

The first step in this upward movement was the fixing of services. In 1303 the *questaux* of Sainte-Croix were bound to carry corn and wine and give hospitality to the Abbot for a day and a night. In the Customs of Lesparre (1317) the serfs were not to be freed from labour dues, but were to perform those duties only to which they were definitely bound. In 1349 the men of Caudeyran, Bouscat and La Vâche, whilst remaining *hommes questaux,* were to have the number of their labour services fixed at thirty a year.

The next step was to change the arbitrary *quête* into a fixed sum. As early as 1282 an agreement was made with the *questaux* of Saint-André of Bordeaux (a property where the peasants were more advanced than on ordinary estates) to pay 10,000 sous for *quête* each year ; and in 1343 the serfs of Sainte-Croix had their annual *quête* fixed at sixty sous. When added to this fixing of *quête*, services were commuted for money payment, it was often considered as equivalent to an enfranchisement. The Terrier of the County of Gaure, for example, enters as *quondam questales* men of a rural community whose dues and services have been commuted to fixed money payments : they were to pay, instead of *quête*, an annual sum of £50, instead of individual dues for the use of the lord's oven £15, for a toll £28, and for small labour services a little over £6.

Besides these means of gradual amelioration which enabled the serf at last to claim actual freedom, there were many cases of immediate enfranchisement. The methods of acquiring freedom in Gascony were similar to those elsewhere : gift, purchase, taking of holy orders, residence in a chartered town or bastide.

Freedom through holy orders was the earliest in date of all the methods adopted. The Church was not a respecter of persons, and there was nothing to prevent a serf from reaching high dignity in its ranks. Hence the regulations against entering religious orders without the lord's leave. If, however, a lord had plenty of tenants to feed him and to work for him this leave was in all probability not very difficult to obtain, and fairly often a lord, as a pious deed, would himself bestow a serf upon a religious house, to be admitted as a member of that house and to rise to freedom. A serf with relations in high positions in the Church was by no means unusual.

Freedom through escape to a chartered town must have been fairly easy for a *questau* sufficiently rich to pay the dues expected from a burgess. In Bordeaux a month's residence was sufficient. to secure freedom, but in most cases a year and a day unclaimed was the rule in Gascony as in England. So great, however, were the opportunities where bastides were created all over the country that, as has been seen, many charters excluded from freedom the serfs of those lords who were seigneurs in the neighbourhood, and the King had constantly to add a clause forbidding the reception of *questaux* who came unlicensed by their lords.

Apart from these ways of escape from a too dependent position, numbers of charters of enfranchisement seem to have been granted, either as free gifts or in return for money payment, especially towards the close of the fourteenth century. Gifts of freedom were very usual in wills. A man on his deathbed was often more anxious to make his peace with God and to reward his servants than to keep his property intact for his successor. Such gifts were often quite unconditional : the tenant was simply declared to be free and discharged from all servitude and *quête*. There are also cases of freedom granted *inter vivos*, generally in reward for some special service ; but as a rule such a grant imposed a fairly high *cens* in place of the arbitrary *quête* renounced by the donor. The greater number of charters of enfranchisement were, however, given in return for money payments, and whatever the legal theory might be, there was certainly no hesitation on the part of the lords in allowing a serf to pay his own money for his own freedom, although they were ready enough on other occasions to claim that all the chattels of their *questaux* belonged to them. In any case, again and again serfs escaped from their position by offering a considerable sum of money paid down, and an annual *cens* for the future. Occasionally the fact that their services were already commuted for money was urged by the tenants as equivalent to enfranchisement, but the recognition of such a claim and its confirmation by charter always required a fresh payment on the part of the claimant. A written title in proof of freedom was very necessary if the future was to be rendered secure.

There was obviously a marked tendency towards freedom in the fourteenth and fifteenth centuries, as is witnessed by the increasing number of these grants of enfranchisement ; and there were other ways also by which the ranks of the freeholders were gradually being augmented. Wastes and forests were being brought under cultivation, and when new land was let out to a tenant who undertook to make it productive, it was practically always granted in return for a *cens* in money, or a fixed portion of the produce. Thus small free holdings were constantly being formed as population increased, and estates were more extensively cultivated.

By the fifteenth century there is no doubt that a number of serfs had gained their freedom in one way and another, or if not nominally free, they were living in security on the lands which they held in return for fixed dues and services; or were even living on little pieces of their own land, and adding to their income by working occasionally for a money wage.

The accounts of the Archbishop of Bordeaux show how much the practice of hiring labour prevailed, even in the fourteenth century, on a prosperous estate in Northern Gascony. The Archbishop had still some serfs and some labour services, but far the greater part of the cultivation on his own lands was done by wage-paid labourers, in some cases his own servants, in others men hired by the day or the piece. His permanent officials and household servants were generally paid a regular salary once or twice a year, and this consisted more often of corn, wine and clothing than of money. Such payments were rather in the nature of extras than of actual wages, for these men were lodged and fed at the Archbishop's expense and had little need of much remuneration. Other workers on the estate were very frequently hired and paid by the day or the job. Transport was almost always paid for and was a heavy item in the expenses of the estate, whether it was by road or river. Ox wagons, mules, donkeys, or men with packs on their backs took goods from place to place where water transport was impossible, and carriers were able to make a considerable amount by their labour. But besides cartage, day labourers were constantly employed on the ordinary farm work : digging, haymaking, reaping, carrying, and all sorts of different processes needed in viticulture. Women were employed a good deal about the vines, where there was much fairly light work to do, but they were paid considerably less than the men, occasionally only half the

ordinary wage of a man by the day. The uncertainty as to
money values makes it difficult to estimate the real cost of a
day's work ; but reckoning in the money of Bordeaux, the
sum of two sous six denarii was a very fair average for the
day's work of a man at the close of the fourteenth century,
on the Archbishop's estates (see page 205 for money values),
and there was a slight tendency for this to increase. Most
of these *laboradors* also did not live exclusively on what they
could earn, but had some lands of their own to fall back on,
when their hired work was not regular. It is impossible,
however, to take the condition of so rich an estate as that
of the Archbishop of Bordeaux as necessarily typical of all
lay property, or of the scattered lands of the poorer seigneurs.
Here old conditions must have prevailed much longer, and
many serfs must have thought it scarcely worth while to become
free men, for *cens*, though fixed, was apt to be heavy, and they
could not always afford the purchase money which was needed
in the first instance.

Thus, despite the very distinct movement towards freedom
in the fourteenth and fifteenth centuries, serfdom had certainly not wholly disappeared until long after the English
were driven out of Gascony. The Customs of Bordeaux,
when reconfirmed in 1520, declare that lords are to exercise
the usual rights over their *questaux*, unless the *questaux* came
in person and prove the contrary within two months.

One feature of this movement towards freedom is also
very marked and distinguishes social progress in Gascony
from that in England.   There was amongst the Gascon peasants
a passion for ownership which did not appear to the same
extent amongst their English contemporaries. The existence
of old allodial property, which had practically died out with
us, and the subdivision of the land which created the system
of small holdings, opened a way of advance to the French
peasants leading in a contrary direction to that followed by
the English serf. The first thought of a prosperous Gascon
peasant was to purchase permanence of tenure at a fixed
cens or a portion of the produce, and if possible to buy a piece
of allod, however small. So that when freedom came at

last, it was as peasant-proprietors, or *métayers*, rather than as landless labourers, that the serfs emerged, and small holdings continued to prevail rather than large farms held at money rent and cultivated by landless wage-paid labourers.

CHAPTER XII

SERFDOM IN THE MOUNTAINS

CONDITIONS of life were so very different in the Pyrenean provinces from what they were in the more fertile region of Northern Gascony that they have to be studied to a great extent separately. The mountaineers, isolated in their valleys, were less likely to be reduced to the lowest stage of serfdom than the peasants of the plains; but, on the other hand, they had less opportunities of changing their condition, and of taking advantage of the economic progress and economic facilities of the more accessible regions.

Many things combined to affect country life and to produce rather special characteristics in the Pyrenees. Throughout Bigorre, Béarn, and the Pays Basque, the tendency to keep property intact by primogeniture, instead of to split it up into tiny holdings by subdivision amongst the children, was very general, and led to more continuity of custom and more complete family union than in other parts. Many places, and even some families, had their own individual rules of succession, so that no statement can be accepted as really exact for the whole region. There was very little arable land, corn was only grown for immediate needs, vineyards existed at the foot of the mountains, but their culture was not the staple occupation, and therefore pasture and the care of flocks and herds, with all that it entailed, was the most usual means of livelihood.

And finally the old theories of freedom, the customs, or *fors*, which the lords had to obey, and the many instances of rural communities (see Chapter IX) all helped to stamp certain features on the life and character of the peasantry.

For example, in the Pyrenees, instead of the *baux a fascen-dura*—the land leases of Northern Gascony—we find more frequently *baux a cheptel* : i.e. the leasing of animals to be held for a term of years in return for certain payments.   Horses, mules, but more commonly oxen, were granted out in this way, at the end of the lease, profits being shared and often the beasts themselves.

Rents in kind, in these parts, although occasionally paid in corn and wine and oxen, consisted most frequently of sheep, lambs, or cheese made from sheep's milk.   Goats, pigs and poultry were also kept, but flocks of sheep seem to have formed the chief part of the peasant's wealth.

Pasture rights were, therefore, very important, and the life of the peasant was actively occupied in the care of his live-stock.   The usual practice was to keep the beasts in the valley farm during the period of frost and snow, to turn them out into fields as soon as might be, and in March to take them up to the common pasture, advancing farther up the mountains as the weather became warmer, and bringing them back to the meadows when the harvest was over.

Some of the flocks were not kept in the mountain valleys at all during the winter, but taken farther from the mountains into warmer regions.   The men of the Valley of Ossau, for example, had the right to drive their flocks freely through the whole of Béarn, and to pasture on the open country north of Pau, known as Pont Long, still uncultivated and unenclosed to a great extent.   Endless quarrels and actual fighting took place between the Ossalois and the men of Pau, who sometimes interfered with the beasts of the strangers and sought to pasture their own beasts at the same time, or even to plough up the soil.   A life of this sort, moving from mountain to valley, responsible for the flocks, and ready to hold their own against interference, must have tended to engender a spirit of independence and freedom amongst the shepherds and cowherds of the mountains.

Nevertheless, despite the free mountain life and despite the theories of liberty asserted in the *fors*, there are traces of *hommes questaux* in the Pyrenees as elsewhere, although these *questaux* often possessed some elements of freedom. To reconcile the old theory of freedom with the existence of *questaux*, it has been suggested that though land may have been servile, serfdom by status was unknown. This is not, however, true. There were certainly serfs by status as well as by tenure, and as elsewhere the two conditions were generally combined. That duties, disabilities and personal rank were based on tenure is usual here as in all feudal countries, and there are plenty of records of it. The *Censiers* of Béarn and of Bigorre are full of notices of servile houses and servile lands— *ostaus questaus* and *terras questaus* ; and in 1374 the Count of Foix frees the place and holding of Casanave from all " questalitat e subjugacion." But on the other hand we find, in 1318, a man who was a serf " tam ratione corporis quam ratione tenentiarum suarum " ; and the same Count of Foix, in 1371, gives a charter of enfranchisement to one of his tenants freeing " his body and person " from all serfdom and subjection. Amongst the younger children of a family, indeed, it is not at all uncommon to find serfs holding no land at all, since they did not inherit any of the parents' property. In a fourteenth-century *Censier* of Béarn we read of *questaux* who live in a sister's house and work for their living, and others who had no houses nor land, but paid *quête* for their bodies.

There were serfs, therefore, in the Pyrenees as in the rest of Gascony : serfs by birth as well as by landholding, but they seem more independent than the usual *questaux*, from whom they differed in various other ways. They were often protected by the old customs of the different districts. The *Fors* of Morlaas, which were more or less in force throughout Béarn, assert that all *questaux* must have enough to live on, that their lord must see that they have sufficient land to nourish themselves and their families, and that the *quête* which they have to pay is not excessive—they must never be forced to sell beasts in order to raise the amount due. A charter granted to Bigorre in 1098 allowed the serfs to resist their lord if he burnt their houses or seized their beasts : though it also noted that they were bound to the soil and debarred from hunting and fishing. The most striking proof, however, of the unusual character of the *questaux* is the fact already noted, that in the valley communities they could become members of the *beziau* and take their share in local government and administration. It seems also indicative of a certain respect that *questaux* at the head of the family are spoken of in documents as *senhors* and *daunes*, a sort of equivalent to messieurs and mesdames ; and sometimes the prefix *en* is affixed to their names, a term generally used elsewhere in the case of nobles.

Another peculiarity of this part of the country is the formula which so often couples together the payer of *cens* with the payer of *quête*, " ceyssau e questau," instead of *cens* emphasizing the distinction, as in other parts, between the free man who owed *cens* and the serf who owed arbitrary *quête*. *Ceyssau* in this connection does not, as a matter of fact, mean the free rent-paying *censitaire*, but the serf paying rent in money or kind, but it does tend to give the impression of a closer linking up of classes. What is more, *quête* here is by no means always arbitrary. Even in early *Censiers* mention is often made of a fixed amount of *quête* either from a man or from a whole village, and this to the overlord, not *questa* to the King ; perhaps, however, there is here rather more the idea of tribute than of an actual servile condition ; but there is altogether a tendency to change many of the dues into definite sums of money. Even though feudal conditions and servitude are general, traces are constantly found of the idea that the natural condition of man is to be free, and that this freedom is a question of status and of free parentage. In charters of enfranchisement it is very usual to find inserted a clause that the tenant who is being given liberty " returns to the state of nature in which all are free, as though he had been born of a free father and mother."

Everything seems to point to a condition of modified serfdom in the Pyrenees, with frequent fixing of services and dues, with protection by law, and with possibilities of independence and of a share with the freeholder in local business.

The essential characteristic of a serf in the Pyrenean provinces seems to be that he was tied to the soil. It has even been suggested by Paul Raymond, sometime Archiviste of Pau, that this is the meaning of *quête* : " If *questare* means to seek," he writes, " *homme questal* may mean a man subject to this search, a dependent whom his lord may seize if he attempts to go elsewhere." Certainly this liability to be reclaimed is a very universal condition of serfdom all the world over : here it assumes special prominence because there are fewer of these universal disabilities, and because it usurps the place of those arbitrary dues which are made so very essential a feature in other parts. There are, indeed, instances in which free men also promise not to leave the estate, but it is never omitted from the *reconnaissance* of a serf. Thus in 1324, a man and woman *serfs e questaus* of the Seigneur of Clavaire, born and bred in the *cazau* of Cammeron, a servile place and holding belonging to the said lord, promise that they will never leave his seigneury " to dwell, marry, or establish themselves elsewhere without his consent " ; and in 1404 a man and woman, acknowledging that their children are serfs, agree that they may not leave the seigneury and promise that they shall come whenever required. A very constant clause in charters of enfranchisement grants the tenants leave " to go and come, to live and settle in whatever place they may wish, as free men are able to do." Naturally serfs were not allowed to give away or sell their land without the lord's licence, and theoretically at least they were not allowed to make wills nor to sit in judgment.

As for other servile conditions, there are a considerable variety, some falling on one tenant, some on another : occasionally it is not very clear whether the duties are necessarily demanded from serfs, or whether they can equally be imposed on the men who were free ; the distinction between free and unfree was very vague. Sometimes arbitrary dues were imposed. In the Red Book of Bénac, leave to marry outside the seigneury had to be purchased by a sum at the will of the lord, and payments on birth and burial may likewise be enforced. But this is rare. It is much more frequent to find a list of fixed dues in the rules drawn up for tenures, or where land is conveyed : so much for *oublies*, so much for *arciut*, so much for *aubergade* (both words mean the provision of hospitality), so much for *quête*. The one duty which is frequently left vague is that of castle guard, which was often demanded from the *questau*, but left, as a rule, to be arranged according to the lord's need or discretion. Various " odd jobs " for the lord's benefit are demanded from time to time from his serfs. In Bigorre some had to beat the water to keep the frogs quiet at night, others made bread, carted wood and washed tablecloths. A due known as *presentia* was something which had to be brought in person by the tenant, which would make certain his actual presence in the estate ; and in Béarn every boy of fourteen and every girl of twelve had to give one year's work to the lord, though a money payment was often taken instead of service, which must have frequently not been needed.

Conditions, on the whole, do not appear to have been very oppressive, and the payments and services when fixed were far from being severe. The lords needed to get food, any services they required, and to be boarded and lodged as they rode forth about the country : but settled cultivation on well-regulated manorial estates was little known : scattered hamlets and pastoral communities round the castles of the seigneur, or in the independent valleys, was the usual form of rural settlement ; and the peasants lived in family groups on the small holdings, to which the eldest son or daughter succeeded on the death of the father, and where he inhabited the principal house or *cap-cazau*.

There is no doubt, however, that the peasantry could be very poor, as well as independent, and that their general well-being depended a good deal on the character of the overlord, who could make the lives of his tenants a burden to them on occasion, whether they were free or unfree. The right to resist did not necessarily bring with it the power to do so, and there are some flagrant cases of cruelty and ill-treatment attributed to the well-known Gaston Phébus of Béarn.

A very good picture of Béarnais serfdom is given from the record of an inquest held in Béarn in 1388, when the Viscount commanded a house-to-house visitation to be made, in order to discover the amount of money which the unfree population was ready to offer in return for the privileges of freedom. This shows a considerable amount of poverty and distress, especially amongst the younger children, who often went out to work, as they could not inherit any of the land ; when a younger son married a younger daughter it is very usual to find that they had neither house nor lands, and were often badly off. Numbers of the serfs answer that they have nothing to give for their freedom ; some add that they have " no ox, nor cow, nor other beast " ; or that they are " poor men who live by the labour of their hands " ; one old woman of seventy, with no husband nor child, says that she has many dues to pay, and no money to offer. In every village there were abandoned holdings, families having either died out or deserted the hard life of the farm for more lucrative employments. There is little proof here of the theory that a serf was well looked after by his lord as being a valuable chattel. The absence of the lord's home farm and dependence on regular villein labour helps to account for this ; there was little direct intercourse between these peasants in the wild country with their overlord, who preferred to gain booty from fighting rather than profits from his estates. In 1305 complaints were sent up to Edward I by certain men of Dax " questaus e homis per son linadge," that their lord and his companions had killed four men and burned all the houses in the parish, and had carried off all their goods and all their beasts and taken all their clothing.

Beside this proof of frequent poverty, the Inquest and many other documents show how very close was the connection between free and unfree and how impossible it is to draw any very distinct line between the two classes. The disputes in court between lords and serfs are especially frequent throughout the whole of this region, and show how extraordinary was the uncertainty at the time upon this subject of social standing. The tenants themselves were constantly confused. One man, in 1388, says that his two holdings are not *questal*, but " vassal et censitaire," although he has to confess to paying *quête*. Another claims freedom because he has never paid *aubergade*, a fact which has certainly nothing to do with the question, as his neighbours do not fail to point out. The difficulty was increased by the absence of any documents to prove one thing or the other. A father, wishing to marry his daughter to a free man, was so doubtful as to her status, that having no written title to show, he promised to purchase her freedom that all might be comfortable and secure. The free men and serfs of Montanerès had a great dispute in the fourteenth century on the payment of *quête*. The *questaux* declared that the free men ought to help them to make up the joint sum that was due to the lord, whilst the free men asserted that it was definitely a servile payment ; and the decision imposed it eventually on all the old holdings. A good deal depended on prescription. Servile duties performed for a number of years were almost impossible to shake off. Thus, in a dispute between the Abbot of Saint-Savin and his men in 1436, the Abbot said, in support of his claim, that he had received servile dues for twenty, thirty, forty, fifty or sixty years and within the memory of man there had been no contradiction ; whilst the tenants asserted that *quête* and other payments had been added in recent times and that they ought to be free men.

All this uncertainty was tenfold increased by the complication of mixed marriages and the doubt as to the effect they produced on status. Marriage with a freeholder was certainly in itself no help to freedom ; according to the Fors of Morlaas, " the husband cannot enfranchise men nor lands which he has from his wife " ; nor does it seem necessarily to have enfranchised the children. In 1388 a serf, who had married a free man, offered ten florins to free herself and her children ; and in another case, a man who was the son of a free man and a *questal* wife, offered thirty florins to free the whole family. One difficult case which arose, in the same inquest, was that of a free man and a free wife who had servile land and did not know what their children would be ; the father considered that they should be free, but offered six florins to make it sure. Occasionally freedom was claimed through the father, though not always with success ; and in one instance, at the instigation of the curé, the children of a serf who had married a free woman were declared free " because the child follows the condition of the mother."

The only security for freedom was a written title, and some who had already purchased the privilege at an earlier date were still considered as serfs by the inquirers, because they were unable to find the record of their former transaction. Charters themselves were not always explicit when obtained. For example, one woman who had married into a servile family, which was afterwards freed, thought that she herself was included in the grant of liberty, but was ready to offer three florins more if she were still a serf.

The general conclusion to which the documents of the time seem to lead is that serfdom was well known in the Pyrenean districts throughout the Middle Ages, though on the whole less widespread, less oppressive and less complete than in many other parts of France, or indeed of Gascony : that the distinguishing and universal characteristic of the *homme questau* was his inability to leave the seigneury ; that his dues, services and payments were frequently fixed, and that at a fairly moderate figure ; and that he had greater opportunities of holding his own, of disputing with his lord, of managing local affairs, and of shaking off dependence than the majority of his class ; but that life was harder and conditions poorer than in the fertile plains and agricultural settlements of Northern Gascony.

CHAPTER XIII

CONCLUSION

IT is difficult to estimate the full extent of the influence exercised on England by her Gascon possessions; but no period of English history from 1154 to 1453 was untouched by the happenings in that distant province. In the reign of Henry II the problem of French relations was different from what it became later, since he had to deal with very vast territory from the Channel to the Pyrenees, and the greater part of his reign was actually passed in France; but already the south-west, under Richard Cœur de Lion, was showing what difficulties could be caused by its turbulent baronage, and its possession was bringing England into closer touch than would otherwise have been probable with the Princes of Spain. When the losses of John's reign and of the early years of Henry III left Gascony alone in English hands the problem of ruling a foreign dependency was limited, but no less difficult.

Shirley's collection of Royal Letters in the reign of Henry III illustrates very strikingly how much the attention of the home government was called to Gascon affairs, and how impossible it was to meet expenditure from the resources of the country; and the Gascon rolls from Edward I's reign onwards show how many matters, small as well as great, were brought before the ruler in England. The fact that a special body of triers for Gascon petitions was regularly nominated in Parliament proves how important this part of parliamentary business was expected to be. Gascon affairs formed a very large section of state business, and policy at home and abroad was constantly influenced by the need for incessant supervision and

236

by the drain on men and money which sudden emergencies entailed.

The intercourse between the two countries became much closer as a result of Edward I's reign, and we find English living in Gascony and Gascons in England. Englishmen who settled in Gascony could become burgesses of Bordeaux under the ordinary conditions laid down by the customs, and a few of them are found receiving houses and lands and pieces of forest round the town to bring under cultivation ; so that some at least were prepared to remain there as regular inhabitants. Gascons, ever ready for adventure, constantly fought in English armies against Scotch and Welsh, and were sometimes in reward given grants of lands in England. Young Gascon nobles were brought over to get some knowledge of English ways and administrative methods before being given official positions at home. Piers Gaveston was only one of several young Gascons who came to visit the English court. Deputations were frequently sent over to England, not only from the seigneurs of Gascony, but equally often from the towns, and occasionally even from the peasants. Considering the distance and expense of the journey the amount of going and coming was really astonishing.

Did England gain or lose by her possession of this distant province ? That she was brought into constant conflict with the French King was the most obvious result. From the time of Philip Augustus onwards, each King of France in turn set before himself the ideal of consolidating France, of reducing to submission the very independent feudal states of which she was composed and of bringing them more closely under central authority. Naturally the English Duke of Gascony was the most hated of·all his dangerous vassals and, since he had England at his back, one whom it was very difficult to subdue ; fraud as well as force was often resorted to in the effort to oppose him. The English Kings, as has been seen in the narrative chapters, were constantly fighting for their lands in Gascony, whether England and France were nominally at war or not. If they were not fighting the French for the possession of Gascony, they were fighting the native nobles for the tranquillity of Gascony. But evidently the value of the Duchy compensated in the minds of the English Kings for the difficulties which it involved, and also in the minds of the English people, so far as they thought about the question at all. The trade connection was undoubtedly an asset of the greatest importance to the home country ; and although Gascon merchants were looked upon as foreigners, and strict rules had to be laid down for their protection and good treatment, they and their goods would have been very much missed in England had the countries been separated before the fifteenth century.

Office in Gascony gave many a man the opportunity of making or marring his reputation. Simon de Montfort may have learnt something there of the importance of towns and the trading classes, which inspired him to seek the support of English boroughs, and to add burgesses to Parliament in 1265. Edward I undoubtedly gained much valuable experience from his apprenticeship in Gascony. Soldiers, such as the Earl of Derby, Chandos and the Black Prince, won their military renown in the south-west of France. On the other hand, many of the Gascon Seneschals succumbed before the difficulties of their position, held office but a short time and fell into insignificance if not disgrace.

The possession of Gascony has certainly to be reckoned with, throughout the whole period, as a factor in the political history of England. Commercially England benefited greatly by the connection, and English ships were increased in numbers and English sailors improved in their seamanship by the constant passage from one country to the other. Socially it is doubtful whether Gascon conditions, so well deserving of study for their own sake, had much direct effect on English life. Town life was progressing in both countries as a result of ordinary economic causes, but the advanced communal system in the south-west was due chiefly to local conditions and to the urgent need for support which made the Kings unusually generous and long-suffering. The communal movement was international, and English towns were obtaining their charters of privileges at the same time as those in Gascony ; but though prosperous and privileged, ordinary English towns never gained so much independence as did Bordeaux, and probably English burgesses knew little or nothing of Bordelais privileges : they looked to London or other great centres for their examples. English and Gascon nobles were not very unlike one another in the Middle Ages, and there was often friendship between them as well as rivalry, but English merchants were not ready to welcome Gascon merchants as fellow-countrymen, and peasants had naturally no intercourse nor knowledge of each other's ways of life.

Social conditions in Gascony are worthy of study for their own sake, not for the influence they exercised on life in England. Thus the old ideal of allodial property and the growing strength of feudal tenure makes territorial conditions especially interesting ; whilst in the north of the province the influence of commerce on social life is illustrated, and in the south the influence of geography. But the development of wage-paid labour in the north and the strength of local custom and independence in the south were matters of no concern to the English government. Gascony was a dependency administered from above, and the central government paid little heed to life among the peasantry, unless appeals were made and arbitration was necessary to settle some of the many disputes which arose between lords and tenants.

After so many years of connection it is curious how little England did to avert the severance, and how little she seems to have felt the final loss of Gascony. In 1453 affairs were in such an unsettled condition at home that neither King nor nobles could pay much heed to the victory of the French, and it was the towns of Gascony which most lamented the end of the long connection with the English.

The growing feeling of nationality which was springing up in England, and which Joan of Arc did so much to awaken in her own country, would soon have shown the undesirability of a large English province in South-western France ; in any case, the great movements of the Renaissance and the Reformation were enough to absorb the energies of both peoples in the century that was coming ; and as new avenues of trade were thrown open to English ships, the merchants of England had little reason to pine for the old wine-trade with Gascony. As for Gascony herself, although she long retained, and still to some extent retains, her distinctive language and her natural characteristics, her definite inclusion in the Kingdom of France was essential to her own welfare in the future and to the building up of that strong spirit of national unity and national patriotism, which was to become so marked a feature of later France.

BIBLIOGRAPHY

EVERY student of Gascon History should procure Monsieur Bémont's invaluable little book, *La Guyenne pendant la domination anglaise*, in the series of "Helps for Students of History" (S.P.C.K. 1920). This gives some account of the main authorities and printed sources for the period 1152–1453. The *Histoire de la Gascogne*, by Louis Puech (1914), has a list of books at the end of each chapter; and Barrau Dihigo, in an article entitled "La Gascogne" in *La Revue de Synthèse historique*, Paris, 1903, has given critical information upon some of the sources and a certain number of modern works published before that date.

Some modern books are valuable on certain portions of the subject : such, for example, as Kate Norgate's *Angevin Kings* (1912), *John Lackland* (1902), and *Richard the Lion Heart* (1924), in which she has constructed a vivid history of the periods of which she is writing from chronicles and printed documents. The reigns of John and Henry III, with special reference to the policy of the Kings towards the towns, are fairly fully treated in *English Rule in Gascony*, by F. Burr Marsh (1912) ; while for Edward I's rule and the war of 1295, the introductions of Monsieur Bémont to the published volumes of the *Gascon Rolls* are of the greatest value. For the period of the Hundred Years' War there are many books, but none that take Gascony as their main subject, with the exception of *Le Prince Noir en Aquitaine* by the Abbé Moisant (1894), which now needs supplementing with fresh material. W. Longman's *Edward III* (1869), Dunn Pattison's *Black Prince* (1910), and S. Armitage Smith's *John of Gaunt* (1904), all have chapters devoted to the subject or information interspersed with general history. A little help is given on English administration by D. Brissaud in his *Les Anglais en Guyenne* (1875), and by Professor Tout in his *Chapters on Mediaeval Administrative History* (1920). The social and agricultural history of the Bordelais has been treated by F. Barennes in *Viticulture et Vinification en Bordelais au moyen âge* (1917), and by E. C. Lodge in *The Estates of St. André of Bordeaux* (1912). Numerous monographs on town history have also appeared : notably Guinodie's *l'Histoire de Libourne* (1845), Gauban's *La Réole* (1873), Gaudet's *St. Émilion* (1841), Balasque et Dulaurens' *Essais historiques sur Bayonne* (1862–75), and Jullian's *Histoire de Bordeaux*

241

(1895), which should be read in connection with Bémont's *Les institutions municipales de Bordeaux au moyen âge* (1916). The book on bastides by Curie Seimbres, *Essais sur les villes fondées dans le Sud-Ouest de la France* (1880), needs supplementing by the review of Monsieur Giry in *La bibliothèque de l'Ecole des Chartes* (1881), and Giry also throws light on Gascon Communes in his *Établissements de Rouen* (1883). Very interesting details are given of Pyrenean customs and life by Bascle de Lagrèze in *Histoire de Navarre Française* (1881-2), and *Histoire du droit dans les Pyrénées* (1867), and by Haristoy in *Le Pays Basque* (1834) ; and of internal administration in Cadier's *Les états de Béarn* (1888). A careful handbook for the economic historian has been supplied by Monsieur Brutails in *Recherches sur l'équivalence des anciennes mesures de la Gironde* (1912).

Many more French works of varying degrees of merit could be mentioned, but the student must primarily depend on the original authorities themselves, and of these there are an abundance. The more important only can be dealt with here. Those already printed will be first considered.

Chronicles are unfortunately chiefly conspicuous by their absence : chronicles, that is, dealing primarily with Gascony. She played, however, too large a part in the fortunes of England and France to pass unnoticed in the contemporary records of either country, so that few chronicles of either country can be wholly neglected, although their information has generally to be scrutinized very closely. The few writers from the South-west itself can be dismissed in a very few words. No history, but nevertheless valuable for the reign of Richard I, are the poems of *Bertrand de Born* (edited Thomas, 1888), a warrior as well as a poet, and for the first part of his career a bitter opponent of Richard Cœur de Lion. *Geoffroi de Breuil, Prior of Vigeois*, a contemporary of Bertrand (Dom Bouquet, Vol. XI, Père l'Abbé, a seventeenth-century edition), tells us mostly of local Church matters, and only deals very sparingly with public events ; *Bernard d'Itier*, 1163-1225, Treasurer and Sacristan of Saint Martial of Limoges, has some information upon provincial nobles (*Chronicles of Saint Martial of Limoges*, Société de l'Histoire de France), and there is a *Petite Chronique de Guyenne* by an anonymous writer of the fifteenth century (published by Lefèvre-Pontalis in *Bibl. de l'école des Chartes*, Vol. 47), which gives a few original details from 1405 to 1442, and careful information for an earlier date on the siege of Bergerac and Battle of Auberoche, 1345-77. There is a so-called *Chronique Bordelaise* from earliest times to 1590 by *Gabriel de Lurbe* (1594), which, however, is purely a compilation from earlier writers, with a few additions from the Archives of Bordeaux, and another with a similar title by *Jean de Gaufreteau*, 1240-1638 (1877-8), which is of little value to history. Thus it will be seen for narrative history we have to fall back on the general chroniclers and their occasional notes of Gascon events.

Rigord and *Guillaume le Breton*, 379–1223 (Soc. de l'Hist. de France, 1882) give some account of the quarrels between the French King and Richard Cœur de Lion : *Joinville* recounts the Battle of Taillebourg, but he was not himself present, "not having yet put on knightly armour," and *Guillaume de Nangis*, 1113–1300, and his continuators, 1300–68 (Soc. de l'Histoire France, 1843), have furnished considerable information about Gascon affairs. Guillaume de Nangis was a monk of St. Denis, and though not an eye-witness had good opportunities of acquiring information. One of the continuators—Jean de Venette—travelled to Auvergne and Provence, but not apparently to Gascony, and though he helps a little for Gascon history, this part of his work is less important than the rest. The *Grandes Chroniques de Saint Denis* (1836–8) are very valuable for the years 1350 to 1377, during which years they were written or supervised by the Chancellor of the kingdom, and contain various official documents : they tell in some detail the victories of the French after 1368.

Far the fullest account of Gascon affairs in the fourteenth century is, however, to be found in the pages of *Froissart*, 1307–1400 (the best edition is that edited for the Société de l'histoire de France by Luce and Raynouard, 1869–97), who relates at length Derby's campaign in 1345, the Black Prince's raids and his subsequent period of rule, the Gascon revolt and the loss of the English possessions. Later he tells of the coming of John of Gaunt in 1394, and the refusal of the inhabitants to submit to anyone but the King himself ; and of the lamentation in Gascony on the death of Richard II—Richard of Bordeaux, as he was called from his birthplace. Froissart is bound to be interesting ; he is unfortunately less certain to be accurate ; he had, however, far more opportunity than the other chroniclers for acquiring information on the history of the South-west. Apart from the fact that when in England as clerk to Queen Philippa, he must have heard much from those who had taken part in the wars, he was himself at Bordeaux from 1366–7, and could have verified his knowledge by local investigations. In 1388 he visited Gaston Phébus, Count of Foix and Vicomte of Béarn at Orthez, with the definite intention of collecting information ; and when in 1394 he was once more in England, he learnt of the ill-success of John of Gaunt's expedition from Gascons who were over at the time, consulting with the King's council on the affairs of their country. Froissart makes some bad mistakes, his chronology is apt to be wild, and his place-names are spelt in a way that makes them hard to identify : but all such difficulties can be obviated by the use of the latest and most excellent edition of his works.

The end of the English rule is vividly described by *Gilles le Bouvier*, *dit Berry*, Herald-at-Arms (Godefroy, *Charles VII*, 1661), the Battle of Castillon by *Mathieu d'Escouchy* (Soc. de l'Hist. de France, 1863–4), and Leseur in his *Gaston IV, Comte de Foix* (edited by Courteault, 1893). The English writers, as is but natural, have perhaps on the whole devoted more time to Gascon affairs than have the French chroniclers, and the volumes of chronicles published in the Rolls Series should be looked through for the facts which can occasionally be gleaned from them ; but they treat of French affairs generally, rather than of those of Gascony in particular. The fullest information can be gleaned from Benedict of Peterborough (ed. Stubbs, 1867) for the turbulent period of Richard's rule ; and from the *Historia Majora* of *Mathew Paris* (Rolls Series, 1872–83) on the reign of Henry III and the rule of Simon de Montfort. Paris was a careful as well as a copious writer, and he seems to have written more or less contemporaneously with the event which he recounts. His friendship with the King does not prevent his outspokenness, and he tells us of his great extravagance in Gascony, of his unfairness to Simon, and of the resolute character of Richard of Cornwall, so marked a contrast to that of his royal brother.

For the reign of Edward I the best narrative information is gained from *Walter of Hemingburgh* (1848–9), but it is for the Hundred Years' War that authorities become most valuable. *Adam of Murimuth* (1889) has some contemporary information ; *Robert of Avesbury* (1889) inserts most interesting documents, such as a letter from Derby in 1346, letters from the Black Prince and Sir John Wingfield, concerning the campaign of 1355, and another from the latter in 1306. *Galfridus le Baker of Swynbroke* (edited Sir E. Maunde Thompson, 1889) is said to be from first-hand information for 1345, 1355 and 1356; and so is the poem written by the Herald of Sir John Chandos (edited Pope and Lodge, 1910), which is, however, essentially important for the campaign of the Black Prince in Spain. Later chroniclers have but little to tell us of Gascon affairs, but in 1442–3, the *Journal* of one of the suite of Sir Thomas Beckington, Secretary to Henry VI (edited Nicolas, 1828), throws interesting light on the general conditions, political and social, of the country, and especially of Bordeaux.

This sparseness of narrative history throws the researcher back upon documents of all sorts : state documents, municipal documents, feudal registers and ecclesiastical cartularies.

Of State documents the most famous are the *Gascon Rolls*, which can be consulted at the Public Record Office. Four volumes of these have been printed in the collection of "Documents Inédits sur l'histoire de France," and cover the period from 1242 to the close of Edward I's reign, though with some gaps. The first volume (1242–54), edited by Francisque Michel (1885), should not, strictly speaking, be included in the series of Gascon Rolls, since it does not comprise strictly Gascon records, but represents orders of all sorts emanating from the King's chancery, which had accompanied him to Gascony. These Rolls are, therefore, Rolls issued in Gascony, not Rolls concerned primarily with Gascon business. Monsieur Bémont has brought out a supplement to this first volume which supplies the index, notes and explanations which the former editor had not done before his death, and has edited the three following volumes in a manner which leaves nothing to be desired (1896–1906). The description of the Rolls is given very fully in his Introduction to the second volume : they contain copies of Charters, Letters Patent and Close, Liberate, Fines, and many other records.

The historical value of such a collection hardly needs emphasizing ; no true idea of the conduct of affairs in Gascony could be obtained without it. The Rolls give the names of officials, they give the royal instructions to these officials, they contain grants of privileges to towns and to merchants, they illustrate English policy, the difficulties with which the King had to deal, the disputes and arbitrations between subjects, and many other matters. They form an important addition and corrective to the narrative history told by the chroniclers.

Further material can occasionally be added to these from the Calendars of Close Rolls and Patent Rolls, which make it less necessary to go to the actual documents themselves ; and from Rymer's *Foedera et Conventiones*, which should of course be consulted, and which contains many transcripts of those Gascon Rolls not yet published in full.

Besides the *Rôles Gascons* Monsieur Bémont has also edited a document known as *Recogniciones Feodorum* [Recueils d'Actes relatifs à l'administration des rois d'Angleterre en Guienne (1914)], a register which once belonged to the archives of the Constable of Bordeaux, the head of the Gascon financial administration. The most interesting part of this register is the record of an inquest made by Edward I in 1273–4 into the tenures of all royal tenants, whether nobles, townsmen, burgesses, or villeins. They were summoned to appear before notaries and to declare what they possessed in abode or in fiefs, what homages and tenurial duties they owed to the King, whether they held by military service or by money rent and so forth. The methods of landholding and the casual vagueness of many of the landholders are well illustrated by a study of this volume.

W. W. Shirley's *Royal Letters illustrative of the Reign of Henry III* (1862–6) has a considerable amount of information concerning Gascony ; Joseph Stevenson's *Letters and Papers illustrative of the Wars of the English in France during the Reign of Henry VI* (1861–4) has disappointingly little, and Champollion-Figeac, in his *Lettres de rois etc. tirés des archives de Londres* (coll. des docts. inédits, 1839–47), has not much beyond a few copies of material from the Rolls. Delpit has furnished some new material from the Exchequer Archives in his *Collections des documents qui se trouvent en Angleterre* (1847), and the first volume of Denifle, *Le Désolation des églises en France pendant la guerre de cent ans* (1899), contains documents from the Vatican illustrating the state of the different French dioceses when the long struggle was drawing to an end.

The most wonderful collection of documents, however, is contained in a vast publication still being brought out, and of which over fifty volumes have been already published by the *Société des Archives historiques du département de la Gironde*. These documents have been excellently transcribed with all the analyses, footnotes and necessary explanations which the French know so well how to do, and the volumes are a perfect mine of information for the student of Gascon history. The sources for their publication are very various. There are some documents from the Record Office and British Museum, others copied from MS. volumes of Bréquigny in the Bibliothèque Nationale, and a few from the Archives Nationales. Most, however, are from local dépôts, not only from the rich Archives of Bordeaux and Pau, but also from private collections, which would not be accessible in other ways, and which are particularly important for the study of feudal conditions, since as a rule they come from the old castles which abound in this region. So varied and extensive is the material in these volumes that it is impossible to say more than that it illustrates all sorts of history—political, municipal, feudal, economic—and that it contains glossaries which are of great help to the understanding of the Gascon texts.

The documents concerning municipal history have perhaps been more fully published in France than those on any other subject, and the Gascon towns, and even bastides, can be studied fairly completely from printed material.

The whole publication known as the *Archives Municipales de Bordeaux* is of the greatest value. Five volumes have already been published (1867–90). Vol. I, *Livre des Bouillons* ; II, *Livre des Priviléges* (almost entirely concerned with a later period than that of the English occupation) ; III and IV, *Registres de la periode* ; and V, *Livre des Coutumes*. The *Livre des Bouillons*—so called from the five great copper ornaments or *bouillos* which originally adorned its cover, has been called by its editor " a monument of the English dominion in France."

The history of Bayonne is not quite so fully documented as that of Bordeaux, but we have the fullest collection in the *Livre des Établissements de Bayonne* (1892), and for Dax in the *Livre Noir et les établissement de Dax*, which fills Volume XXXVII in *Archives Historiques de la Gironde*. The various monographs on towns and bastides contain almost always *pièces justificatives* from the municipal archives, and besides the charters to bastides to be found in Gascon Rolls and printed in the *Archives Historiques*, others can be found in Bladé's *Coutumes du Gers* (1864) and in the last volume of Monlezun's *Histoire de la Gascogne* (1846–50). The customs or laws of various districts have been also largely printed. The *Fors de Béarn* have been edited by Mazure and Hatoulet (1841–5), the *Fors de Bigorre* are included by Bourdette in his *Sept Vallées de Labéda* (Argelès, 1898), the *Fors de la Soule* by Haristoy in the second volume of his *Pays Basque*.

Much can therefore be done from the printed page, but much remains to be gathered from unpublished material. In England we have sources in the British Museum and the Record Office. In France State documents are in the Archives Nationales in Paris, but all the important information concerning local conditions and social life has been retained in the localities ; chiefly in the departmental archives, of which the richest and best catalogued in Gascony are to be found at Bordeaux and Pau.

The British Museum material is mainly in the collection of documents made by Sir Robert Cotton in the seventeenth century and bound up into volumes named after the Roman Emperors. *Julius E I* has been called " a veritable cartulary of Aquitaine " for the reigns of Henry III and the first two Edwards. It is a stout volume containing State documents, royal letters, records of homages and various *rentiers* useful for social history. It has been largely utilized by writers on this period. *Caligula D III* has also a few documents concerning chiefly the political and commercial history of Gascony from 1209 to 1407.

In the Public Record Office, besides the whole series of *Gascon Rolls* (to 1460), there are *French Rolls* which are occasionally useful for the South-west (catalogued more or less insufficiently by Carte, and for the later Rolls in Volumes 44 and 48 of the Report of the Deputy Keeper), and there are also *Gascon Petitions* (Files 281–293 of Ancient Petitions, and also scattered through them) which well repay study. Nobles complain of towns and other nobles : towns clamour for redress and compensation, merchants demand privileges, and even country people send up complaints of the violation of pasture rights and of damage to their crops. The Gascon business which went up to the King, or at least to the officials of his Chancery, was very miscellaneous, and the connection between Gascony and the government of its distant suzerain was closer than is often realized.

In Paris the information in the Bibliothèque Nationale chiefly consists of copies made in the eighteenth century from many different sources. *Bréquigny* has made many extracts from *Julius E I* and the *Gascon Rolls* ; the *Fonds Doat* is a vast collection of copies from Archives in the south of France, sometimes useful for the administration of the Black Prince, and there are a few original documents also helpful in the *Fonds Latin*, of which an Inventory has been made by Léopold Delisle.

In the Archives Nationales are some State documents of importance, especially in what is known as the historical section under the letter J, which indicates the *Trésor des Chartes* (in the numbering of these Archives double letters stand for Registers, single letters for detached documents collected into cartons). The *Trésor des Chartes*, according to tradition, dates from the time when Philip Augustus was surprised at Fréteval by Richard I in 1194 and lost all the important royal·documents, which up till then had been carried from place to place wherever the King went.   To avert such disasters in the future it was decreed that all such acts should be guarded in some central place, and the Chamberlain and Keeper of the Seal was given charge of the collections.   The *registres du Trésor* correspond to our official Rolls : they are copies of the acts sent out from the King and his Chancery.   The *layettes du Trésor* (coffers) are the originals of the pieces addressed to the King or deposed in his Chancery for any special reason.   The *Trésor* contains useful information for the history of the wars in Gascony and also for the history of French encroachments and for the administration of those parts of the country which fell one time or another under the government of France.   A few pieces in K (Monuments Historiques) are also useful for the wars in the South-west and for the reduction of Bordeaux in 1451.

The real study of Gascony, however, cannot be made in Paris. Local archives are absolutely necessary for any thorough piece of work, especially one concerned with social conditions.

The *Archives Départementales* were originally composed of the documents rescued during the Revolution from the monasteries, seignorial courts, corporations both civil and ecclesiastical, and any private collections which survived the War of the Châteaux and were not concealed by their owners ; the proceedings of local parliaments were added later, and now annual dossiers are sent from the administration on all local affairs.   Inventories have been made for all these local dépôts, in some cases admirable in quality, in others mediocre, but on the whole extremely useful volumes, which enable the researcher to find out the material which will be useful and to get hold of it without difficulty.   These can all be consulted in the British Museum. The student of Gascon history is particularly fortunate in his departmental archives.   The more permanent part of the English dominion was in the modern department of the Gironde, and the *Archives Départementales* of Bordeaux are as rich and well-catalogued as any in France. After the Gironde, the Basses Pyrénées with its dépôt in the Préfecture of Pau has the next richest collection in the South-west, and these documents have been excellently catalogued by Raymond, sometime *Archiviste* there.   These archives are particularly valuable for the history of Béarn, but there are documents there concerning all the Pyrenean country as well as some on other parts.   The other departments in Gascony—Gers, Hautes Pyrénées and Landes—have little to contribute to this early period.   There are also interesting documents to be found in the Archives Municipales—especially of Bordeaux and Bayonne, but a great many of these can be utilized in print.   Anyone who has to use manuscripts in France should procure *Les Archives de l'histoire de France* by Langlois and Stein (1891), which describes the nature of the sources to be procured at the different dépôts, and indicates those which were published at that date.

The cartularies in which the record of great ecclesiastical estates have been entered are the most important among the materials for social history, and have been better kept than the *terriers* of lay lords. Volumes of accounts, occasional inquisitions into properties, feudal extents and rent rolls are invaluable for the study of landholding, or agricultural conditions and of labour-services ; but the analyses in the printed Inventories give a clear idea of the nature of this unpublished material.

It must be remembered that there is a certain difficulty to be overcome by the student of documents in the language which is often used. State documents are usually in Latin, but nearly all local records, old customs and seignorial matters are in Gascon or Béarnais, and there are great varieties of both, according to the locality. The different glossaries which occur in many of the collections of documents are often more useful than actual dictionaries. These are to be found, amongst other places, in Vol. XI of *Archives Historiques de la Gironde*, and in Luchaire, *Recueil de textes de l'ancien dialecte gascon* (1881). There is a good Béarnais dictionary by Lespy and Raymond (1880), and a much less useful Gascon one by *Cénac-Montaut* (1863). *Mistral* (1878) is concerned with Provençal and not Gascon, but nevertheless he is often helpful and gives a certain number of the local varieties which often render the form of a word very puzzling. The easiest way to begin such reading is to collect words from any translations which are given in books, such as *Les Fors et coutumes de Béarn* by Mazure and Hatoulet, and in the very full epitomes given of some of the most important documents in the *Archives Historiques de la Gironde*.

INDEX